# Ethnicity and Machine Politics

### Jerome Krase
Brooklyn College of the City University of New York

### Charles LaCerra
The College of Staten Island of the City University of New York

UNIVERSITY
PRESS OF
AMERICA

Lanham • New York • London

Copyright © 1991 by

# University Press of America®, Inc.

4720 Boston Way
Lanham, Maryland 20706

3 Henrietta Street
London WC2E 8LU England

**Library of Congress Cataloging-in-Publication Data**

Krase, Jerome.
Ethnicity and machine politics / Jerome Krase, Charles LaCerra.
p.   cm.
Includes bibliographical references and index.
1. James Madison Club (Brooklyn, New York,
N.Y.)—History—20th century.
2. Democratic Party (N.Y.)—History—20th century.
3. New York (N.Y.)—Politics and government—1898-1951.
4. New York (N.Y.)—Politics and government—1951-
5. Brooklyn (New York, N.Y.)—Politics and government.
6. Minorities—New York (N.Y.)—Political activity—
History—20th century.
I. LaCerra, Charles, 1928-  .   II. Title.
JK2319.N56K73   1991
91-11342 CIP

ISBN 0–8191–8235–4 (cloth : alk. paper)
ISBN 0–8191–8236–2 (paper : alk. paper)

The paper used in this publication meets the minimum requirements of
American National Standard for Information Sciences—Permanence
of Paper for Printed Library Materials, ANSI Z39.48–1984.

# Acknowledgements

During the decade-long process of researching and writing this book, many personal debts have been incurred. Although it is impractical to cite all those who have made the completion of this work possible, the authors must acknowledge those whose contributions have been invaluable. We are especially grateful to Lawrence Hayden for reading and extensively commenting upon the many drafts of our ever-changing manuscript. Robert J. Kelly must be similarly cited for his editorial advice when the book was taking on its present form. The organizational suggestions of Suzanne Krase made our final draft as concise as possible without losing the historical flow of events which we had envisioned for the book. Sylvia LaCerra, in addition to providing the authors with supportive critiques, played a major role in proofreading all versions of the manuscript. Finally we are indebted to the Professional Staff Congress/City University of New York Faculty Research Award Program for a grant which supported our early investigations into the history of the Madison Club.

It is, of course, impossible to give proper recognition to all the members of the Madison Club and the community residents who allowed us to interview them or otherwise contributed to the success of our research. There are a few people, however, who the authors repeatedly called upon over the course of the years and whose help demands commensurate notice. The assistance of Anthony Jordan, Jr. was crucial to the success of our project. As a past president of the Madison Club and Justice of the Supreme Court of New York State, his experience and insight gave us a direct connection to the reality of day to day political life. Three people who were often called upon to identify important persons and issues at the Madison Club were Anthony C. and Rose Nicoletti, and Salvatore Jordan. Finally we must acknowledge the help of the late Stanley Steingut without whose cooperation a truly open and honest view of ethnicity and machine politics would never have been possible.

■ ■

# Table of Contents

## Tables

## Maps

# Introduction

In American urban history and folklore, the images of the sleazy local political "Boss" and the corrupt big city "Machine" are quite common. So much so, in fact, that Bosses and Machines are part of the American literary and film traditions. Two of the best examples of this public fascination for the more romantic and seamy side of politics were Edwin O'Connor's 1956 novel, *The Last Hurrah*, and Frank Capra's 1939 film classic *Mr. Smith Goes toWashington*. Despite the almost commonplace ideas of urban politics, there is still much to learn about the dynamics of these pervasive forms of city political life. A brief reading of our nation's history during its many and varied periods leads to the conclusion that the machine, and the corruption related to it, have always been with us. Periodically recurring headline stories in newspapers about political scandals in major American cities indicate as well that urban political machines are still with us and are likely remain on the city scene for the foreseeable future. Familiarity with the studies of cities outside the confines of the United States breeds the conviction that urban political machines are not a unique American invention. The machine is a universal type of political organization crossing political, racial and cultural boundaries. Like a virus, machine politics is comfortable in many host societies. Therefore the study of the political machine in all its forms will occupy the attention of social scientists for many decades to come.

In order to better comprehend the machine, research efforts should be broad and multi-disciplinary. City politics must be studied from top to bottom and *vice versa*, and political organizations ought to be looked at by more than one pair of eyes at a time so that different perspectives can be generated and compared. Ideally, we should be able, like genetic engineers, to theoretically take the machine apart and put it back together again. This would be no mean achievement. For example, it is not an easy task to obtain a comprehensive view of city machines from the existing literature. The study of American politics has been dominated by those who emphasize large scale and mass events. It is easy to find studies which focus upon major political institutions, movements and ideologies. Relatedly, biographers find it more profitable to limit their efforts to the most prominent and well-known political actors whose impact on the political scene has been most obvious and significant. Although the literature on American political machines is considerable, it also focuses on the highest strata of political activities at the expense of giving needed attention to local life and everyday persons. Biographies of presidents, big city mayors and governors abound, but very little attention has been paid to the smaller scale political operations which comprise the majority of what can be called "normal" political activities upon which the political "big shots" depend. These activities include such mundane things as getting out the vote and managing the inter-personal and intergroup relations within local political organizations that take place in unique neighborhood environments.

According to C. Wright Mills the proper focus for the study of all aspects human society is the intersections of biography, history and social structure.[1] Unfortunately, the rarity of comprehensive micro-political studies which trace the relations between high and low level organizations, and those that look closely at local political organizations, makes it difficult to connect major political events and personalities of the past and present to the more commonplace, but equally important, social lives and histories of local voters, activists, constituents, interest groups and communities. Ultimately, it is these ordinary people who are the actors who determine the fate of elected officials. They are also the ones who are the life blood and foundation of the national political parties, presidential campaigns and ideological movements which have shaped the history of nations. To recognize the importance of ordinary people, one need only consider, for example, the work of Gustave Le Bon whose study of "The Crowd" during the French Revolution gave a different interpretation of this earthshaking event by focusing on the motivations and psychology of the ordinary participants in revolutionary events rather than on the conflicting ideologies and acts of prominent political leaders and thinkers.[2]

Ethnicity, race and religion, in conjunction with organizational factors such as group dynamics, and social stratification, are the major social forces in the creation and operation of urban political machines. Acting upon and through each other they account for the rise and fall of these pervasive, and sometimes peculiar, local institutions which influence all levels of social and political life. Their impact can be seen in the back rooms of smoke-filled local clubs, as well as in the media nuances of presidential campaigns. The tactical problems of Al Smith's or John F. Kennedy's Roman Catholicism as presidential candidates in a Protestant American nation, have counterparts in the sometimes deft, but more often obvious strategies of local politicians to "balance" their tickets to reflect the prejudices of their constituents, or, in some cases, to take advantage of them.

One of the most powerful political myths in the United States is that of ethnic succession as "improving" the integrity of urban politics. Throughout American urban history, impoverished minority groups have seen their salvation in the election of one of "their own" to high positions such as the mayor's office of the city in which they lived. Regardless of the political advancement of any particular group, however, history has consistently revealed that the hoped for "improvement" in the character of political operations does not occur. Although some members of the ethnic group may become more successful, the general tone of urban politics remains as it was despite a period of high expectations for "reform." The pattern has been that the newly empowered group slowly becomes part of the old guard and joins in taking advantage of any new minorities who later come upon the urban scene.

In America the building blocks of national political life are local political associations which vary greatly in degree of their formality, longevity and influence. They are the small-scale units which bind political parties to government and the electorate. In recent years, local associations appear to have lost power because of the increased use of mass media and other direct appeals to voters by candidates and parties, especially at the national level. However, the "old fashioned" political party apparatus continues to rely upon its small scale organizational bases, if for nothing more than stability, continuity and "tradition." One reason for the continuation of this style of politics is that, for most people, political activism does not make much sense without personal involvement and personal gain. For example, even the most sophisticated and elitist political activists seem to shape themselves into club-like political associations not only to more effectively influence political processes but to experience a sense of *camaraderie*.

Although many older ethnic machines, led by stereotypical cigar-smoking Irishmen, Poles, and Italians, may have declined in visibility, if not importance, in cities like Boston, Chicago, Cleveland and San Francisco, the institution is by no means extinct. Generally speaking, the traditional machine has adapted to the changing political climate. Coalitions between ethnic and interest groups, once seen as diametrically opposed, appear with regularity as power bases wax and wane. Once politically Neanderthal, political bosses have now adopted modern techniques for exercising control, and have continued to mediate between the broader and narrower, more local, political levels. The image of the new style ethnic political boss is likely to be that of a non-smoker with an advanced degree. His or her campaign war chest is also more likely to dole out funds to media experts and political think tanks than to distribute turkeys at Thanksgiving. More importantly for the survival of the political machine, in cities across the country, recent immigrant groups, as well as native Hispanics, Blacks[3] and nonwhites, have developed their own political consciousness, sophistication, local clubs, and their own machines. It is to these newcomers that the traditional forms of machine politics have been directly bequeathed.

To get a better angle on the numerous transformations in the constant evolution of urban machine politics, this book focuses upon a single, local Democratic political organization in Brooklyn, New York. At one time one of the most powerful political organizations in the country, the James Madison Club was overshadowed in New York City only by the legendary Tammany Hall, which has attracted

almost all of the attention of historians and political commentators.

Since the 1920s, Brooklyn, or Kings County, has been
one of the largest Democratically enrolled counties in the
United States. Until the 1970s, only Chicago's Cook County
organization and Manhattan's Tammany Hall surpassed
the Brooklyn machine in national prominence. The club
and its members had established a record of achievement
in national, state and city affairs for nearly seventy-five
years beginning at the turn of the century. From the ranks
of the Madison Club emerged Democratic party county
bosses, leaders and speakers of the State Assembly,
Members of the Assembly, State Senators, Members of
Congress, a State Attorney General, Judges, a District
Attorney, a Mayor, Comptroller of the State, and many
other elected and appointed officials of local, state and
national government. Equally important, the Madison
Club produced the crucial votes in party primaries, caucuses, conventions and general elections which helped
put hundreds of people into office ranging from lowly
election district captains to U.S. Presidents.

The period, 1900-1980, in American city life was characterized by the struggle of ethnic, religious and racial groups
to obtain and then preserve their share of political power.
The source of the far-reaching power of the club had
always been the success of its ethnically sensitive local
operations. Ethnic awareness, organizational know-how,
the strength and popularity of its leaders and the club's
direct relationships to the neighborhood communities
combined to maintain its power within ever changing
political and demographic environments.

Basically, the Madison Club was a selective social group,
and a study of the interconnected histories of its members
and its neighborhoods helps to explain how their political
achievements were obtained. The interrelated fates of

members and communities also explain the eventual failure of the club even while its members and friends continued to hold lofty political positions.

Political organizations do not live in a sociological vacuum. They must struggle for survival in a highly competitive and occasionally violent human environments. For party organizations, the most important elements of this volatile system were the different ethnic, religious and racial groups who have successively entered into the political arenas in most American cities since the turn of the century. The story of the Madison Club tells how ethnic, religious, racial and generational transitions affect decisions, group cohesion and the success of political organizations at all levels from block captain to city wide candidates.

A major goal of this work is to bring to life the actors and events of machine politics by describing in detail some of its "nitty gritty" of everyday activities. By showing how the one political club - the Madison Club - responded to social changes in one urban place - Brooklyn, New York, the authors of this book believe that the normally invisible connections between the highest and lowest levels of political activity will become apparent. This is important because despite the eventual demise of the Madison Club, its story demonstrates the resilience of political "machines" and "bosses" in the face of periodic "reform" movements.

The authors would like in the course of this work to lessen the credibility of two interconnected myths. The first, already mentioned, is that of the automatic "improvement" in urban politics by the advancement of particular ethnic groups. The second, which is perhaps more of an "Old American" bias than a myth, depicts big city machine politics as a "foreign" cultural element and an historical aberration rather than as an enduring and integral aspect of the American democratic political system which continues to enable disadvantaged groups to work out alternative ways to obtain political power.

We hope then, in the following pages, to accomplish all of these interrelated tasks through a close examination of a particular local political organization over three generations of political life which we believe to be exemplary of local politics nation-wide. To do this, *Ethnicity and Machine Politics* is divided into four historically and theoretically successive, but also overlapping, parts. These divisions reflect major periods, or stages of development, in the political climate and ethnic composition of New York City. Each of the parts is introduced by a "theoretical" chapter which discusses what the authors feel is the most pertinent theory of urban political life for that particular historical period. The theoretical introduction is followed by an historical description and analysis of the Madison Club during that time period. These historical discussions are reinforced by selected demographic, geographic and political data collected for each time period which are reported in the Appendices.

The first section describes the Madison Club as a "Traditional Machine" from the turn of the twentieth century to the middle of the Great Depression and employs the near classic "Social Structure and Anomie" theory of Robert K. Merton for analysis of the club's first leader, and Brooklyn Boss-John H. McCooey.[4] During this time, the Madison Club sat at or near the top of a monolithic county-wide political organization.

The second period with which we deal is from the Depression into the decade of the Sixties when the highly centralized Brooklyn organization devolved into a contest between competing local clubs. Here the organizational theoretical orientations of Edward C. Banfield and James Q. Wilson on city politics are most appropriate as ethnic power in Brooklyn began to shift from Irish Catholic to

Jewish leaders and the fate of the group became associated with that of Irwin Steingut.[5] Although during this time the machine became more complicated, it did not adopt a universalistic credo. Neighborhoods, voters and politicos retained their ethnic, racial and religious foundations.

The third major era of city politics, from the vantage point of the Madison Club, was from the 1960s until the end of the club in 1978 when ethnic and racial population shifts radically changed New York City's political arenas. During this time, the fate of the club was closely associated with its political "stars" Abraham Beame and Stanley Steingut. The insights of *Beyond the Melting Pot* by Daniel Patrick Moynihan and Nathan Glazer are brought to bear upon the even greater impact these changes had on the rapidly integrating neighborhoods surrounding the Madison Club in Brooklyn.[6]

The fourth section provides a more politically and historically "unconventional" view of the Madison Club and New York City's political machines. The theoretical chapter outlines the radical approach of Jack Newfield and Paul DuBrul in their analysis of the fiscal crisis which brought the city to its knees during the late 1970's.[7] This chapter also shows how the fate of the city and the club were inexorably intertwined. The final chapter is a 1978 participant-observation study by one of the authors (Jerome Krase) of the "Last Campaign" of Member, and Speaker of the New York State Assembly, Stanley Steingut when, after seventy-years of political domination, the Madison Club was no longer able to survive in the radically changed ethnic and political environment. It takes a first hand look at how interpersonal and intergroup relations determine the fate of local elections. The personal narrative is intended to describe the Madison Club, at that time, as an example of the intersection of "biography, history and social structure."

# Footnotes

1. C. Wright Mills, *The Sociological Imagination*. New York: Oxford University Press, 1959, p. 143.
2. Gustave Le Bon, *The Crowd*. London: Unwin, 1916.
3. After considerable discussion, the authors have decided to capitalize the term "black" when it is used as an equivalent to the designations of other groups in the United States such as Italians, Jews etc.. It should be noted that prior to the recent employment of terms such as "Afro-American," and "African-American, American Blacks were referred to, in scholaraly literature, as "Negro" or "Colored," both of which were dignified by capitalization. In much of the text presented here, "Black" is preferred as a reference because of its "racial" connotations, as opposed to the "ethnic" meaning of African-American. This is necessary due to the special racial context for Blacks and other nonwhite groups in machine politics.
4. Robert K. Merton, *Social Theory and Social Structure*. Glencoe: The Free Press, 1967.
5. Edward Banfield and James Q. Wilson, *City Politics*. New York: Vintage Books, 1966.
6. Daniel P. Moynihan and Nathan Glazer, *Beyond the Melting Pot: The Negroes, Puerto Ricans, Jews, Italians and Irish of New York City*. Cambridge, Mass.: M.I.T. Press, 1970.
7. Jack Newfield and Paul DuBrul, *The Permanent Government*. New York: The Pilgrim Press, 1981.

# The Madison Club as a Traditional Political Machine

Robert K. Merton in his modern classic, *Social Theory and Social Structure*, provides us with the clearest and must useful analysis of the urban "Political Machine."[1] His discussion of the history of the American machine and the functional approach he employed is especially well suited for an analysis of the Madison Club and the Brooklyn Machine under Boss John H. McCooey for the first third of the twentieth century. During that time Brooklyn was a burgeoning city and the destination of hundreds of thousands of immigrants, ripe for political exploitation by the traditional machine. The theory, adapted for different historical realities, is helpful in explaining the operation of urban political organizations in later periods as well.

The general form of the functional argument in social science, and indeed all science, is that there exist *a priori* certain basic needs of all social systems and the structure and operation of the system acts or reacts in such a way as to meet those needs. As needs change so does structure. As structural change creates new needs, or modifies old ones, the system continues to evolve. Throughout this process, however, it tries to maintain the "balance" or stability of the existing structure. A common criticism of this perspective is that it relegates human beings to mere cogs in societal machinery. Merton states very simply that: "The social functions of an organization help determine the structure (including the recruitment of personnel in the structure), just as the structure helps determine the effectiveness with which functions are fulfilled..."[2] His discussion of the political machine is based on an assumption that these types of political organizations are immoral or undesirable in American society even though they are "functional." Others, such as Richard Hofstadter have added that machine politics is opposed to the "indigenous Yankee-Protestant democratic ethos of individual political action and conciousness which leads people to act unselfishly for the common good. To people like Hofstadter, the new European immigrants threatened American political life by their emphasis on personal loyalties as opposed to law and morals.[3]

If we accept this view of American political and social morality, then we must agree with Merton that the machine is not a product of the "manifest," or intended, needs and functions of American society but rather one of its "latent" (unanticipated, accidental, and secondary) productions. Simply put, White Anglo-Saxon American society manifestly produced the ideal American political ethos, while latently it produced the antithetical machine: If it were not for non-Anglo-Saxon-Protestant immigration, there would have been neither political machines nor the corruption associated with them. Hofstadter and others seem to have overlooked the history of cities in Anglo-Saxon-Protestant nations and also to have neglected to mention the considerable corruption evident in colonial and early American cities such as New Amsterdam, New York, Boston and Philadelphia. In any case, there is at least a theoretical equivalence between manifest and latent organizational types. That is, the theoretical rules for operation of both are the same.

Large segments of the American population see political machines as undesirable. This evaluation is based on what people see as the organization's most publicized, and least palatable, activities: corruption, graft, fraud and patronage. What is not apparent to the causual observer are the latent needs of the social system and its parts which are met by the machine and are its *raison d'etre*.

Manifestly, the machine violates the moral codes of the dominant society. For example, "political patronage" goes against the well accepted notion that all applicants for jobs, for example, should be evaluated on the same basis.[4] "Bossism" rejects the idea that voters should elect candidates based on issues and honest appraisals of qualifications.[5] It is clear that the bribery and "honest graft" of the machine contradicts the laws and mores of society.[6] Yet political machines persist and even when periodically "destroyed" by reform movements and good government campaigns, they have the "phoenix-like quality of rising strong and unspoiled from their ashes."

According to Merton's structural-functional analysis, the political machine exists and perseveres because it performs needed positive functions which are not being done by existing, more legitimate organizations.[7] Alternately, political machines fail when they no longer perform those functions; other structures replace them when the needs they cater to are eliminated or reduced. Therefore, the creation and rise of the Madison Club ought to be found in the historical record as a product of serving these unmet needs, and its decline and demise should be understood in the context of more successful competing structures and the changing needs of its constituents. The competing structures could be government itself, private agencies, or similar but more effective political organizations.

Seeing political machines, bosses and clubs as organisms in a larger community or ecological environment highlights the need of the organization to survive by preventing change and the rise of competitors. Adding the element of conscious planning by machine politicians who are quite aware of their power bases, modifies structural-functional analysis and removes the naive notion that political machines are merely systematic products rather than socially created and maintained entities. The Madison Club, and other clubs, were not accidental "natural" consequences of divine, demonic or impersonal forces. They were consciously created and maintained and thrived as long as they did because they served the needs of individuals, groups and, it can be said the existing power structure of the society as a whole.

One must also realize that it is possible for organizations like the Madison Club to operate as machines at one time and not at another. For example, Madison Club officers and candidates had been touted at times as "reformers", especially during the rise of Franklin D. Roosevelt in New York State. This raises the issue on the contemporary scene of the "life cycle" of urban political organizations. Perhaps in the 21st Century, scholars will be retracing the growth of non-white minority "machines" which came into existence in the 1980's touted as altruistic champions of political reform.

Merton's functional approach also makes it possible to study machines which are "innovative" and not easily recognized as such because they do not fit the historical stereotype. In all societies groups and individuals are presented with goals and the means to attain these goals. Some are blocked from legitimate means and use illegitimate ones to attain the same goals. In this paradigmatic view, machine politics is a more or less a form of illegitimate means to attain political, social, and economic ends. Although machine politics is "deviant," it is no less understandable in sociological terms.

The political machine should be defined by its functions and the needs it serves, and not primarily by a moral evaluation of its assumed ethos. For example, a political organization could operate quite morally, and indeed commendably, by fulfilling the unmet needs of certain groups in society as do philanthropic and charitable groups. The operation and structure of the organization is a response to the available means and the social context, and not necessarily the result of evil intent. Some political and social scientists continue to imply that bossism is a type of "subversive" politics which is radically different from, and opposed to, a pristine model of American political behavior. Even though the first Tammany organization in New York was run by Anglo-Saxons, the "machine" label has been reserved for Catholic, Jewish, Italian and Eastern European political groups in urban America.

The machine is a more or less common and generic type of social organization and the key structural-functions of the boss are organizing, centralizing and maintaining the power not taken up by legitimate political structures. The power is obtained by meeting the needs of people that the legitimate groups are unable or unwilling to address.[8]

In order to understand the role of bossism and the machine, it is necessary to consider two types of sociological variables. The first of these is the societal context which makes it difficult, if not impossible, for morally approved institutions to fulfill essential needs. For example, during rapid industrialization and mass immigration to American cities at the turn of the century, government was unable to quickly adjust to the new economic and social realities. This situation left the door open for political machines or other structural equivalents, such as ethnically-based organized crime, to fill the vacuum. The second variable are the subgroups, such as immigrants, the poor or minorities, whose distinctive needs are left unsatisfied, except latently by the political machine and other illegitimate organizations.[9]

To Merton, American government is a dispersed human system in which all people and groups try to get around government, either legally or illegally. Government cannot fill the needs of all groups, especially when there are competing interests for scarce resources. Therefore, "alternative," or "unofficial" structures are likely to be created.[10] From a sociological point of view, machines and bosses are a natural outcome of an operant system and are by no means "aberrant" although, perhaps, abhorrent. Business corporations, doctors, lawyers, private and public agencies, lobbyists, political and other "legitimate" actors are just as active in attempting to get around the structure of government as the illegitmate actors such as political machines and organized crime.

In order to understand how machines are created and maintained it is necessary to understand the sub-groups they serve. Merton identifies four types of sub-groups: "The Deprived," "Those For Whom Social Mobility Would Otherwise Be Blocked," "Legitimate Business," and "Illegitimate Business." It is obvious that interrelations between these subgroups are possible and most probable. We shall consider in this section primarily the needs of the "Deprived" and "Immobile" during the first period in the life of the Madison Club; 1905-1935. It was during this time that the club was most machine-like in the classical sense. The deprived and immobile groups were essentially the same people. Other than the considerable Irish Catholic population, the constituents for the organization were recent arrivals to the city; Southern Italians, and Eastern

European Jews. Most of these people were low- or un-skilled workers, under- or uneducated, and poor. These groups also shared the experience of ethnic discrimination and political oppression in their home countries. Each group presented both prospects and problems for the maintenance of the power of the club which had to adapt both internally and externally to changing demands placed upon it.

Within a short period of time after he established the Madison Club in 1905, John H. McCooey, became the Chairman of the Kings County Democratic Committee, or Brooklyn "Boss." New York City then was still controlled by Tammany Hall in Manhattan, but both the rapid growth of Brooklyn's population and changes in New York State party rules led to the loss of its absolute control of party matters. Before the turn of the Century, Brooklyn already had a Democratic Party machine led by "Boss" Hugh McLaughlin. His organization "was accused of engaging in electoral frauds, diverting city funds, selling street railway franchises, filling the city payroll with political appointees, and other similar illegalities and inequities, charges not unlike those made against machines in other cities."[11]

There was, however, considerable Republican Party and Reform Democratic opposition representing Brooklyn's substantial business and middle class population. These groups and Brooklyn's prominent families, led for some time by Brooklyn Republican Mayor Seth Low, championed the cause of reform and were instrumental in the consolidation of New York City in 1898. The consolidation is easily seen as an attempt to bolster Republican opportunities in the State. The city charter revision was written by a commission appointed by Republican Governor Levi P. Morton, and it was approved in 1897 by the Republican dominated State Legislature, headed by Republican "Boss" Thomas C. Platt. The fate of Brooklyn as an appendage of Manhattan had actually been sealed in 1883 with the completion of the Brooklyn Bridge. This intercity transportation revolution was engineered by the same coalition which favored political consolidation.

Despite the bridge, consolidation, Republicans, and reformers, Brooklyn became dominated by a Democratic political machine. From 1905 into the Great Depression, the Madison Club and the Kings County organization fit closely Merton's model of the ideal-typical "machine." During that time the Brooklyn machine was a highly centralized operation which controlled virtually every election in the county and took on increasing importance in city, state, and even national party elections, conventions, and caucuses.

The development of the club as a powerhouse from the turn of the century is summed up in a 1932 *Brooklyn Eagle* newspaper article which declared that Madison Club and County Leader John McCooey had defeated Tammany Hall by accomplishing the nomination of Herbert Lehman for Governor of New York State.[12] In the same year, Governor, Franklin D. Roosevelt was quoted in the *Eagle* as saying that he was "indebted" to Brooklyn and McCooey because they were the largest Democratic voting unit in the country.[13] This compliment was made by the President despite the fact that McCooey had not supported Roosevelt initially in the 1932 Presidential convention in Chicago. McCooey had lent his support to Al Smith for the nomination, perhaps in part because of their shared Catholic background. McCooey's erroneous calculations in 1932 did come back to haunt him when Roosevelt, as President, cut the Brooklyn machine off from Federal patronage during the New Deal until the Kings County leaders, realizing the McCooey liability, deposed him and set up a more "acceptable" county alignment of power under the guise of "reform." In 1934, shortly after his defeat in the County leadership battle, John McCooey died, and the Madison Club's status was relegated to that of one of many powerful clubs in a shifting coalition of regular organizations in Brooklyn. The club did, however, continue to wield enormous power via its new leadership in the person of Irwin Steingut. The elevation of Steingut represented not merely a change in the source of patronage through the New Deal, but also the movement of Jewish politicians and constituents to the forefront of Democratic politics in the City and State. In the 1930's they pulled alongside the Irish and ahead of the Italians as an ethnic power bloc.

Changes in New York State Democratic organization rules helped bring an end to "old style" machines. For example, the introduction of primaries which replaced restrictive party convention, or caucus systems for choosing candidates made it a great deal more difficult for machines to operate with impunity. "Reform" movements essentially limited the power of bosses to make decisions unilaterally, and opened the party to wider participation. Also, over the years there were changes in the mechanisms by which people registered their party membership, and the introduction of quasi-independent Boards of Elections eliminated the absolute control of bosses over local elections. Federal agencies and civil service reform additionally reduced local patronage and the "favors" that could be dispensed at local club houses.

In 1880 the county of Kings contained 599,495 persons, already quite large for a county division, and by 1910 the population had almost tripled to 1,634,000. This incredibly rapid growth continued for two more decades. Brooklyn was 2,018,356 strong in 1920 and in 1930 the population stood at 2,560,560. (Brooklyn's population peaked in 1950 at 2,738,000.) For most of the twentieth century, Brooklyn, if a city, would have been the third or fourth largest in the nation. The speed of this growth for the first three decades and the fact that most of the new borough residents were immigrants fostered the growth and determined the form of the new Brooklyn machine. Adding to Brooklyn's suitability for "Bossism" was the fact that many of the new Brooklynites were already indoctrinated by Tammany style Democratic politics in Manhattan. A good example of this was Madison Club power broker Irwin Steingut whose father Simon had been a Jewish local "mayor" on the Lower East Side.

If we consider the population of Brooklyn and the Madison Club Assembly District, we get some indication of how the machine operated to assist the "Deprived" and "Immobile." In the early decades of the twentieth century, the main ethnic groups in the club's orbit were Irish Catholics, Italians and Jews. Each of these groups, as new immigrants, was greatly impoverished and exploited. As they improved their basic social and economic situations, with the assistance in many cases of the machine, they graduated to a higher, but still limited levels of social status and prestige. Naturally, over time, these groups also competed with one another for rewards in the political arena.

The two main religio-ethnic groups making up most of Brooklyn's increase in population from 1900 to 1930 were Italians and East European Jews. Prior to this invasion, Irish Catholics had formed the bulk of the Democratic voting population, and, long after the Irish lost their demographic hegemony in the borough, they continued to dominate in party leadership and high level patronage appointments. They were particularly at an advantage over the Italians as they controlled the Roman Catholic diocese which could have otherwise been a source for Italian power. Besides lacking an institutional base, Italians also had little in the way of ethnic solidarity and were extremely suspicious of government in general. Eastern European Jews probably had the worst experiences in their home countries with regard to government, but this also taught them the importance of concern for political matters.[14]

The machine both served the needs of the new immigrant groups and at the same time took advantage of their vulnerabilities. Merton noted that the machine realizes that voters are particular individuals who have particular problems, needs and concerns.[15] The organization then operates on this basis and tries to reach the voter face to face, or otherwise directly and not through abstract, impersonal appeals. In this way, elections are won at the small scale local level. The machine operates through the establishment and maintenance of networks of elaborate personal relations with ordinary people which tie together their needs with those of the organization. By this process "politics is transformed into personal ties."[16]

Interviews with long time Madison Club members such as ex-Mayor Abraham Beame, State Supreme Court Judge Anthony Jordan, Jr., and Speaker of the Assembly Stanley Steingut indicated that in the early years of the club it was "the place to go for help" in the community. Less able people might have gone for handouts of coal, food, or small favors, but for those with education or a business, political contacts were needed for advancement. Madison Club old-timer Abe Beame was a school teacher and a practicing accountant and Jordan's father was an Italian plumber. The different needs of each ethnic group and of particular individuals or families were dealt with by the club and it expected a return on its investment.

The Irish, Italians and Jews in the club's domain lived separately, and, in order for the boss to reach and control them, a network of smaller neighborhood and ethnic clubs were tied to the Madison Club through a series of local leaders or "Captains." In feudal terms, the boss was a king and the captains were his vassals. In Brooklyn, the Irish were on the verge of "respectability"; Jews were seeking occupational, business, and professional access; and Italians, for the most part, were seeking opportunities in the skilled and semi-skilled trades. All three groups faced various obstacles and different degrees of discrimination.

The Madison Club had many captains and lieutenants to connect itself to the communities. For example, eighty percent of the "Pig Town" section of the district was Italian and ninety percent of them were registered to vote for McCooey's choices. The captains and club members registered the voters, helped them through the required literacy tests, and they also helped them to vote the "right way." If necessary, captains and lieutenants brought people to the polls or reminded them of their obligations by personal visits on election day after checking the voter lists to see who had not shown up. The club in those days had so much power and control of the polling places and booths that they could even "vote" dead people if they wished. Some report that the Holy Cross Cemetery was one of the best political districts. In return for voting, people received work and help with their many problems, such as citizenship for relatives, housing, health care, legal advice and assistance, and education. The old clubs were very much social service centers as well as meeting places for business and other contacts.

Merton describes the precinct captain in this way; "The precinct captain must be a friend to every man, assuming if he does not feel sympathy with the unfortunate, and utilizing in his good works the resources which the boss puts at this disposal."[17] The captain fulfills the function of humanizing and personalizing all manner of assistance in our impersonal society.[18] The way help is provided is often as important as the service itself. Given the traditional suspicion of Southern Italians toward government, in Pig Town, a local friend or relative was the best vehicle for contact. In fact, ethnic neighborhood political obligations are easily transformed into family ones and reach across generations. Among the more religious Irish and Jews, churches and synagogues, rabbis and priests, were appropriate vehicles for contacting the various communities.

After the turn of the century, public agencies and private philanthropies reached into lower class ethnic communities through settlement houses, community centers, schools and clinics. But most local people still preferred the more personal and less "official" contact at the club or the visit of a club worker which allowed them to feel less shame and where workers were less constrained by rigid rules and regulations regarding such things as eligibility requirements for assistance.[19] In later years, political club houses would begin to refer constituents to public and private agencies where the organization had its own contacts and established ties. This enabled them to continue taking credit for help.

Organizations like the Madison Club had long histories of service to the community prior to the establishment of public programs. The needs of unique communities are seldom exactly translated to an agency's standards and operating procedures. Community needs also change more quickly than the policies of public agencies creating a "lag," or gap that can be filled. The machine fills the void because of its organic relationship to the community, responds more quickly, specifically and sensitively to the day-to-day challenges and problems of individuals and groups.

Long before the Great Depression, rough times existed for the inhabitants of the multitude of "Little Italies," "Jew Towns," "Pole Towns," "Irish Shanty Towns" and other immigrant or similarly deprived commmunities in urban America. Clubs like the Madison provided local people with all forms of assistance, and naturally took advantage of their vulnerability. The way in which such services were performed is basic to the survival of machine style politics. Abraham Beame related that the Madison Club gave out Thanksgiving food baskets, turkeys for Christians on Christmas, and similar kosher food to Jewish constituents on Passover. In those days, the club tradition was for the needy to come to the headquarters and be handed their gifts in large brown bags by Boss McCooey himself. It is clear that the recipient could not forget where the gift came from. Those who couldn't make it on their own to the club received a visit from their local captain. Everything was done on a person-to-person basis. Every person who asked for and received a benefit from the club, whether it was small or large, was assumed to have made a "contract." They received something in return for something else. Most often these contracts were not explicit, only an expectation that when the time came; the *donee* would reciprocate.

The Brooklyn Democratic organizations did many other things to "humanize" politics. They ran parades, sponsored ethnic celebrations, held rallies, lit bonfires, sponsored dances and parties, and congratulated people on birthdays, weddings, births, Bar Mitzvahs, Christenings and the other meaningful personal events in the lives of constituents.

Before consolidation with New York City, Brooklyn ran its own municipal services and if one controlled the county, one controlled a vast array of patronage opportunities. Following consolidation many of the borough services continued to be controlled locally. Each reform in the city tended to centralize power in city hall. Despite this centralization, powerful county organizations still maintained their share of city-wide and in most instances, virtually complete control of local patronage. Until the New Deal, the Madison Club and McCooey had considerably more to "hand out" in the way of favors than mere bags of food for the needy.

Even after McCooey's run-in with President Roosevelt, the Madison Club received a good share of Federal patronage including WPA jobs and other handouts. The best jobs from any source, and the "no-show" jobs, as always, went to the most politically active and valuable. "Reform" and civil service requirements put somewhat of a damper on the Madison Club, but through its network of satellites and "alumni" already placed in important city and state positions it continued in its central role in county politics and patronage. The major effect of political changes was that the most glaring abuses were diminished and people often had to be more "qualified" for the jobs, services and other assistance they might receive than before. The Democratic County Organization's control over the Office of the Borough President continued to be of especially great patronage value until later city charter revisions. This executive office wielded great power in making contracts for such lucrative activities as construction and maintenance projects for water supply and sewers, schools, highways, and other services which were, at that time, decentralized by borough.

## The Machine Adapts to Change

Although the emphasis in most analyses of the machine is on the role that it plays in meeting the unmet needs of the disadvantaged, there are other groups whom the machine also serves, who are by no means "deprived." Some observers had predicted the demise of the machine because of the social and economic mobility of ethnic populations.

However, the machine can serve even advantaged populations and survive the transition from deprived to more affluent constituencies and interest groups as did the Madison Club.

In his discussion of the machine, Merton allowed for the functioning of boss-types to serve the needs of both legitimate and illegitimate business enterprise.[20] Despite *laissez-faire* ideology, American government at all levels has been highly involved both directly and indirectly in individual and collective economic pursuits. One argument has been presented that the decline of the machine came about as government expanded its efforts into social services and local community issues. The Madison Club history shows however that as government expanded into the areas served by the machine it eventually adapted to the new situation by infiltrating and, in some cases, taking over its assumed "competitor" for local support.

Although important strategic issues such as operating policy for national, city-wide and state wide agencies are not determined at the local level, it is well to remember that the higher policy-makers are usually collections of former local politicians connected by a web of party affiliations. Therefore it may be expected that decisions made by these self-interested individuals would not result in the conscious destruction of their own personal bases of support. The change toward more government involvement in the provision of direct local services merely adds a level to machine politics and demands greater sophistication of party and elected officials who must bargain amongst themselves for part of the largesse. These larger scale activities do however decrease the apparent dependency on the locality for overall success, although one must still be re-elected to remain in the game. The increase of government activity and the centralization of authority, characteristic of the periods following the Great Depression, and the "professionalization" of social services required that the semi-feudal machine also adopt a more bureaucratic form.

Even before the great transformation of the New Deal, machines served the function of providing political privileges and favoritism which entailed the immediate economic gain for entities such as public utilities, franchises and other organizations which were either regulated by government or could benefit or suffer because of government actions. For example, local government has long been involved in the granting of concessions, allocating public funds for construction, ruling on zoning variances, building public facilities such as schools and hospitals, issuing licenses and setting fees. Not to be forgotten, government offers jobs and positions of influence and prestige to aspiring individuals. Special attention must also be paid to the areas of law enforcement and ajudication. Political connections appear to be helpful in obtaining favorable court rulings where discretion is allowed. Lawyers seek judgeships, clerkships and opportunities to serve as public prosecutors. All these opportunities provide for both legitimate and illegitmate personal gain. The laws themselves and their interpretation are the focus of interest group attention. Civil and Surrogates Court positions are highly desirable as are the custodianships, receiverships and collections that are effected. City Marshalls, auctioneers and others can also benefit from court proceedings. In other words, even after "reform," there remain significant rewards to distribute through the political system. Furthermore, it must be noted that the judicial-political system has the power to investigate and to prosecute as well as ignore and conceal. Each positive sanction has a corresponding negative sanction; most simply, in the denial of the "favor."

Political opportunities for "favors" continued in the

form of laws governing regulated business activities, concessions, licensing, pricing regulations, tax policies, and franchising. The machine cannot survive and prosper based on the small number of votes of individuals and special interests of those who benefit by favors, but it can enjoy the financial and other supports that such entities can more easily provide such as campaign contributions and the use of resources. More directly, people involved in politics are also concerned with their economic self-interest and can individually benefit in the return of favors-- a kind of reverse patronage.

Business "arrangements" between politicians and private enterprises have a long history in American urban politics, not all of which has been seen as illegitimate. For example, "Good Government" political types have usually been business people who seek control of local government to better represent their economic interests. This is especially true of the legal professions, banking, finance, insurance, industry, real estate and transportation areas in New York.

Very little of this considerable interaction between business and politics is illegal or even unethical, but it does make for weaknesses in the operation of government for the general public interest. Whether one refers to this activity as graft, corruption, "dirty" campaign contributions, conflict of, or mutual interests, it has been the "grease" that makes the politic wheels turn more quickly and efficiently. Private business is not the only player in this influence game. Since the 1920's unions and professional associations have also been active participants in the politics of New York. It is easy to see, for example, why municipal workers and their organizations would be especially concerned with who is elected. Despite attempts on the part of private industry and the Republican Party to limit their influence, unions of public and private sector workers provide a great deal of support for the operations of the Democratic Party in New York.

## The Iron Law of Political Survival

Although Merton and others have strongly argued that government often makes the legitimate demands of subgroups difficult to meet, and that the machine serves the function of making life easier for them, they tend to ignore the obverse. That is; the machine can also create problems for subgroups. This can be done as a punishment, as an inducement or as a threat. The machine in effect can create or maintain the need for its services. We must not forget that the machine reasons, correctly or incorrectly, what is in its own best interest. A sociological axiom is that organizations, once established, attempt to maintain themselves. The mere change in the socio-economic character of the American urban population did not guarantee that the urban political boss system would simply roll over and die. The machine was in position to be *against* streamlining bureaucratic mechanisms and increasing the competence and efficiency of government that would diminish the need for their services. They were also in position to insure that the providers of new services were either themselves, in new guises, or their friends.

In any case, the new providers of social services, for example, had to go through the existing political structure for legitimation and funds. Naturally, such help was contingent upon "playing the same old game of politics," and the "good guys" themselves were not immune to political necessity. One might say in New York that after reform, the Tammany Tiger didn't loose its stripes; it merely changed them to better match the times. The smoke-filled room where political decisions were made was replaced by a corporate board room. Irwin Steingut bore little resemblance to John McCooey, and Irwin's son Stanley even less so. For the Madison Club and other machine type organizations, as the stakes and interactions in the political arena were raised to higher levels, they slowly became more distant from the local communities that had made it possible for them to stay in the game.

## The Machine and Illegitimate Business

Besides the political machine, another, closely related route for the advancement of the "Deprived" and "Immobile" was organized crime. It is natural that these phenomena would bear some relationship to one another. They both stem from the same causes and rely on the same conditions for continuity. Crime and politics can benefit each other by cooperation, if not collusion. Merton noted: "Within this context, even the corrupt political machine and the racket represent the triumph of amoral intelligence over morally prescribed failure when the channels of vertical mobility are closed or narrowed in a society which places a higher premium on economic affluence, (power) and social ascent for all its members."[21]

In William F. Whyte's classic study of "Cornerville;" a neighborhood in Boston's North End during the Depression which was similar to those in the Madison Club district, the rackets and politics were given extensive treatment. To him they were the major local institutions which connected the "Big Shots" to the little people in the area and served as a connection between the disadvantaged community and the society at large.[22] Whyte said that; "The sociologist who dismisses racket and political organizations as deviations from desirable standards. . . thereby neglects some of the major elements of slum life." He argued that sociologists studying slums did not recognize the functions these organizations performed for their members and the local community.[23]

In discussing the connection between Italian organized crime and machine politics, Daniel Bell noted that support from racketeers helped win "a political voice for Italians in the power structure of the urban political machines...well illustrated by the career of (Frank) Costello and his emergence as a political power in New York."[24] From a comparative ethnicity perspective, Bell stated that "men of Italian origin appeared in most of the leading roles in the high drama of gambling and mobs, just as twenty years ago East European Jews were the most prominent figures in organized crime, and before that individuals of Irish descent were similarly prominent."[25]

Because of the romanticism and ethnic sensitivity associated with studies of American ethnic groups, although we recognize the fact that the Irish-Catholics and later immigrants had great difficulty initially finding places in our urban social and political structures, the tendency is for ethnic scholars to downplay the illegitimate routes by which upward mobiliy was attained. It is obvious that despised immigrants and their children could not have achieved their present level of social status without gaining control or substantial influence in the urban machines of American cities.[26] Similarly, the rackets provided otherwise unavailable opportunities for social mobility and were closely allied to machine organizations as noted by Whyte and many others.[27] The conditions which cause the rise of political machines and the rackets are the same and it should not be surprising or embarrassing that by their concomitance and cooperation each has served the interests of the other.

In many respects illegitimate businesses and legitimate businesses operate the same way. They have products, services, markets, competition, etc., and they need favors which are legal and/or illegal. Both make contributions to maintaining the machine and both need its protection. Merton noted that both types of business are identical in the: market demand for goods and services; the concern for maximizing gains from their enterprise; the need to influence control of government which might otherwise interfere, and the need for an efficient and powerful centralized agency to provide a liaison between business and government.[28] As for reforming the urban political environment, he warned that unless alternate legitimate structures and opportunites are provided, machines and rackets will survive, as in fact they have.

Although it would be next to impossible to accurately document specific relationships, if they existed, between the Madison Club in its early decades and, as Whyte would call organized crime, the "Rackets," one can be reasonably certain that some relations did in fact exist. Brooklyn was the site for large scale organized crime activities in vice such as gambling and, during Prohibition, bootlegging and illicit alcohol related enterprises. These operations require political cooperation and for a long period of time, the Madison Club was the fulcrum of political leverage. In general, however, the Madison Club and its leaders were seen by most political commentators as relatively "clean" for political bosses. Most accusations of corruption at or through the club focused more on shady legitimate business deals than on relations with stereotypical organized criminals. For example in the 1920s and 30s McCooey was accused of "cozy" relationships with Brooklyn realtors with reference to property condemnations and school construction.[29]

There were also several investigations into the finances of his successor, Irwin Steingut.[30] In discussions with old time club members, references were casually made to local bookmakers, and at least one club member ran a speakeasy during prohibition which was regularly frequented by politicians. These activities, it must be remembered, were viewed by local residents as a "natural" part of the community life of the time. During the period of Madison Club dominance in Brooklyn the less palatable forms of racketeering were much in evidence such as "Murder Incorporated" in East New York and the notorious Brooklyn waterfront groups who dealt in illegal alcohol, drugs, extortion and prostituion. In fact, the Madison Club, from McCooey through Stanley Steingut, who led the club decades later, was seen as in the forefront of reform in these areas of corruption. It cannot be said, however, that it was without blemish. Political corruption in Brooklyn, *vis a vis* organized crime, was at its peak during Prohibition. Its repeal in 1933 and the initiation of the New Deal coincided with the end of the old style monolithic Brooklyn machine.

Merton argued that what he thought was the "end" of the urban political machine was not so much due to the efforts of reformers as it was a consequence of the changing structure of society. The needs of subgroups in society began to be met by alternative, legitimate structures such as the "welfare state" and increased opportunity for social and economic mobility of disadvantaged populations.[31] Concluding his discussion on the machine and the rackets, Merton quotes from Daniel Bell:"But big, organized city crime, as we have known it for the past seventy-five years, was based on more than these universal motives. It was based on characteristics of the American economy, American ethnic groups, and American politics. The changes in all these areas means that it too, in the form we have known it, is at an end."[32]

The following chapters will show how wrong both Merton and Bell were, as the borough-wide Brooklyn machine and the Madison Club responded to these changes with varying degrees of success. Despite the fact that their hopeful prognoses were wrong, the theoretical approach they employed--structural-functionalism--continues to have a great deal of explanatory, if not predictive value to social scientists who wish to study urban political systems.

## Footnotes

1. Robert K. Merton, *Social Theory and Social Structure*. Glencoe: The Free Press, 1967, pp. 125-36.
2. *Ibid.*, p.136.
3. Richard Hofstadter, *The Age of Reform*. New York: Vintage Books, 1955, p. 9.
4. *Ibid.* p. 9.
5. *Ibid.* p. 9.
6. Merton, *Op. Cit.*, p. 125.
7. *Ibid.* p. 126.
8. *Ibid.* p. 126.
9. *Ibid.* p. 126.
10. *Ibid.* p.127.
11. David Ment, *The Shaping of a City: A Brief History of Brooklyn*. Brooklyn: Brooklyn Educational and Cultural Alliance, 1979, p. 64.
12. *The Brooklyn Eagle*, October 5, 1932.
13. *The Brooklyn Eagle*. October 7, 1932.
14. See: "The Missed Step: Italian Americans and Brooklyn Politics," in Francis X. Femminella (ed.) *Italians and Irish In America*. Staten Island, New York: American Italian Historical Association, pp. 187-198.
15. Merton, *Op. Cit.*, p. 128.
16. *Ibid.* p.128.
17. *Ibid.* p.129.
18. *Ibid.* p.128.
19. *Ibid.* p. 129.
20. *Ibid.* p. 132.
21. *Ibid.* p. 131.
22. William F. Whyte, *Street Corner Society*, Chicago: University of Chicago Press, 1943.
23. W.F. Whyte, *American Sociological Review 8*, pp. 34-39.
24. Daniel Bell, "Crime as an American Way of Life," *The Antioch Review*, Summer, 1953, p. 147.
25. *Ibid.*, pp. 150-151.
26. Merton, *Op. Cit.*, p.132.
27. See for example, Irving Howe, *World of Our Fathers*. New York: Harcourt, Brace and Janovich, 1976, and Stephen Birmingham, *The Rest of Us: The Rise of America's Eastern European Jews*. Boston: Little, Brown and Company, 1984.

28. Merton. *Op. Cit.*, p. 134.
29. *The Brooklyn Eagle.* February 23, 1926, July 1, 1930, September 2, 1930, September 4, 1930, July 30, 1931, October 29, 1931, February 2, 1932.
30. *The New York Times.* January 27, 1932, December 4, 1942, *The Brooklyn Eagle,* May 22, 1941, December 3, 1942.
31. Merton, *Op. Cit.*, p. 247.
32. Bell, *Op. Cit.*, p. 154.

# John H. McCooey and the
# Early Years of the Madison Club

Out of necessity, colorful and controversial Brooklyn Boss John H. McCooey was an independent and ambitious man from his earliest years. Born in Williamsburg, Brooklyn's Irish ghetto in 1864, he was the oldest of six children. After living in Brooklyn for several years, the McCooeys moved out of the state. While John was still a teenager, his father died and he had to contribute to the family's support. When McCooey finally returned to Brooklyn as an adult, it was to the same Irish ghetto he left. There he was to plant the political seeds needed for the growth of what was to become the Kings County Democratic Party machine's most powerful local unit, the Madison Club.

At the age of twenty-four, McCooey entered the postal service where he chose his friends wisely and established key friendships. One life-long friendship that he was to establish during this time was with the politically ambitious John Hylan, who later became Mayor of New York City. While his political skills were being honed, McCooey became secretary and later president of the New York City Civil Service Commission from 1899 to 1903.

Brooklyn's County leader Hugh McLaughlin, the first to have the label "Boss" bestowed upon him, retired from politics in 1904.[1] Powerful New York County leader Charles F. Murphy, the man considered to be the leader of Tammany Hall of New York City, had tried to his extend his power over the newly absorbed borough in the Greater City of New York. He was not completely successful because Brooklyn had been an independent city before the merger and was not so docile. McLaughlin's absence now created a power vacuum and an opportunity for someone to assume the leadership for the borough. McCooey founded the Madison Club in 1905 because he saw there was an opportunity for himself and that one way to gain power was to establish his own local political base.[2] A neighborhood political club would serve this purpose very well.

The Madison Democratic Club of Brooklyn was the brainchild of John H. McCooey and four other charter members, Henry J. Dougherty, Ernest Eggert, Andrew T. Sullivan and William L. Collins.[3] After the establishment of the Madison Club in 1905, McCooey continued his upward climb serving as Deputy Comptroller of New York City from 1906 to 1909, when he was finally able to establish control of Kings County.[4] As a member of the Municipal Club, the Brooklyn Club, the Kings County Democratic Club and of course the Madison Club he made the all-important political contacts that were needed to build his power base. He cultivated ethnic and religious allegiances as a member of the Friendly Sons of Saint Patrick and as president of the Emerald Society, two organizations that were the meeting grounds for important and wealthy Irish-Catholics.[5]

It had become a pattern after 1900, that Irish party leaders were frequently recent arrivals to Brooklyn, coming from cities like Philadelphia along the Eastern seaboard, and not from overseas. McCooey, and later Frank V. Kelly, his successor, came from outside New York State as adults to start their political careers.[6] Like the others, McCooey wisely chose an area that was known for its Irish constituency to make his bid for political power.

The first home of the Madison Club was located at 1519 Pacific Street and McCooey established his residence close by at 1426 Pacific Street. From this time forward, as the 18th Assembly District shifted as a result of rezoning, he would move so that he remained within the district and not very far from the clubhouse itself. In this way his contact and control could be more easily maintained. McCooey felt at home in these kinds of ethnic neighborhoods and the environment, in turn, enhanced his opportunities for political ascendancy.

Of course McCooey's power was not based merely on the number of Irishmen he came into contact with. Although the Irish began to decline as a proportion of Brooklyn's population during the first third of this century their power in Kings County actually increased. For example, while McCooey rose in power from 1910 to 1930 the number of Irish Foreign-born decreased from just over 70,000 to a little more than 45,000. During the same period, Italians and Russians (usually given as an indicator of Jewish population growth) almost doubled.[7] This situation was not peculiar to the Irish as the pattern in American cities has been that dominant ethnic groups hold power long after their members are no longer a majority.

## Political Philosophies

McCooey was to base the philosophy for his club upon the Tammany Hall model. No doubt he had met George Washington Plunkitt, the almost mythic member of Tammany Hall, a district leader, and strong advocate of machine politics. Plunkitt was very bold in stating his concept of the "ideal" politician. He was one who did not practice dishonest graft, because "there is so much honest graft lyin' around." For Plunkitt, honest graft meant using knowledge to make a profit: "I'm tipped off say, that they're going to lay out a new park at a certain place...I go to that place and buy up all the land I can in the neighborhood...I seen my opportunities and I took 'em."[8] It was a disgrace to him for a person to work for the party and not have a job after the party won: "There's no crime so mean as ingratitude in politics."[9]

The way to control the vote, Plunkitt held, was by helping people in distress. He said the party had to accommodate both Jews and Christians alike. He felt he had a moral right to take from the public pie because he helped unfortunate people who were ignored by those in office. Plunkitt agreed with Lincoln Steffens in that, "Philadelphia, ruled almost entirely by Americans, was more corrupt than New York, where the Irish do almost all the governin'...The Irish was born to rule."[10] Finally, what further vindication of the boss-system was needed then to see the gratefulness of the Irish who had a job soon after they arrived. Tammany, for Plunkitt, was the most perfect political machine on earth.[11] McCooey easily slipped into this tradition of urban Irish politics.

Long after McCooey had risen to the exalted position of Brooklyn Boss, New York Times reporter S. J. Wolfe was able to get an interview with him, which was an extremely rare event. McCooey told Wolfe: "Man is a gregarious animal and he can't expect to live by himself and get on. He must help others and others in turn will help him."[12] The Democratic Party, McCooey maintained; "... does more than look after the political welfare of the community, it goes to the root and looks after the material welfare of the individual."[13] McCooey's approach was typical of the kind of personal touch that the Irish brought into politics. Wolfe posed the question to McCooey as to whether or not these times called for new leadership. McCooey responded, "The old personal contact that the leader enjoyed with his constituents has to some extent been lessened by the telephone. A number of friends telephoned me this morning, when years ago they probably would have dropped in to see me. But again taxis and the subways have brought people closer together so that in many ways one thing counterbalances another."[14] For McCooey, the days before all this technology had their advantages in that talented people were sponsored and promoted by others: "Of course, those were the days before the efficiency craze had struck us. People were regarded as human beings and not machines."[15] The Brooklyn boss sought to maintain the human element in politics through personal contact. To him, friendly relations were crucial to success. Wolfe said that McCooey had been a dean of politics. "That open door is the secret of his political success, it is never closed; everyday he is in that room [at the clubhouse] to see all comers and to permit all comers to see him."[16] Wolfe's impression was that McCooey was a sentimental, sincere man, who inspired one's confidence instinctively and read responses of human beings well.[17] David F. Soden, who had been a very close associate of McCooey, recollected that McCooey's success was due to many things but most often to his widespread geniality and thoughtful philanthrophy.[18] People lined up by the dozens to see McCooey. From Hollywood's standards at least, he would indeed become Brooklyn's *Last Hurrah!*[19]

## McCooey's Rise

Including McCooey's thirty year reign as county boss, Brooklyn's Democratic Party produced only three leaders between the years of 1867 and 1934. This was a tradition of stability which suggests that local organizational structure was quite impervious to the political system-at-large and the enormous changes that were taking place between the Civil War and the Great Depression.

Within the first years of its founding, the membership of the Madison Democratic Club grew quickly to over a thousand people.[20] The club was off to a good start but it took McCooey a number of years to overcome several obstacles in order to consolidate his power base.[21] One major problem for McCooey was the dominance of the Brooklyn organization by upstate forces led by State Senator Patrick M. McCarran. In 1905, *The Brooklyn Citizen* reported that Kings County was like a personal possession of Senator McCarran and the Democratic County Committee. McCarran, borough leaders contended, did not listen to their grievances and they called for a new county organization.[22] Against McCarran and his entrenched "mandarins," McCooey had to move cautiously. In addition, New York County was dominated by the powerful Tammany Hall leader Charles F. Murphy who had his eye on extending his control over the Brooklyn machine.[23] Generally the Democratic tickets downstate were the result of an agreement between Murphy and McCarran. But Murphy was very ambitious and resented the influence of the uptate politicians. He knew if he could absorb Kings County, McCarran's power over him would be drastically reduced. Murphy's aspirations made McCooey's task of establishing a power base all the more difficult.

Up to this time, State Senator Patrick M. McCarran had vigorously fought with his Brooklyn opponents. In the face of Murphy's grab for power, he held out an olive branch to his foes. Early in 1909, the Brooklyn's County Committee named five of its members to try to bring about harmony in the Democratic Party. McCarran named

Brooklyn leader Henry Hesterberg from the 18th Assembly District to speak for him on what came to be known as the Harmony Committee. The choice of Hesterberg was no accident since the base of the Madison Club was in the 18th district and Hesterberg was a powerful ally of McCooey. McCarran was trying to pull the followers of McCooey and Tammany over to his side as he realized that he had to make some concessions.[24]

Four months later, in May of 1909, the clans of the Democratic Party were still at war. The Harmony Committee, recommended "that a provisional committee be appointed to exercise power and advisory functions. This committee is to propose candidates to various nominating conventions after listening to the wishes of the delegates."[25] Objections were raised against the committee's authority to call caucuses and to make their will binding on the caucuses. Attempts to bring about a peace movement were all but shattered.

Brooklyn leaders James P. Sinnott and Thomas F. Byrnes refused to agree to a peace program. Byrnes said McCarran wanted to make "wooden men" of the delegates to conventions and force his views on them. This would be a strong argument in favor of the direct primaries that New York Governor Charles Evans Hughes had proposed. Naturally, Tammany Hall was strongly opposing the growing call for reform proposed by advocates of good government for direct primaries wherein the nominating process would be wrested from the hands of the machine.[26] Sinnott and Byrnes believed that the power of the Harmony Committee to call caucuses and make them binding would not help downstate control and would play right into the hands of the dreaded Progressives.

As the Fall, 1909 elections approached, and the Democrats became increasingly anxious about all the infighting, Senator McCarran died. Many expected a major political battle in Kings County after McCarran's death, but McCooey had things well under control and took charge of the Democratic organization. While there was no great enthusiasm for McCooey in the Brooklyn machine, he had managed to survive six years of factional political warfare. He pledged political autonomy for Brooklyn and warned Tammany about "crossing the bridge" into Brooklyn. The powerful Executive Committee of the county selected him, and he remained its Chairman until his death in 1934.[27]

McCooey's troubles did not end with his election, he still had to come to terms with Charles Murphy, leader of New York County and Tammany Hall. Traditionally, New York County, going back to the days of William Tweed, was the base for Tammany Hall. Brooklyn was an independent city with a history and prominence of its own until 1898, when it became incorporated into New York. It had had its own indigenous Tammany-style politicians, like Brooklyn Boss Hugh McLaughlin, who controlled the Democratic political machine from 1857 to 1904, and who had amassed a fortune in Brooklyn real estate.[28] Soon after the Civil War Brooklyn's city fathers had planned to link New York City (Manhattan Island) and Brooklyn, first by a great bridge, and then politically. At the same time it was hoped by the Tammany men on the other side of the East River in Manhattan, that the Brooklyn's large voting bloc help would tip the political scale in favor of downstate Democratic machine-men over the Republican upstaters. Brooklyn Democrats, however, had a tradition of being independent, and McCooey wanted to preserve some of that distance from the New York County group in order to run his own show.

## Population and Power

At the turn of the century, Brooklyn had become a huge collection of flourishing ethnic communities. The census reading of the borough in 1900 showed a population of 1,166,582. Five years later, *The Brooklyn Citizen* commented on the large growth of population in the borough, estimating the population at a million and a half. It further projected that by 1915, Brooklyn would be the most populous borough in the city.[29] Over in Manhattan, Tammany Hall leader Charles Murphy understood the population projections and feared Brooklyn's potential voting strength.

Population figures for 1920 and 1930 show the extraordinary growth of Kings and Queens Counties in the third decade of the century. This growth marked the shift of dominance, in voting strength, from New York County to Kings County. Kings County's population increased from 2,018,356 in 1920 to 2,569,401 in 1930, while that of New York County, due to the change in the recording of The Bronx' population, decreased from 2,284,103 to 1,867,312. In approximately the same period, Queens County's rate of growth was five times that of Kings', but far behind it in terms of population and potential voting strength.

Party registration and voting data for New York City by county from 1900 to 1935 shows the growth of political power wielded by McCooey during his reign. Presented by five-year periods, Democratic Party enrollment in Kings County increased over Republican enrollment in all periods noted except for 1920 when the county swung to the right. The figures also demonstrate the emergence of Kings over the other counties as the stronghold of registered Democrats. In 1900, Kings had 34% of all registered Democrats in the city. The percentage of Democrats varies only 2% during these years, reaching 36% in 1935. Despite the small variation in percentage, Brooklyn's strength relative to New York County voting dominance tipped in the former's favor by 1925. It was to McCooey's and the Madison Club's credit that Brooklyn was turned into a Democratic stronghold.

Surprisingly, until 1920 in the 18th Assembly District, where the Madison Club was located, more voters were affiliated with the Republican than with the Democratic Party. But from 1925 on the district shows that an overwhelming number of voters chose to be associated with the Democratic Party. In this regard the district followed a change in voter registration similar to what was transpiring throughout the borough.[30]

Publicly, McCooey disavowed ties with Tammany Hall, warning "the Tiger not to cross the Bridge," quoting a phrase Senator McCarran had used to refer to Tammany's attempts to rule Brooklyn. Yet, The New York Times observed in 1925 that McCooey played golf regularly with Tammany leaders Charles Murphy and George Olvany. The needs of New York and Kings Counties were not so disparate that they would not want to work together. The Times noted: "It's time also that the very growth of Brooklyn and its immense and expanding area of that part of the city make it conscious of its relations to the State and the legislation passed in Albany."[31] McCooey, the pragmatist and accommodator, knew this and played ball not only with the Manhattan bosses but with the forces upstate.

Two months after this editorial appeared, McCooey was formally initiated into the Tammany Society.[32] This organization was originally a social, benevolent and patriotic group, but now was allying itself with the Tammany political organization. The Brooklyn organization was very pleased with how McCooey had increased party power during his tenure. During his initial years as county leader, Brooklyn had frequently gone Republican. But under his leadership, Brooklyn became as solidly Democratic as the other boroughs of New York City.[33] Tammany paid tribute to McCooey's organizational triumphs at a banquet on April 15, 1928, celebrating his nineteen years as Chairman of the Kings County Executive Committee and leader of the Brooklyn Democratic party.[34]

It was always in the best interest of both Murphy and McCooey to end the power struggle and close party ranks. In 1933, the *New York Post*, regarding McCooey, observed: "In his time he has been pro-Roosevelt, pro-Walker, pro-Olvany, pro-Curry. It is all the same to Uncle John if he's on top. He finds no virtue in lost causes."[35] According to Aaron Jacob, a close associate of McCooey at the Madison Club, the Brooklyn leader would call his lieutenants together and ask "What will benefit us the most?"[36] McCooey saw no profit in fighting if he could avoid it. He established a model for later clubs and county leaders. He ran the Madison Club as a pragmatist. He wanted independent power, but also wanted to survive. Thus he was a consumate accommodator, giving something if there was something in it for him. Despite his comments to the contrary, he obviously had recognized Murphy's leadership of Tammany Hall in the City and State. Making peace with Murphy also meant that McCooey would remain boss and share in city-wide patronage in the form of jobs, contracts and kickbacks.

## The Madison Club Expands Its Power

McCooey built the Madison Club and his Brooklyn machine into a powerful entity. Over his thirty-year reign as county boss, he was able to sustain support and consistently get out the vote. McCooey distributed power to his captains and respected their judgment. They were McCooey's crucial links between the voters and the organization. It was they who selected the location of polling places which would produce the most votes for their candidates. They also selected those in their districts who would receive financial and other aid from the club such as food, and coal. Captains spoke on behalf of the voters who needed a favor from McCooey.[37] McCooey, however, reserved the right to appoint or remove his leaders, summarily if necessary. In this way, McCooey kept a tight grip on his assembly district.

One of the most important political mechanisms were "satellite" clubs which were formed to extend the control of the Madison Club over the whole county.[38] Newly arrived immigrants, and others who had moved to Brooklyn, were welcomed into the Democratic fold at these local ethnically-based social organizations which were tied into the machine in various ways.

One arm of the Madison Club which helped McCooey sustain his power extended into the southern area of Crown Heights known as "Pigtown." Established there in the populous 18th A.D., the Three Leaf Club, later known as the Three Leaf Democratic Group, aided newly arrived immigrants and was nourished by the power of the machine. Through this structural arrangement the disenfranchised entered the political system.[39]

The name "Pigtown" for the community was somewhat of a misnomer; former residents and the *Brooklyn Eagle* recall that there were "more goats than pigs" in the neighborhood, but the name gave a more accurate sense of the deplorable health conditions in the area.[40] When in 1906, a riot broke out between the Italian community and the authorities because a patrolman tried to apprehend an Italian who was dumping "a cartload of dirt on a public highway."[41] Other Italians came to their countryman's aid, led by Antonio Pope, the acknowledged "mayor" of the neighborhood.[42] Pope, had "for years been employed as a special officer for the section," and worked with authorities, as did dozens of other ethnic mayors throughout New York City, to keep order in their ghettos.[43] Generally, Pope was heeded but he obviously was not successful in keeping sanitary conditions acceptable to the city authorities.

One Italian resident still living in the Wingate section of Brooklyn's Crown Heights in 1987, recalled that many of the Italians had small farms in the area where chickens and other fowl roamed about freely with the goats and pigs. At the time, local streets were unpaved and there were also many vacant lots. After a heavy rain or snow, he said, he would have to put on his hip boots in order to walk, laboriously, from one place to another.[44] It would be at least a generation before Pigtown improved its image in the minds of outsiders. The community attempted to replace the pejorative "Pigtown" label with "Crown Slope," then the name of the southern most part of Crown Heights.

In addition to its unsanitary conditions, the district had also been stigmatized by a nearby penitentiary, but by 1921, the prison was gone along with the goats. Brooklyn real estate developers "discovered" the area and a large number of substantial homes with rear garages appeared, indicating prosperity had come to the ghetto. In 1924, a reporter for the Brooklyn Eagle, John H. McCandless, wrote of the area: "It looks as if the Pigtown of 1916 is doomed in a few years to merge itself into the surrounding middle-class neighborhood and be transformed into what perhaps may by described as a more tidy and respectable, if less interesting, Flatbush home section."[45] More densely populated now, Pigtown was ripe for political absorption by the Madison Club which up until had generally ignored it.

The story of how Pigtown became tied to the Madison Club is interesting. It seems that on one Sunday in 1924 John H. McCooey urgently needed a plumber and could not get his usual Irish plumber. He then called upon the services of Anthony Jordan, Sr., who had established a plumbing business in the area, to do the job. McCooey was so impressed with Jordan that he asked him to act as liaison to the Italians in Pigtown.[46] Anthony Jordan, Sr., ("Pappa" Jordan), an active member of the Three Leaf Club became captain of Pigtown in 1925. An important attraction for the members of the club and the community in the early days was the promise of getting jobs through the Madison Club.[47] It was also expected that Jordan would help fix tickets for traffic and other municipal violations and aided the residents with their other legal problems. Being literate and bilingual he was especially effective, and his role in the Madison Club made him feel part of the whole political machine: he rubbed elbows with the politically prominent, and personally knew all the commissioners in the city. Like other ethnic leaders, Jordan would try to use his position as a launching platform for his family's upward mobility.[48]

After the repeal of Prohibition in 1933, Jordan "officially" opened his bar and grill in Crown Slope and frequently held parties before and after elections. Besides McCooey, many of the prominent-to-be's frequented Jordan's place such as Mayor Abe Beame, Judge Leon Healy, Judge Nat Sobel, and Judge Murray Feiden. The bar was a social and political center for the area where candidates would come to discuss politics and sometimes seek Jordan's advice. The establishment was also a frequent haunt of the Brooklyn Dodgers baseball team which played at nearby Ebbets Field.

Pappa Jordan's children recall how their father, to keep politically up-to-date, was frequently on the phone with McCooey, and, in later years, with district leaders Irwin and Stanley Steingut.[49] As a neighborhood captain, Jordan would engage people in the Pigtown neighborhood and go from door to door, as he did, to get out the vote. One of

Jordan's helpers recalls that they would tell people which Democratic candidate to vote for on election day. They would rally to get the people out, but this was no small task. Many of the Italians in the neighborhood would not readily got to the polls. In some cases Jordan would supply car service for anyone who needed transportation and make sure that they voted. Local politics was a family as well as an ethnic pastime. All the Jordan children can recall their participation from adults helping turn out the vote at the polls to youngsters standing on shoulders to hang political posters.[50] It was with these personal attachments and methods that McCooey (and later Irwin Steingut) held absolute control.

Under McCooey, Irish style machine politics was raised to an art form. Through the Madison Club, the machine served the purpose not only in extending a warm hand to the Irish but also to other immigrant groups coming into Brooklyn. Because many thought of the newcomers as "riffraff," and regular political channels could not or would not serve their needs, the Madison Club always had a line of people waiting to gain a favor.[51] McCooey made governmental services and authorities accessible to the so-called "riffraff" of the big, congested city. It is said that McCooey sometimes saw as many as two hundred people a day. His ready availability and the immediate help he offered was what made him so effective as a leader.

## The Power of the Club Expands Beyond Brooklyn

McCooey's machine and the Madison Club made their power felt throughout the state, and as far as Washington D.C.. Franklin Delano Roosevelt had made his appearance on the political scene in New York when he was elected State Senator from Dutchess County in 1910. For the next several years Roosevelt was at odds with Tammany Hall of

New York City and spoke out against certain political practices. President Woodrow Wilson, however, having taken Roosevelt under his wing, advised him against this: "Use as much influence as possible but say as little as possible."[52] Wilson was speaking from experience and on the advice of Joseph Tumulty, his long-time friend and confidant. Tumulty, who advised Wilson on New York politics, was afraid that the Republicans would sweep New York after the successful impeachment of Democratic Governor of New York State William Sulzer in 1913.[53]

Tumulty saw no chance for Progressive reformers like Roosevelt to unseat Tammany and, therefore, did not want to alienate the local bosses. He did however, find that the New York machines were amenable to concessions; Charles Murphy and McCooey were "willing to adopt pro-Wilson candidates in their organizations in return for a share of patronage and a guarantee of administration neutrality in local affairs."[54] Wilson, like many high-level officials in the American system, knew he had to cooperate with local politicians who sometimes operated on the fringe of the law in order to sustain their own local political bases. Agreements were usually negotiated through Wilson's aides so that he appeared untainted by contact with the bosses lest he lose his "good government" supporters. Wilson pretended not to see all this, but nonetheless continued to dole out patronage to Tammanyites and Madison Club members.[55]

Apparently, Wilson's advice came too late because Roosevelt, a United States Senatorial candidate in the 1914 Democratic primaries, took a trouncing. The machine candidate, James W. Gerard, crushed Roosevelt throughout the state, 210,765 to 76,888. Results in the city showed Gerard led Roosevelt 87,404 to 23,244; but most overwhelming were the results recorded in Kings County, where Gerard bested Roosevelt by a margin of almost four to one (31,910 to 8,762).[56] During the following year, Roosevelt was willing to live and let live, and in his position as Assistant Secretary of the Navy continued to offer patronage in the form of jobs to some of the very congressmen who had attacked him so bitterly the year before. He buried the hatchet with Tammany and was to tread carefully with the organization for the next twenty years.[57]

By 1932, when Roosevelt was serving his third term as Governor of New York, McCooey was at the peak of his power. McCooey, operating on a strictly *quid pro quo* basis, used his personal hegemony over the Madison Club to obtain jobs for his Brooklyn barony. Over the years, however, McCooey became more and more intractable: "He was very smooth, very arbitrary, and totally disinclined to take advice from anybody."[58] Now with 125,000 more Democrats enrolled than Tammany, he was in a position to call the shots. McCooey sought a judgeship for his son in a favorable political atmosphere, as he had the ability to call out the largest army of voters in the state for his party.

The Republicans, however, hoped to corner Roosevelt in the fall election for Governor on the corruption issue and on his cooperation with Tammany bosses. Roosevelt found himself in a "Catch-22" situation: if he cracked down on the New York and Kings County machines, he might lose election support from the organization; and if he failed to do so, he would be dubbed a Tammany power.[59] Roosevelt straddled the fence, as he so often had done, and he never allowed himself to be directly confronted in any of the investigative attacks on the machine.

Under these circumstances, a bill supporting the addition of twelve new judgeships came to Roosevelt's desk. The public was outraged. Many of the City's civic leaders warned Roosevelt that a corrupt deal was in the making.[60] Throughout 1932 the *Brooklyn Eagle* fought vigorously against the bill, urging Roosevelt to veto it. But local Democratic as well as Republican bosses backed the candidates for judgeships.[61] Roosevelt, feigning ignorance of the implications of the bill, signed it into law. John H. McCooey, Jr., thirty-one years old and having little experience, became a Justice of the Supreme Court of New York State. The power of the Madison Club and John Sr. appeared invincible.

## The "Boss of Kings" and the Spoils of Politics

For someone who had no formal education, and was never elected to any office, John H. McCooey Sr. had prospered immensely from his involvement in politics. He worked in appointed offices such as chief clerk in the court of Surrogate Frederick Ketcham. It was the prerogative of the surrogate to make the appointment of his clerks and he did not ignore the needs of the machine. Surrogate Ketcham earned $10,000 a year, and McCooey's appointment brought him $9,000 annually. In 1911, this was a large salary and it indicated the extent of McCooey's power.[62] Lawyers at the time noted that the position required legal knowledge and that McCooey, unlike his predecessor in the job, had no legal training.

Another source of income for McCooey was the favors he did for people in tight situations. On one occasion, McCooey wrote a letter for one of his constituents named Henry Holtman, stating that if Holtman transgressed the law it was done unknowingly, and he gave assurance to the authorities that the man's record was clean. McCooey asked for fifty dollars, as he was often to do, "in behalf of his constituents."[63]

Years before running for Mayor, Fiorello La Guardia publicly attacked McCooey as the "Boss of Kings" showing how members of his family lived off the public treasury. In addition to the $9,000 a year job McCooey held as Chief Clerk of the Surrogates's Court, he had his sister Margaret appointed Associate Superintendent of Schools in Brooklyn. The job paid $12,500 annually which was a great leap from her former salary of $4,750 as a school principal. Complaints were also made that she was appointed over others with greater seniority and qualifications. In 1931, the records regarding her appointment were subpoened by Sidney Handler, assistant counselor to the Hofstadter legislative committee.[64] This good-government effort was of no avail as she was reappointed in 1934 to the position for her third six-year term.

La Guardia also attacked McCooey's brother-in-law James J. Byrne, Borough President of Brooklyn where he controlled millions of dollars legislated for public works projects. La Guardia pointed out that McCooey's brother, Herbert, was a lawyer in the construction bonding business. With the assistance of "Papa McCooey" and "Uncle Jim" Byrnes, Herbert had no trouble convincing contractors who did business in the borough to place their bonds through him. LaGuardia noted that between 1926 and 1929, 868 bonding contracts were placed with Herbert McCooey in Brooklyn compared to only 100 for all other bonding companies.[65]

John McCooey, Jr. was in law practice with his brother-in-law Gardner Conray. La Guardia said the two received twenty to thirty times the normal number of referrals from the Surrogates' Courts for an individual law firm. Their appointment fees as referee or guardian ran as high as $8,000- a huge award in 1929. Their firm also worked with the Board of Standards and Appeals, which, among other things, issued garage permits in Brooklyn. Since the Irish were highly involved in the Teamsters and trucking businesses this was a gold mine for Tammany and McCooey. La Guardia said that the issuance of garage permits was "racketeering," not practicing law.[66] A number of writers of the period made serious innuendos and accusations against McCooey. In *What's the Matter with New York*, the authors implied that doing business with insurance salesman John McCooey could have its advantages: "What ambitious young contractor doing business with the City could fail to see the advantages of such useful contacts?"[67] They added that if legal propriety was overstepped, Tammany-appointed judges would come forward to defend the rights of Tammany stalwarts. McCooey sold land at inflated values and if questions on the legality of his business dealings arose, he was not fearful as he had many friends on the bench.[68]

Democrat James E. Finegan was outraged at McCooey's practices as early as 1921. He spoke out against McCooey's brand of politics and hoped to organize Democrats to oppose the Tammany men in the primaries. He also hoped to form anti-McCooey groups in each assembly district in Kings County; but he could not gain much support. In *Tammany at Bay*, Finegan noted that Tammany men had the power to vote on applications for city tax remissions and that these discussions were usually surrounded in secrecy. In one publicized instance, Coney Island resort properties were given these remissions. It "just happened" that several of the owners of these resorts were clients of McCooey.[69] These tax allowances were not regularly made for such commercial properties. Also, certain judges were known as "liberals" (generous) because of the awards made to some claimants.[70] In most of these hand-outs, from a fifth to a half of the cash returned went to a lawyer or other "fixer." McCooey in the decade of the 1920's, succeeded in getting reductions in taxes of over $125,000 for clients, which was a huge sum of money for the times.[71] Naturally, McCooey would expect favors in return.

In another investigation in 1911, McCooey was called to

testify about certain accusations made against him that he sent a man with "stubby thumbs" to threaten a pharmacist named Dr. J. Rohrer. Dr. Rohrer was brother-in-law to State Assemblyman Louis E. Goldstein who was investigating McCooey. The threat to Dr. Rohrer was that Goldstein would lose his post as steward in one of the county buildings if he pushed his investigation. Also, Goldstein was up for renomination and if he did not stop he would lose support from McCooey for his possible renomination in the Fall. McCooey denied that he ever sent a "goon" to speak to Dr. Rohrer or that he later made a deal with Goldstein concerning his renomination to the Assembly.[72] Nothing came of the investigation nor was anything revealed concerning a "deal" between McCooey and Goldstein.

In other ways, however, McCooey learned a certain restraint from Charles Murphy about keeping his "orchards clean." In fact, one of the unique features of Murphy's leadership was his steadfast opposition to any graft in connection with gambling, saloons, or prostitution in his own district.[73] When it became known that gambling was taking place in Pete McGuiness' Club in the 15th Assembly District, McCooey assisted Police Captain Lewis J. Valentine in stopping it in order to keep the political clubs of Brooklyn beyond reproach.[74] Either it was an insult to his Irish and Catholic sensibilities, or, more likely, this was not "honest graft" and McCooey therefore would not allow it.

McCooey was a master at urban politics and knew how local machines worked. It also is quite conceivable, and perhaps likely, that he had his hand in the public till. The fact that accusations and charges against him were never pursued through the courts attested neither to his innocence nor his guilt. Adler and Blank found in their study of political clubs of New York that alliances between criminals and politicians crossed factional and party lines.[75]

Perhaps this was why McCooey's political "opponents" never pursued him vigorously.

## McCooey's Pragmatism

In 1925, Tammany Hall and Mayor John F. Hylan were in a tug-of-war to win McCooey's favor in the upcoming mayoral election. Hylan went so far as to name a city ferryboat after McCooey to get the support for a third term from his old, and presumably loyal friend. This made some Tammany members angry because McCooey had only been recently admitted to their club. *The New York Times* noted: "Everybody in Democratic circles knows that McCooey has it within his power to compel the nomination of Mayor Hylan for a third term. It is known also that a word from Mr. McCooey would lead to the elimination of Mr. Hylan for a third term in the Mayor's office."[76] McCooey gave Hylan as much support as he could, his loyalties running very deeply. His support demonstrated how independent McCooey could be from Murphy and New York County.

However, this same year Charles Murphy died, and George W. Olvany took his place.[77] Tammany, with Governor Alfred E. Smith behind them, was now beginning to push for State Senator James J. Walker in the mayoral primaries. When McCooey continued to support Hylan, Smith spoke to Olvany in June about reconciling their differences and getting behind the new candidate.[78] McCooey then met with the rank and file of his organization to determine the advisability of again naming Mayor Hylan to head the Democratic ticket.[79] In September of 1925, eleven days before the primaries, Brooklyn leaders were ready to bolt; only their loyalty to McCooey held them in the Hylan column. Suddenly, McCooey said he had become less interested in the fight for Hylan's renomination and went off to vacation in Bretton Woods, New Hampshire.[80] After Hylan lost the primaries, McCooey came out in support of Walker. McCooey, the eternal realist and pragmatist had seen Smith's handwriting on the wall and knew how to survive.

Walker's plurality in the primary was 95,543, with almost 400,000 Democrats voting. He had a huge plurality in New York County, seat of Tammany, winning 103,596 to 27,942. In Brooklyn, however, the vote was 65,584 to Hylan's 60,959. So despite the strong backing of Walker by Governor Smith and Tammany, thousands in the Brooklyn machine remained loyal to McCooey. Although it appeared as a defeat for McCooey, *The New York Times* reported that this would not disturb McCooey's leadership position.[81] This judgment was to be substantiated as McCooey's strength grew during the remaining nine years he lived to head the Brooklyn machine.

McCooey's power as Boss was often the subject of press commentary. And newspaper editorials often described the open cooperation between New York City's Tammanyite Mayor Joseph V. McKee, who completed Walker's term after his resignation, and McCooey. Judge Samuel Seabury, of the famed Seabury Investigations, examining charges of corruption in Walker's administration, realized how beholden the politicians were to the district leaders. In 1932, Seabury called the district leaders "the essence of the Tammany system of governments," and accused McCooey of the grossest mismanagement and waste, saying he was almost as bad as Boss Tweed. Seabury thundered that the city was "machine-made, machine-controlled and machine-operated."[82] After McCooey's death in 1934, a *Times* editorial pondered the significance of the Irish Boss. McCooey, it stated, was not brutal or brazen, aloof or secretive: "Yet he understood and protected the art of political control in much of the same terms as Tammany had always done." He unblushingly gave government positions to family and friends. He put the Brooklyn organization up for the highest bidder, but always with an eye toward perpetuating his own strength. He was an attractive exponent of the system, it continued, but still must be condemned.[83]

Only a political novice would have wondered how McCooey earned the huge estate he left at his death in 1934. At first, attempts were made to disguise the extent of his holdings, as his personal property was assessed at $10,000 and real estate holdings at "no dollars." But a year later, more of the truth of his wealth was revealed; he had an estate with a net worth of at least $650,000.

Inside rumors had fixed McCooey's wealth at two million dollars and the $20,000 inheritance tax paid on the estate would probably have been enough to cover the larger sum.[84] In terms of dollar values of the time, it was an extremely large holding. This was the estate of a man who had no professional training and was never elected to political office. Indeed, one might conclude that McCooey had seen his chances and "took them."

Political scientist James C. Scott, could have been talking about the Madison Club under John McCooey when he observed that machine organizers acted like entrepreneurs and not as representatives of their constituents: "The machine is rather a non-ideological organization interested less in political principle than in securing and holding office for its leaders and distributing income to those who run it and work for it...the machine may be likened to a business in which all members are stockholders and dividends are paid in accordance with what has been invested." The machine sought individual commitments from their constituents and voters in exchange for favors generated by business and governmental activity. The success of the machine, Scott stated, depended upon the benefits accrued and the sustenance of a voting base. He also concluded that the machine served latent functions converting "parochial demands into a system of rule that was at once reasonably effective and legitimate."[85]

## Conclusion

The first objective of McCooey's machine and the Madison Club was the aggressive mobilization of its electoral base. Without organized support the club could not survive, and therefore, neither would its leaders. McCooey was, at best, ethically evasive, but the whole political system supported him, including the opposing party. McCooey's estate shows that he profited personally while serving the various interests of immigrants and other constituents. Under McCooey, the Brooklyn machine was "apolitical" in that it struck deals with any government or clique in power as long as its prerogatives were not threatened. It was guided by the norms of reciprocity, negotiation, and accommodation. These are the golden rules in politics and are ideologically ambivalent as well. From a deeper historical perspective, the Madison Club--not withstanding the corruption and venality of its leaders--symbolized perfectly the Jeffersonian ideals of Republican, i.e. "representative" democracy at work.

McCooey was at the height of his power when the country readied itself for the coming Presidential election of 1932. Going into the Presidential National Convention as a national committeeman from New York, McCooey supported the nomination of Alfred E. Smith over Franklin Delano Roosevelt as Democratic candidate for President. Besides being a fellow Catholic, he did so because Smith had greater allegiance to Tammany and the machine still did not always trust Roosevelt. It also must be mentioned here in passing that Roosevelt clearly reached out more to Jewish constituents in New York, perhaps as a counter to the Irish Catholic dominance in the state's Democractic machines. By July 3rd, both McCooey and Manhattan Tammany leader John F. Curry decided to throw their weight behind Roosevelt when Smith failed to get the nomination.[86] After Roosevelt was elected President, McCooey adopted a policy of reconciliation toward Roosevelt. McCooey gave orders to his members in the House of Representatives to support the administration's legislative efforts.[87] Federal patronage for his minions was at stake.

In May of 1933, with hats in hands, McCooey and Curry went to Washington to pay their respects to Roosevelt. But the President was "not available;" as he wanted it to appear that he had divorced himself from the machine. They met instead with Louis Howe, Secretary to the President: "The inference was drawn that the two leaders had emphasized the fact that Democratic workers in New York City, especially the Tammany group, had not been rewarded for their jobs." The policy of the new administration was to give patronage only to those who helped the Roosevelt in the primaries.[88] The following month, Postmaster General James A. Farley was named "patronage czar" of New York State by Roosevelt. He also put off seeing McCooey. It was to be expected that more important posts would go to those friendly to Roosevelt *before* his nomination. It was also clear that State Secretary of New York, Bronx Democratic Boss Edward J. Flynn, an early supporter of Roosevelt, would have "important veto power on local appointments."[89] The distribution of Federal patronage, a source of membership inducement and control, was taken away from the Madison Club. The only thing left was personal loyalty which had limited currency in the new politics.

Although Roosevelt as New York Governor had "played

ball" with Tammany, he was one of its traditional enemies. He believed that powerful urban political machines had to be eliminated because they stood in the way of good government. Now as President and with the support of the Reform Movement in New York City and elsewhere, he tried to undermine some of the local organizations. It seems that Roosevelt's efforts were not aimed merely at McCooey but at the power of organizations. But in order to destroy the system he had to dethrone McCooey. However, one can assume that Roosevelt's ego was bruised by McCooey's support of fellow Irish-Catholic Smith at the Presidential Nominating Convention. One can also assume that he enjoyed helping to topple McCooey from power.

Ironically, just at the time his power was being challenged McCooey's health failed, and he died soon after Roosevelt came to power. Therefore there is no basis upon which to judge if he would have rallied around the new federal programs of relief to regain his leadership of the Brooklyn machine. His death, however, accelerated the collapse of his particular Irish-Catholic brand of boss politics, already weakened as a result of patronage now being generated from Washington D.C. and channeled through Farley rather than through McCooey and the Madison Club.

There are no records as to the number of people John McCooey was able to assist, but a number of old time club members have attested that over the years "thousands" came to see him. His generosity was well known. The fact that he controlled Kings County for thirty years proves that the Brooklyn Machine must have kept large numbers of people satisfied, both in and out of office. Without that, the Madison Club could not have survived.

## Footnotes

1.  David McCullough, *Brooklyn and How It Got That Way*. New York: Dial Press, 1983, p. 115.
2.  *New York Times*, December 31, 1924, p. 1:2.
3.  Other charter members were Henry J. Dougherty, Ernest Eggert, Andrew T. Sullivan and William L. Collins. *New York Times*, June 19, 1925, p.14.
4.  *Ibid.*, p. 1:2.
5.  *Brooklyn Life, 25 Years of Brooklyn, 1890-1915*. LI, No. 1317, May, 1915, p. 142. (Brooklyn society magazine.)
6.  Henry C. Wells, *"Political Development in Urban America: The case of the Brooklyn Machine,"* Paper presented at the CUNY Conference on Political Science, New York, New York, December 15, 1978. p. 20.
7.  See the tables in the Appendices for data on population and party registration. The figures presented here and in the text come variously from: *Population of the City of New York 1890-1930*. Cities Census Committee, Inc., Compiled and edited by Walter Laidlaw, 1932.; Registration figures have been compiled from the *Manuals* of the New York State Assembly and the *Reports* of the Board of Elections of New York City.
8.  William L. Riordan, *Plunkitt of Tammany Hall*. New York: Dutton, 1963, p. 3.
9.  *Ibid.*, p. 33.
10.  *Ibid.*, p. 30.
11.  *Ibid.*, p. 40.
12.  *New York Times*, March 23, 1930, V., p. 10:3.
13.  *Ibid.*
14.  *Ibid.*
15.  *Ibid.*
16.  *Ibid.*
17.  *Ibid.*
18.  *The Brooklyn Eagle*, August 2, 1945.
19.  John P. Walsh, *"John H. McCooey: Brooklyn's Last Hurrah."* Paper presented at the Brooklyn Historical Seminar, St. Francis College, Brooklyn, New York. April 26, 1965, pp. 5-6. Interview with Jacoby, December 18, 1964.
20.  Madison Club Ball Journal, 1906. Courtesy of Stanley Steingut. Interview March 21, 1981. Club originally located at 1519 Pacific Street.
21.  *The Brooklyn Citizen*, September 20, 1905.
22.  *The Brooklyn Citizen*, July 23, 1905.
23.  *The Brooklyn Citizen*, August 1, 1905, p. 3. See also: Nancy Joan Weiss, *Charles Murphy, 1858-1924: Respectability and Responsibility*

*in Tammany Politics.* Edwin H. Land Prize Essay, Smith College, Northhampton, Mass., 1968.

24. *New York Times,* November 12, 1909, p. 6:2. and *The Brooklyn Citizen,* September 20, 1905.
25. *New York Times,* January 13, 1909, p. 7:2.
26. *New York Times,* May 19, 1909.
27. *New York Times,* November 12, 1909, p. 6:2.
28. McCullough, *Op Cit.,* p. 115.
29. *The Brooklyn Citizen,* October 2, 1905.
30. Francis T. White, *County Government, A View Point from the Second Most Populous County in the U.S.A.,* 1934. White was a judge and a member of the New York Bar Association.
31. *The New York Post,* May 8, 1933, p. 3.
32. Walsh, *Op cit.,* pp. 5-6.
33. *New York Times,* August 22, 1925, p. 10:1.
34. *New York Times,* June 2, 1925, p. 1:6
35. *New York Post,* May 9, 1932, p. 3.
36. *New York Times,* April 15, 1928, p. 22:5.
37. *New York Times,* June 2, 1915, p. 5:1.
38. Interview with Abraham Beame, May 19, 1981. Beame formed the Haddingway Club in Crown Heights, one of six satellite clubs. See also: *New York Post,* October 20, 1965.
39. Crown Slope Democratic Club Brochure, Annual Entertainment and Ball. April 1, 1932. Many ads appear in it for the Three Leaf Club. Salvatore Jordan, Rose (Jordan) and Anthony C. Nicoletti confirmed this in interviews.
40. Interview, Joseph DiGiovanni, July 14, 1982. See also: *Brooklyn Eagle,* April 6, 1921.
41. *Brooklyn Eagle,* June 14, 1906.
42. *Ibid.*
43. *New York Times,* March 5, 1905, III, p. 6:1. Max Hahn was spokesman for the East Side Mayor's Association. He made general observations about the city's ethnic mayors.
44. Interview, J. DiGiovanni.
45. *Brooklyn Eagle,* September 14, 1924.
46. Anthony Jordan Sr.'s children confirmed this story.
47. Interview, Anthony Jordan, Jr., May 23, 1980.
48. Interview, Rose (Jordan) Nicoletti, July 7, 1981.
49. Interview, R. Nicoletti.
50. Interview, J. DiGiovanni.
51. Richard Hofstadter, *The Age of Reform.* New York: Vintage Books, 1960, p. 178. See also: Robert K. Merton, *Social Theory and Social Structure.* New York: The Free Press, 1967, p. 126.
52. James Mac Gregor Burns, *Roosevelt: The Lion and the Fox.* New York: Harcourt, Brace and World, Inc., 1956, p. 56.

53. John Morton Blum, *Joe Tumulty and the Wilson Era*. Boston: Houghton-Mifflin Co., 1951. The Riverside Press, p. 78.
54. *Ibid.*, p. 79.
55. Burns, *op. cit..*, p. 56.
56. *New York Times*, November 3, 1914, p. 1:8. The results are based on all but 28 of 1780 districts in New York City.
57. Burns, *op. cit.*, p. 59.
58. Allan Nevins, *Herbert H. Lehman and His Era*. New York: Charles Scribner Sons, 1963, p. 125.
59. Burns, *op. cit.*, pp. 120-21.
60. Paul Blanshard and Norman Thomas, *What's the Matter with New York: A National Problem.*, New York: Macmillan Co., 1932, p. 22.
61. James E. Finegan, *Tammany at Bay*. New York: Dodd, Mead and Co., 1933, p. 21.
62. *New York Times*, August 1, 1911, p. 16:4.
63. *New York Times*, October 15, 1911, p. 29:2.
64. *New York Times*, October 19, 1929, p. 1:4, and October 11, 1931, p. 1:2.
65. *New York Times*, October 19, 1929, p. 1:4.
66. *Ibid.*, Note: In the *Brooklyn Eagle* there are many more references to the ways that McCooey and his friends profited through their control of the Brooklyn machine. For example: "Patronage in Condemnation" and "Fees to Real Estate Experts," February 2, 1926; "Partner in Property Deal," July 1, 1930; "Site Owner in School Grab," September 4, 1930, July 30, 1931, October 29, 1931, and February 1, 1932; "Bay Ridge Gas Tank Site," October 29, 1931; and "Brooklyn College Building Site," December 8, 1933.
67. Blanshard, *op. cit.*, p. 45.
68. *Ibid.*, pp. 234-6.
69. Finegan, *op. cit.*, p. 150.
70. *Ibid.*, p. 34.
71. *Ibid*, p. 152.
72. *New York Times*, August 8, 1911, p. 5:3.
73. Weiss, *op. cit.*, p. 22.
74. *New York Times*, September 25, 1931, p. 20:5.
75. Norman Adler and Blanche Davis Blank, *Political Clubs of New York*, New York: Praeger, 1975, p. 22.
76. *New York Times*, June 5, 1925, p. 1:5.
77. *New York Times*, June 9, 1925, p. 1:7.
78. *New York Times*, June 17, 1925, p. 1:2.
79. *New York Times*, June 20, 1925, p. 15:3.
80. *New York Times*, September 25, 1925, p. 5:1.
81. *New York Times*, September 17, 1925, p. 1:8.
82. *New York Times*, December 10, 1932, p. 1:5.
83. *New York Times*, January 23, 1934, p. 18:3.

84. *New York Times,* August 15, 1935. Some estimates place it as high as two million dollars.
85. James C. Scott, *"Corruption, Machine Politics and Political Change,"* *American Political Science Review,* XLIII, No. 4, 1969, p. 1144.
86. *New York Times,* July 3, 1932, I & IV, p. 10:6.
87. *New York Times,* March 22, 1933, p. 13:4.
88. *New York Times,* May 10, 1933, p. 12:4.
89. *New York Times,* June 25, 1933, p. 4:1.

# From City-Wide Machine to Competing Clubs

The 1930s was a transitional period for the Madison Club and the Brooklyn Democratic machine. By this time many politically important changes had occurred and the old machine could no longer operate in the traditional fashion. John H. McCooey's ouster as County Leader and his death were literally the "Last Hurrah" for the mono-lithic form of party politics in Brooklyn. The older, highly centralized and autocratic political organizations of the traditional machine variety required a large mass of poorly educated, vulnerable constituents. Although the Great Depression had insured, for a time, economic dependency for large numbers of people, the National Origins Quota Laws of the 1920s had already ended the massive flow of immigrants who provided the most malleable population base for the old-style machine.

A new Standard Operating Procedure was needed for political organizations. The American foreign born slowly acclimated themselves to electoral democracy, and their literate, middle-class offspring demanded more of the system. In New York State and City, reform and "good government" political movements had reduced the power and scope of neighborhood party leaders while ironically increasing the power of individual county chairmen. City Charter revisions centralized power in City Hall at the expense of the boroughs. City-wide elections, therefore, became more important and city-wide campaigns as a result required more resources. The influence of large-scale business corporations on city affairs also increased. Finally, the New Deal had resulted in direct government involvement in the problems of the poor and began to erode the power of the machine which was based upon direct personal assistance and favors at the local level. The growth of Federal bureaucracies dealing with social and economic problems was mirrored at the state and municipal levels and affected the form and function of political life for everyone. The ultimate result for the machine was a breakdown of central party control which led to the formation of a large number of separate political clubs who competed rather than cooperated for power. Strict party discipline was also lost in the process. The interests of individuals and cliques became paramount as opposed to loyalty to the machine-as-a-whole.

In order to better understand the Madison Club and the Brooklyn Democratic organization after the golden years of the old style machine, it is necessary to introduce some new theoretical notions, and to modify Robert K. Merton's functional model which neatly fit the club under Kings County Democratic political "Boss" John H. McCooey.

These ideas are found in the work of Edward C. Banfield and James Q. Wilson on *City Politics*. Rather than looking at the relationship between the political machine and the system-as-a-whole, as had Merton, they focused instead on the internal operations of the machine itself and its relations to individual members.

According to Banfield and Wilson, a political machine is "a party organization that depends crucially upon inducements that are both specific and material."[1] A specific inducement is one that can be offered to one person (or group) while being withheld from others. A material inducement can be money, a job, a contract, a favor, or some other physical thing to which value attaches. Nonmaterial inducements include especially the satisfactions of having power and prestige, doing good, the "fun of the game," and the sense of enlarged participation in events in a pleasant environment. The machine then, operates on the basis of individual interests and not for the good of the whole. Universal rewards such as democratic principles, the good of the community, etc.. are, to the machine, immaterial and perhaps irrelevant.

As does any type of real organization, a political machine offers a mixture of these various kinds of rewards in order to get people to do what it requires--rewards are the mainspring of its power. But it is distinguished from other types of organizations by the very heavy emphasis it places upon specific, material inducements and the consequent completeness and reliability of its control over behavior, which, of course, accounts for the name "machine." This model, provided by Banfield and Wilson, is instructive in that the range of organizations not ordinarily called "machines" could be quite large. Theoretically, it would be difficult, if not impossible, on the basis of this definition to in fact distinguish a political machine from any other strong organization such as a business corporation. But Banfield and Wilson insist that the machine is a specific type of political organization. To them the implication is obvious; political organizations whose *modus operandi* are "universal," "impersonal" and "unselfish" are "nonmachines." Here we can see an implicit bias in their theorizing, one that we also came upon in Merton's discussion of "Boss Politics." Negatively stereotyped urban political machines are compared to idealized American political organizations akin to the New England "town halls," or midwest agrarian commune models. Banfield and Wilson prematurely claimed in 1966 that, for the most part, old-style, city-wide machines no longer existed. Despite their lack of political foresight, political organizations can be analysed fruitfully by employing their model. To their credit, they also stated that in many cities, large and small, elements of the old fashioned party organizaiton survived as fragments of old machines, operated on a machine-like basis.

Looking at New York City, Banfield and Wilson noted that, "Tammany has been weakened and perhaps destroyed in Manhattan, but Democratic machines are still powerful in the Bronx and Brooklyn."[2] The Madison Club was a significant force in the fragmented Brooklyn machine. Many of the reasons they cite as leading to the decline of old style political machines have direct application to the eventual fate of the Madison Club especially the loss of its absolute control over patronage and other material inducements in Kings County during the New Deal and the mayoral reign of Fiorello LaGuardia. The response of club members to the periodic threats of reform was typified in an interview with the past Treasurer of the Madison Club, an old-timer with the organization. As could be expected, the club fought hard against the LaGuardia's anti-machine campaign for mayor. During her interview she noted with great pride that her own election precinct carried for his opponent. The great battle against cleaning up city government was lost and the club had to adapt to cutting up a smaller patronage pie.

Central to the organizational needs of the machine is the loyalty and efficiency of its workers. Practically speaking, the fidelity of party workers is dependent on the rewards provided by the organization for service. As the needs of the workers, and the rewards available decrease, loyalty and commitment to the machine should also decrease. However there are other rewards or reasons for continued personal involvement which change the content and context of political activity. Nonmaterial inducements for involvement play a much more important role in the life of political organizations than most scholarly commentators have suggested and unfortunately seem to have been left to the political novelist and speculator.

Loyalty and service to the organization are influenced also by subjective factors such as friendships and other kinds of personal, perhaps psychological investments. In the ethnically-conscious urban environment, there are group satisfactions as well such as seeing "one's own" get important visible positions in government, a kind of vicarious success. For example, Jewish club members took great pride in the rise of Herbert Lehman, Irwin Steingut, Arthur Levitt and Abraham Beame even though they may not have personally benefitted from their success. It is common in New York politics for ethnic group organizations to push the candidacy of their members even when particular individuals lack qualifications or are clearly not the best choice. (In the 1980's gender and sexual preference have been added to the more traditional group bases in the competition for political spoils.)

As the needs and functions of constituents, organizations and political club members members change, the boss system, to remain efficient and effective must also change. Effective operation of the club is also dependent upon the learned or innate skills of organization workers such as the traditional election precinct captain who in good times controls a set of block lieutenants either personally loyal to him or dependent upon the captain for a material reward. The machine only operates effectively when these ties from the command center to the periphery are well maintained.

A factor not noted by other observers of the urban political scene, but apparent at the Madison Club, was the generational transition of the most loyal and effective workers. In the declining years of the club some of the most important members were advanced in age and physically could not perform as they had in their youth. At the same time, because of their personal successes, their own dependence on the organization had decreased substantially. Their children were also less in need of the club's services. In the past, members would be expected to stay in the old neighborhood, but many of them no longer resided in the club's assembly district as a result of social and economic mobility.

Not only did the local club not offer oldtimers much in the way of either material or non material inducements, newcomers lacked the sentimental attachments to the club. The Madison Club retained some value to members mainly because of its county, city and state-wide influence, not its local relevance. For example, some members and "hangers on" held city, state or federal patronage positions and were in a sense required to pay their dues by occasionally coming to meetings, or responding to club requests for favors. In the end, oldtimers were tactically useless in campaigning and gathering local support. Additionally, the transfer of skills from the old to the young at the club was also made more difficult because of the drastic changes in the ethnic makeup of the community being served.

Finally, machines depend on the experience of workers and the Madison Club members actually had little experience in electoral politics or political campaigns. Powerful local political organizations survive because they eliminate competition, not, as many believe, because they defeat enemies at the polls. Therefore successful machine organizations seldom have large numbers of experienced campaign workers. If they need them, they hire them.

When reformers, or the opposition, survive challenges to being placed on the ballot, cannot be bought off, co-opted or intimidated, a different set of skills is needed for the organizations--campaign skills. Strangely, machines are at a disadvantage in modern times compared to reform movements which are electorally conscious, more technologically sophisticated and organized with voters, not club members, in mind.

It should also be pointed out that machine politics is essentially "issueless" politics. Those involved in the machine are active primarily because of the potential for personal benefit. Issues are used, only if necessary. The machine relies on its normal day-to-day operations to win elections. Much to the chagrin of the machine, reformers and opposition candidates often run on issues. Issues serve to influence large numbers of people who otherwise are unreachable. Reformers, and the opposition, because they are out of office, do not have material inducements available to them to run a machine type campaign. Issues are, therefore, potentially powerful forces in politics, especially against machines because they can transcend or counter the material inducements offered by the machine. For example, in the final defeat of the Madison Club the issues of corruption, abortion, capital punishment and neighborhood preservation played important roles in the downfall of the club.

Even without being on the "right" side of the "right" issues, a competent machine is still an odds-on favorite to win in an election because of its far reaching influence and access to rewards for loyal service. Undoubtedly changes in election laws and the introduction of government election "watchdogs" have decreased the ability of machines to simply steal elections at the voting booth, but they still try and are sometimes successful at it. After many electoral reforms, their success at unethically effecting elections was dependent in large measure on their influence at higher levels of the political system rather than at individual polling booths. One cannot lose sight of the fact that it is the party organizations in power who appoint and control the election "watchdogs."

For a time, the development of civil service and other more objective and influence-free hiring practices by local governments was also a severe blow to the power of political clubs as it reduced the number of rewards it could give out for loyal service. Politically independent government agencies and commissions, which oversaw the letting of lucrative public contracts, also eliminated, for a short time, more of the material inducements controlled by local clubs. As the party machine recovered from these reform efforts, however, they regained control over these "independent" bodies. After all, are not the members of such groups appointed by elected officials?

Changes in the socio-economic character of electorates have had a much greater effect on the survival of machine organizations. Such organizations are more likely to develop, and to persist in lower class areas, where the sophistication of voters is low and their unmet needs high. Even when changes in the operation of public services becomes a matter of "right" rather than a "favor," especially in poorer and immigrant communities, people lack awareness of their civil rights and continue to go to political clubs for assistance and advice concerning such things as Social Security and welfare assistance.

World War II and the subsequent economic recovery from the Great Depression lifted many people out of poverty and dependence on the local political organization for economic survival. This period also heralded a decrease in ethnic consciousness and separateness which had in the past contributed to the maintenance of the city boss system. After the war, the Federal government's policy of stimulating the building of new housing in suburban areas led to the outflow of the younger generation whose families were in many cases sentimentally tied to the old organization. Eventually the vacuum created by this loss of white middle-class population led to the decline of the inner city and the in-migration of poor nonwhites. The result of all these changes was the creation of a new style of political machine operation, less tied to local constituent needs and demands but still able to operate at some levels with impunity because of the apathy of voters and the growth of a new urban underclass.

Some machines can survive for a time, as did the Madison Club, the transition of the poor and working class constituents to middle-class propriety, but their structure and operation must change in accordance with the new demands and realities. Another factor which initially hurt local clubs was the development of community and neighborhood associations in poverty areas which began during the 1960s. These new groups on the local scene, often spurred by Federal initiatives in urban renewal and later anti-poverty efforts, provided residents with alternative methods for local problem solving. Local organizations were also fostered by the more politically independent New York Mayors Robert Wagner and John Lindsay as a way to circumvent the clubhouse structure in the city. In neighborhoods which are more middle-class, educated and sophisticated voters also produced pressure on old-fashioned clubs to become more democratic in their processes and practices. At the Madison Club, as the electorate and club membership changed, the older workers and leaders found it difficult to adapt and become more of a "community" or "civic" association and less of a closed, smoke-filled room. Interviews with old time Madison Club members gave clear indication of their contempt for liberal community activists in the club who sought to democratize the organization. Because of these changes, machine-type organizations like the Madison Club became increasingly susceptible to challenge by new style political movements and organizations which developed in the 1960s and 1970s, and in some cases new reform and independent clubs replaced them on the local scene.

As in the past, some of New York City's political operators adjusted to the changed environment, but with limited success and a further dimunition in the power of monolithic organizations. As always, the American system of government created opportunities for political entrepreneurs by fostering competition for limited resources. Individuals and groups continued to seek "favors" and special treatment. The political system, by distributing economic and other rewards, remains the focus for entreaties.

Not all who seek rewards are beggars. For example, during the 1960s, control of government-funded social and health services, aimed primarily at the poor, became a major prize sought by national, state and city private secular and non-secular agencies. Providers of services became a new constituency seeking favors. The "Great Society," "Community Action," "Model Cities," and other programs were ripe with patronage and provided new jobs and spoils for urban political machines to distribute. "Independent" local agencies quickly came under the control of local bosses. In New York City, "community control" and "decentralization" efforts such as the Office of Neighborhood Government, Community School Boards and Community Planning Districts were viewed initially as undermining local party leaders. However, because the funding and appointments for these programs were politically controlled, they eventually were taken over by regular political clubs such as the Madison Club. Even those new groups which were "elected" by the community, as

for example; Community School Boards, slowly gravitated toward the usual politics as teacher's unions and
suppliers saw the need to control their actions and joined
with regular political clubs to elect board members sympathetic to their needs and desires.

City newspapers exposed on many occasions corruption in social service and "poverty empires" created by the
"Great Society." Community level corruption is not,
however, limited to poverty areas or minority groups.
Scandals also resulted from private social service contractors, like nursing home operators, and school lunch providers who made pay-offs to get political help in obtaining
lucrative government contracts to serve the poor. Private
hospitals and clinics also vied in the same way for a piece
of the social services pie.

Many local community and development groups were
also funded by the government and therefore had to get
approval from local politicians tied to clubs. The Community Planning Board system requires as well that local
projects be reviewed by borough and city-wide overseers.
Even though the ultimate power to fund projects rested in
the City's Board of Estimate, which was dominated by the
mayor, local political organizations wasted little time in
taking over these "independent citizens" committees.
Members of the boards were chosen by the area's City
Council member and the Borough President, who in most
cases were in turn determined by the Democratic Party
County organizations. These "independent" boards in
turn were given the authority to approve such items as
cable television franchises, housing and economic development projects.

As politics changed and other interests entered the
arena, more adaptation by the fractionalized machine was
needed. The addition of union, professional, health, housing and social service organizations created new needs for

the machine to serve. The machine itself also had new needs. The most important change involved modern election campaign tactics which required more funds for radio, newspaper and television advertising, phone banks, printing, large scale mailings, legions of street workers, huge campaign staffs and expensive political "experts" such as media, public relations and polling professionals. McCooey had merely to deal with the introduction of the telephone. The Steinguts had to struggle with an entirely new political world. According to Banfield and Wilson, the aftermath of the reform movement in city politics created "Factions and Factional Alliances," as opposed to the preceding city-wide boss-dominated machines. These factions, or sub-groups of larger machines, comprise four analytic types according to the nature of their inducements: the machine of less than city-wide scope, the personal following, including ethnic and "natural area" followings, the interest grouping or coalitions such as labor or issue groups, and the club.[3] Our own research on the Madison Club indicates that the groups which participated in the new political arena could also be mixed cases or types.

How does the Madison Club of Brooklyn fit into Banfield and Wilson's typology? Historical investigation shows that the club went through several successful transitions and adaptations before its end. To begin with, the Madison Club was never a city-wide machine because Brooklyn was no longer an independent city at the time of its inauguration in 1905. At most in the beginning it was a county organization and a powerful part of the city-wide apparatus of the Democratic Party which was run from Manhattan. Despite his protestations to the contrary the club, under McCooey, had definite and positive relations with the Tammany Tiger across the East River. New York City, as usual, is also a bit anomalous as a "type." The size of the city, and its congruent county-borough structure could be viewed, at times, as a collection of several semi-autonomous cities.

In its early decades, the Madison Club was very much like the city-wide machine with important reservations. The structure of New York City government, even after consolidation or annexation of the City of Brooklyn in 1898 left much of "local" affairs to the borough government. As the borough grew, it rivaled New York County as a faction in the city-wide machine. Concomittantly, the Madison Club's power increased. Even after McCooey's downfall it became one of the powerful factions within the county machine. As other factions grew in strength, and new ethnic groups entered the scene, independent clubs and reform politics also advanced in Kings County politics. Interestingly, the Madison Club, under the Steinguts was seen at first as part of the "reform" movement as the county organization tried to revive itself from the impact of the New Deal and the LaGuardia mayoralty, which severely wounded the city-wide organization. Many of the Madison Club's "new generation" after Boss McCooey were more closely tied to Franklin D. Roosevelt's political apparatus and therefore survived the New Deal.

Banfield and Wilson's description of "the club" as the lowest level of the machine organization in its devolution in city politics has direct application to the history of the Madison Club. The "club", they define, as an element of the party that is held together simply by the satisfaction people find in being members of it.[4] There was a great deal of satisfaction derived from joining the Madison Club, with its traditions and its aura of power. The value of these intangible aspects of the club, as well as its actual power, diminished by the 1970s because of the many changes in the operations of city politics and the dramatic shifts in its population.

Even before the Madison Club became merely one of several powerful clubs in the competitive Brooklyn organization, there existed divisions within the club itself. As far back as the 1920s there were at least ethnic and personal club factions; one associated with the Irish and McCooey, and the other, newer faction, tied to Irwin Steingut and Jewish constituents. Italians, also a major group, generally played second or third fiddle to either of the two more powerful entities. Naturally, further divisions could be noted such as those between prominent families and cliques. Rifts within the organization became clear when special issues emerged concerning the dispensing of coveted political rewards. One such early conflict resulted from the State Supreme Court Judgeship given by McCooey to his son in 1932 at the expense of others in the club who felt they deserved it more. Disputes like this appeared at regular intervals over the decades and became more vicious as the available spoils decreased. In all instances the club lost important members and their followings; the club festered with resentments for decades to come. Personal followings, ethnic loyalties, economic and political self interests, and conflicting club traditions divided the organization, but its ability to continue to provide sufficient inducements, both material and non-material, kept it together.

Historically, the process of political change in the Brooklyn machine and the Madison Club in particular was one of increasing factionalization and, finally, competition between individuals for limited spoils. This intense competition eventually led to the accusations of "sabotage" during the club's second and final "Last Hurrah" in 1978 when personal slights and intra-club rivalries came back to disrupt campaign efforts.

Another cause producing factions and competition within the Brooklyn machine was the indirect result of the demand for proportional representation in the New York State Legislature. Because of Republican control of the state, voting districts in more Democratic New York City were drawn in such a way that they contained much larger populations than upstate districts. In his study of "The Demographics of Politics" Arthur Klebanoff found, for example, that in 1953 in 38 upstate counties there was one Assemblyman for each 51,203 persons while in New York City there was one for every 135,511.[5] Assembly districts are amended after every decennial census. On three such occasions the Madison Club's Assembly District was greatly reduced in both geographical area and population size; between 1900 and 1910, 1910 and 1920, and 1940 and 1950.[6]

Although one would first assume that its political power would be lessened because of the loss of voters and population, for a time at least, the reverse actually occurred. The creation of the new districts, made of old Madison Club domains, meant that the club, indirectly, controlled more districts. The leaders of the new areas were prominent members of the club and, at least initially, owed their allegiance to it. One new Assembly District leader in 1944 was Alexander Hesterberg, who was the son of Henry A. Hesterberg, a Brooklyn influential at the turn of the century who helped McCooey establish the Madison Club. Al Hesterberg had started his own regular political club, and later became Brooklyn Borough President.

These new districts, or perhaps "fiefdoms," also created potential rivals such as the powerful Assemblyman Max Turshen whose 30 plus years of seniority led him to chair the Assembly Judiciary Committee from 1965-68. Just as did classical empires, when city-wide political machines collapse, they most often break up into feudal factions. "Friendly" competition between the local political clubs is the usual form that the factionalism takes when satisfactory "deals" between competitors cannot be worked out for splitting up the patronage rewards. At least one long-time Madison Club member recalled that Turshen and his friends became angry with Steingut and the club when a later reapportionment pitted Turshen against a highly popular Assembly candidate--Steven Solarz, in a district which favored Solarz. Solarz won and later became a powerful member of the New York State congressional delegation. Undoubtedly Turshen's friends and relatives were not totally disappointed when Steingut lost in 1978.

According to Roy V. Peel, Tammany Hall, the Democratic political party organization of New York County, was a city-wide machine during the period of its greatest strength when it was led by Charles F. Murphy. Then its basic unit was the neighborhood, or district club.[7] These clubs were the local centers for the distribution of patronage and other material inducements. They also offered secondary attractions such as the opportunity to rub shoulders with well known figures in a congenial atmosphere. Over the decades, after many years of reform had washed away some of the patronage and other material benefits of memberships, many clubs had little to offer other than sociability and the opportunity to share stories of what it was like "in the good old days." By 1960, according to Banfield and Wilson, few club members were actually "payrollers." The Tammany Association, at least at the lower ends of the hierarchy, had ceased to be a "real" machine and had become an alliance of clubs.[8] What club members probably knew however, was that political leaders kept more of the available spoils for themselves and distributed less at the lower levels.

James Q. Wilson, in his study of local political organizations in three cities, noted that the loss of patronage power had a definite effect on the operation of any political organization. Efficient precinct work is much harder to obtain when one controls, not a worker's job and income, but only his or her access to a social club. The individual no longer responded as readily to club discipline. Furthermore, attempts to punish workers were likely to disrupt the organization and have further negative consequences. "Firing" a precinct captain from his post, Tammany leaders found, often created resentment and uncertainty among members of the club. In these circumstances there was nothing to do but grudgingly tolerate workers whose only interest was hanging around at the club. As a consequence of lost discipline, Wilson noted that Tammany suffered many defeats in the 1950s and the 1960s at the hand of reform organizations whose members were imbued with missionary zeal.[9] By the 1970s, the Madison Club, Tammany's Brooklyn counterpart, was also on its last legs as grumbling and even open rebellion against the club leadership was not unusual. It, too, fell to a collection of rebels and community zealots.

There were many other-than-"organizational" factors which assisted in the decline of the monolithic party machines in New York City. What had begun in the 1950s in Manhattan (and what has continued to the date of this writing) was the "gentrification" of Manhattan Island as upper-middle-income white collar professionals replaced the lower- and working-class populations, destroying the environment most suitable for the old style machine. The impact of this change was first noticed in politics as the Tammany machine, led by Carmine DeSapio in Greenwich Village, began losing ground in the 1960s to reform and independent insurgents such as future Mayor of New York City Edward I. Koch. This demographic transition of Manhattan to an upper-middle class island, which began in the 1950s, continued up the east and west sides of the island and began to spill over into Brooklyn in the 1980s.

Of special note in the weakening of the New York County Democratic Party machine were the powerful corporate interests which had increased their influence in Manhattan, as well as the city as a whole. The culmination of the growth of this corporate power in political decision making was creation of the Municipal Assistance Corporation which took over the financial affairs of New York in response to the City's much publicized "fiscal crisis" during the mayoral term of Madison Clubber Abraham Beame. Another powerful organizational entity was the New York City Partnership; a private group which became directly involved in many of New York's problems such as housing and education. The direct involvement of corporations in the managment of American cities was not limited to New York. During the same period similar intrusions occurred in many declining urban centers in eastern and midwestern cities such as Cleveland, Detroit and Pittsburgh. As in the past, political reforms were fueled by powerful private economic interest groups.

## Footnotes

1. Banfield and Wilson, *City Politics*, New York: Vintage Books, 1966, p. 116.
2. *Ibid.*, p. 117.
3. *Ibid.*, p. 128.
4. *Ibid.*, pp. 132-33.
5. Arthur Klebanoff, "The Demographics of Politics: Legislative Constituencies and the Borough of Brooklyn, 1950-1955." Unpublished senior honor's thesis. New Haven: Yale University, 1969, p. 17.6. Renderings of Madison Club Assembly District Maps are provided in the Appendices.
7. Roy V. Peel, *The Political Clubs of New York*. New York: G.P. Putnam's Sons,1935.
8. *Op. cit.*, p.133.
9. James Q. Wilson, *The Amateur Democrat: Club Politics in Three Cities*. Chicago: University of Chicago Press, 1962. Chapter X.

# The Power Changes Hands: Enter the Steinguts

The first phase in the life of the Madison Club ended with the death of John H. McCooey in 1934. At the time of his death McCooey was the leader of the 18th A.D., seat of the Madison Club, Chairman of the Kings County Democratic Committee and Democratic National Committeeman for New York State. To his contemporaries, McCooey "understood and practiced the art of political control in much the same terms as Tammany has always done."[1] His prominence and power were attested to by the thirty-thousand people who attended his funeral, one of the most impressive ever held in Brooklyn's history. Political notables such as former Governor Alfred E. Smith and State Democratic Chairman James A. Farley attended, while Governor of New York State Herbert Lehman was an honorary pallbearer.[2] The man eventually to succeed McCooey at the club and lead it through its next period, Irwin Steingut, was also in attendance.

## Simon Steingut and the Shadow Immigrant Political Establishment

Irwin Steingut's father, Simon, was the first to hoist the family's political banner. In 1888 he opened his office at 31 Second Avenue in Manhattan's immigrant crucible, the crowded and colorful Lower East Side. There he announced that anyone in the neighborhood could come and seek his help. His local popularity was reflected in the label of "Mayor," that local businessmen created for him. After that he was known as the "Mayor of Second Avenue"[3]

New York City had about three dozen of these unofficial local ethnic community leaders who helped the elected mayor of the city to conduct neighborhood affairs. As part of the informal structure of city government, the local mayors tied the polyglot neighborhoods of lower Manhattan to both the city and Tammany Hall. The mayors formed an organization called "The East Side Mayor's Association" with Max Hahn as its president. Members of the Association included both Democrats and Republicans. Hahn stated, "We are the only ones to whom they (the immigrants) can come for relief. And you would be surprised how useful they find us."[4]

The members of this group were an important adjunct to city government as, in general, new immigrants were frightened and suspicious of political authority. The ethnic mayors were actually "minority middlemen" who functioned to control the teeming immigrant ghettos. They were the conduits in the symbolic relationships between voters and elected officials. As middlemen for minorities, they acted as liaisons between the elected government of the city and the ghetto, and of course, received favors in return for their service.

People like Max Kahn and Simon Steingut were classic examples of power brokers-not elected officials or even influentials within the party, but agents and representatives of ethnic groups with nominal access to the political machine. It was from these humble beginnings that political dynasties, such as that of the Steinguts' would grow. The neighborhood mayor system represented another form of ethnic political entrepreneurialism which McCooey had represented.

Local mayors were very busy people settling as many as fifteen to twenty neighborhood disputes a day. People tended to abide by their judgments even though they had no real legal standing. Mayors were also helpful in official courts, being available to lawyers and judges for advice. Sometimes they provided coal for the indigent in cold weather or helped put food on the table for the hungry. In general they had the confidence of the their people and advised their constituents on political candidates. Just as importantly, they also served to turn out a large number of voters at election time.[5]

Although a popular local leader, Simon Steingut also earned a reputation as a "slippery fellow" because of some of his business dealings. In one instance in 1901, he was brought to magistrate's court by a representative of the bar association for impersonating a lawyer and collecting a lawyer's fee. It seemed he had a reputation as a counselor-at-law around Houston Street. Most immigrant ghettos had many unlicensed, and untrained "professionals" because lawyers and doctors avoided poor areas of the city. Immigrant ghettos had many people acting as professionals without license.

Simon Steingut was highly indignant over being summoned to Court. As a learned disciple of Sir William Blackstone, the famous English legal theorist, he therefore represented himself at the hearing. Steingut claimed to presiding Judge Mayo that he never held himself out to be a lawyer, stating that "I am a notary and as such draw legal papers strictly within my rights."[6]

But, Assistant District Attorney Monks produced a diagram of the mayor's office showing a sign that it was a "law office." The sign, Steingut admitted, belonged to a lawyer with whom he had once shared the office, a Mr. Hegeman, and he had never removed it. On his promise to take it down, Judge Mayo allowed Steingut to be released.

In 1913, the business community of the Lower East Side celebrated Simon's 25th anniversary as Mayor of Second Avenue. Over the years Steingut had learned, as did other local bosses, that to keep his political position he had be generous. When political rival Joe Levy, "The Duke of Essex Street," tried to oust Steingut's people with an opposition Fusion ticket, he was not intimidated. Steingut said, "I will win. Wait till I open my strongbox when it comes from Europe next week...and I give some presents I promised to bring! Fusion ticket! . . . *Ish gebibble!* . . . We will see what talks the loudest, Fusion or remembrances."[7] Steingut assessed his followers correctly and Joe Levy did not unseat him.

In 1915, Steingut's loyal followers were given another opportunity to demonstrate their commitment to him when he was arrested again for practicing law without a license. Members of the New York County Lawyers' Association were the complaining witnesses against Steingut and six others. This time, in Special Sessions of the Court, Simon was found guilty of unlawful practice. He was sentenced to thirty days in jail, or the payment of a two-hundred and fifty dollar fine. Steingut's friends paid his fine under protest, saying that they would appeal the decision, but they never did.[8]

In December of 1918, Steingut became seriously ill, with cancer of the tongue. Three months later he died at Montefiore Hospital. For thirty years he had held sway as the Mayor of Second Avenue, colorfully dressed in a silk hat

and Prince Albert coat. It was his custom to distribute
Christmas baskets to the poor of Second Avenue. And near
the end, even though deathly ill, he directed his son Irwin
"to see that the usual number of baskets were sent out."[9] A
decade later, the *Brooklyn Eagle* would note that the Mayor
of Second Avenue did much for "his fellow East Siders and
was a good Tammany man in the days that are gone."[10]

### Irwin Steingut's Rise

Irwin Steingut was introduced to John H. McCooey by
Tammany leader Charles Murphy.[11] From this a close
political friendship flowered and, some say, McCooey
began to look upon Irwin as a "son." According to Irwin
Steingut's son Stanley, however, it was Irwin's mother-in-
law, Mrs. Kaufman, who was most responsible for establishing their political partnership. As the story goes, she
and Irwin's mother approached McCooey and asked,
"Why not run a Jew for Assemblyman?" McCooey responded that he had "nothing against Jews" and that it
was a "good thought." It is more likely that, consumate
politician, McCooey was aware that his assembly district
was changing as many Jews had moved into the area,
spilling over from the crowded ghettos of Brownsville and
East New York. Therefore, it would be good politics to let
Steingut run.[12] Murphy gave his approval to the idea and
Steingut was elected to the New York State Assembly in
1921.

### Herbert Lehman as an Ethnic "Role Model"

Irwin Steingut had come from the Lower East Side of
Manhattan with such friends as future Mayor Abraham
Beame and Nathan Sobel, who, in later years, would be
elected Surrogates Court Justice. Judge Sobel remembered,

"Abe and I were living in the Crown Heights section, in the 18th A.D. and in that year (1928) Herbert Lehman was being drafted to run for Lieutenant Governor. Both of us had a very high regard for Lehman because he had always been interested in settlement houses on the Lower East Side. So with Murray Feiden, now a Supreme Court Justice, we formed our own club, the Haddingway Democratic Club in Crown Heights. This was one of six small clubs that were part of the parent organization, the Madison Democratic Club, of which John McCooey was leader, as well as, county leader."[13]

As a member of a prominent German-Jewish family which had concerned itself with the problems of their less fortunate brethren, Herbert Lehman influenced and inspired the young Jewish members of the Haddingway Club. It was he, as Governor in the early thirties, who would give Madison Club district captain Beame, a C.P.A., his first important political appointment.[14]

In an interview, Beame recalled that when he first moved from the Lower East Side to the 18th A.D. it was already an overwhelmingly Jewish area with small pockets of Irish and Italians. In the 1920's the Crown Heights area was considered a major step upward from the Manhattan ghetto. Many Jews, enjoying their recent economic mobility, also wanted to become politically active and make their mark on the system. Beame noted that the programs of Lehman and Roosevelt provided many jobs and aided those groups who were moving from Manhattan to Brooklyn.[15]

At the time there were few organizations to join which would provide opportunity for professional advancement, so Beame, a high school teacher, involved himself in a developing teachers' organization. He was asked by the organization to go to Albany and represent their views, and with Irwin Steingut's help, a bill was passed to aid teachers. Steingut also got Nat Sobel appointed as counselor to Governor Lehman, and it was upon Sobel's recommendation that Lehman signed Beame's bill. Over the years, Beame drew close to Steingut and did accounting for the Madison Club, and for Steingut personally. It was natural that their complementary needs would form the basis of a nucleus of friends who helped each other to get ahead politically.

In 1930, the premature deaths of Assemblyman Maurice Block and Peter Hamill within a week had promoted Steingut's career, as either of them was a more likely choice for minority leader of the New York State Assembly than he.[16] The position gave him greater influence and in 1933, Steingut returned to the Assembly elected under the banners of both the Democratic and Recovery Parties.[17] When the Democrats won control of the Assembly in late 1934, Steingut was named Speaker of the Assembly for the following year.[18] In this position it was easy for him to work closely with his good friend, Governor Lehman.

## Trouble and Ethnic Succession in the Brooklyn Organization

Irwin Steingut's political ascension was not without controversy. In the months preceding his death, McCooey's power in the Brooklyn organization had already been contested because of the refusal of the Roosevelt administration to recognize him as Federal patronage-dispenser for Brooklyn. His death created a power vacuum that many were anxious to fill and a major power struggle ensued. The *Brooklyn Eagle* reported on January 30, 1934 that the Madison Club was making every effort to get minority Irwin Steingut, to fill McCooey's unexpired term as state committeeman. More than half of the electoral district captains in the 18th A.D. and the Madison Club satellite Tally-Ho Democratic Club, satellite of the Madison Club, came to Steingut's support and also endorsed him for district boss.[19]

Resistance to Steingut's succession as district and county leader came from his biggest rival in the county, Harry Walkoff. The rebellious Walkoff was a member of the Tilden Club, another satellite organization which refused to back Steingut. In addition, the Cleveland Democratic Club was promoting Walkoff himself for leader of the 18th A.D. and county chairman.[20]

Unfortunately for Irwin Steingut, just before his death, McCooey had indicated to Daniel Fogarty, president of the Madison Club, that elections should be held in February of 1934 despite his failing health. Fogarty said, soon after McCooey died, that he would conduct elections promptly. Steingut objected to the early timetable, hoping to postpone the vote for a month to gather supporters since Walkoff already had the backing of half the county committeemen.[21]

On February 25, 1934, the Brooklyn Democratic organization met at Alexander Hamilton High School in Brooklyn and Irwin Steingut was selected as leader of the 18th A.D.. The Democratic County Committeemen designated Steingut as their spokesman in county affairs. Steingut received heavy support and was invested with provisional powers so that the county would have a voice until a permanent executive chairman was chosen. The vote in the resolution was 383 for Steingut, 3 abstentions and one vote against him. His drive for county chairman was gaining momentum.[22] In addition, the organization urged the state Democratic committeemen to elect someone as national committeeman to fill the vacancy left by McCooey's death.

On March 2, 1934, the *Brooklyn Eagle* had described the growing struggle within the Madison Club as support swung toward Steingut. At a weekly meeting, violence broke out as Harry Walkoff got into a fistfight with another club member, Billy Maher, who called Walkoff a rebel. In the melee, Maher's fist missed Walkoff and blackened the eye of woman who was standing nearby. Walkoff's said that Steingut was a pawn of Tammany. In a last ditch effort, Walkoff got his lawyer Jack Friedman to try to block the district committee selection of Steingut as new leader of the 18th A.D., but he was unsuccessful. Steingut, on the other hand, declared himself a loyal follower of the well-respected President Roosevelt, Governor Lehman, and Democratic chairman Farley.

Walkoff continued to oppose Steingut's growing strength. He created another disturbance at the club meeting by again threatening violence. According to him, Steingut was not the choice of the 50,000 Democrats of the 18th A.D. for party leader. Walkoff threatened to get a court order to prevent Steingut from attending the executive committee meetings of the county organization. He said he wanted to see the credentials which proved that Steingut had received the endorsement of the Democratic and Recovery Party, as he contended.[23]

Walkoff was not alone in viewing Steingut as a tool of Tammany. In May of 1929, the Citizen's Union, a public service group that evaluated those in office, said Steingut's "work was of poor quality and his record below average."[24] The following year, they rated Steingut as still needing to demonstrate those qualities of true leadership.[25] Steingut, however, persevered and several years later, the Citizen's Union praised him for having shrewd leadership qualities. But they still had serious reservations. The Union noted, "His good work was more than counter-balanced by abject subservience to the local bosses."[26]

Some of Steingut's actions justified the criticism directed at him. In early 1932, he had attacked the Samuel J. Seabury Committee appointed by Governor Roosevelt to investigate corruption in the city, and defended Tammany Mayor James T. Walker. He commented that it was the New York City government's responsibility to correct itself, not the state legislature's.[27] Later, Steingut said the Seabury report did not serve its purpose and again praised Walker. He claimed that Seabury was merely promoting himself as a national candidate for the presidency or the vice-presidency. The New York courts, he asserted, should deal with the problem of derelicts instead of politicians.[28] In February of the same year, Steingut was still berating Seabury for using the investigation he was leading to promote his political career.[29]

As the year 1934 progressed, Steingut's position in Brooklyn improved despite the fact that he was not named county leader. Factionalism was fading but hadn't disappeared.[30] To settle the issue of executive chairman for Kings County, the Brooklyn machine decided on district leader Frank V. Kelly rather than Steingut or Walkoff. At first, Roosevelt and Farley opposed this selection because they believed Kelly would be in alliance with New York County Tammany leader John F. Curry.[31] As Governor, Roosevelt had often been at odds with Tammany Hall and the Brooklyn machine. Now as President, he assessed the reform efforts in New York which could curb Tammany's power. As a result of Washington's reservations, a triumvirate was created to temporarily run the Brooklyn organization consisting of Brooklyn leaders Thomas F. Wogan, Francis J. Sinnott, as well as Kelly. By the end of 1934, however, when Kelly showed he could be independent of Tammany Hall, and pledged to support Governor Lehman and Irwin Steingut, as well as FDR, Washington gave its endorsement and he became county leader.

While the machinations over who would replace

McCooey as county leader proceeded, Irwin Steingut, "Lehman's boy," received support from FDR, Lehman and Farley to become the first Speaker of the Assembly from Brooklyn in the history of the state legislature. Steingut was also the first Jew to hold this position.[32] At the beginning of 1935, Steingut terminated his long-running feud with Mayor Fiorello H. LaGuardia. The two men had been especially at odds after Steingut had accused LaGuardia of deliberately abolishing certain civil service positions and filling them with cronies of his own.[33] Both celebrated their reconciliation with a banquet attended by 500 political notables at the St. George Hotel in Brooklyn.[34] The event, sponsored by the Madison Club, marked the emergence of Steingut as a powerhouse in municipal and state politics. Here the Assemblyman said he accepted the speakership of the Assembly because the Democratic Party, after efforts to reform, was now united.[35]

Reminiscent of Roosevelt's attempts to surround himself with knowledgeable men when he became President, Steingut formed his own "Brain Trust" of college-educated advisors recommended by Tammany leaders. This group would read and check every bill which was introduced in the legislature and provide expert advice from which the Speaker could frame his policies in the Assembly. Members of the Brain Trust were Abraham Brodsky, James McKenna, James Tighe, Peter Eschman, Irwin Davidson and Daniel Kornblum, all of whom were graduates of prestigious American colleges.[36]

Despite his modern approach to politics, Steingut did not forget to bring home the legislative bacon. He publicly stated he would support any legislation proposed by New York City as a reminder to his supporters that his concerns in Albany would not preempt his responsibilities to his local districts.[37] But Steingut recognized that to meet the increasing demands of his constituents, he would have to

rise even higher on the state political ladder. Not inciden-
tally, the rise of Steingut and the Jewish ethnic bloc in
Brooklyn and Albany coincided with the decline of Manhattan's Tammany Hall and the Irish political hegemony
throughout the city.

At first, Steingut had led the Brooklyn organization
much as McCooey had. Former Mayor Abraham Beame,
as well as numerous other club members, relate that they
remember long lines of people waiting to see Steingut for
jobs. Like McCooey, Steingut was very accessible at the
club. In this way, the nucleus of ambitious young Jews
looking to enter the system were able to help each other
and promoted the transition of power to a new ethnic
group in the Madison Club, Kings County and State politics. Beame recalled that in later years as City Comptroller,
and as Mayor he dealt with many people who were former
members of the Madison Club.[38] But the energy of the
Reform Movement, changing times and the new leadership were to steer the Club and the county machine for a
time in broader political directions.

## Irwin's Legacy

By the 1930's the Irish held a disproportionate share of
the power in the 18th A.D., in Brooklyn, and throughout
the City. Increasingly, Jews and Italians, who were more
numerically significant, resented their second and third-
class status in the Deomcratic Party. Therefore, it was not
surprising that when the new opportunities for Jewish and
Italian patronage were created by Mayor LaGuardia,
Steingut was ready, willing and able to take advantage of
them. Politics served his own and his constituents' aspirations as the political process speeded assimilation into the
mainstream of society. He used his power and authority,
plus the power of the Madison Club, to achieve this end.

The New Deal and the Recovery Party introduced new reforms into the political scene in New York City especially, and Steingut was prepared for them also. Out of necessity he also brought more open leadership and wider participation into the Madison Club.

As minority leader of the Assembly, Steingut had said, "I am for anything that Governor Lehman wants." Steingut and Lehman made comfortable bedfellows and before long Irwin became known as "the governor's boy."[40] It came as no surprise when the *Brooklyn Eagle* reported that the "combined influence of President Roosevelt, Postmaster General Farley and Governor Lehman cleared the path for the election of Irwin Steingut of Brooklyn as Speaker of the Lower House in Albany."[41] In a short period of time, Steingut was propelled to the top of state politics.

During the 1930s, Irwin Steingut worked closely with party leaders. He labored side-by-side with Lehman and kept in contact with Roosevelt, pressing Democrats to support them. In 1937, after the Democrats lost control of the Assembly, Steingut showed his astuteness, realism, and brilliance as a tactician. Following the death of Assemblyman Richard B. Smith of Onondaga, Republicans had the exact number of votes in the Assembly as did the Democrats and the legislature was therefore immobilized by partisan politics. Steingut proposed to occasionally "lend" Democratic votes to Republicans in order to get the work of the Assembly completed. The Republicans accepted the offer in good faith so as not to "burden the taxpayers by long, drawn out partisan deliberations on the business before the Assembly ."[42] In this way, Steingut, as minority leader, was an enormous influence helping the Governor realize his programs even without a Democratic majority in the Assembly. By helping the Republicans on some items, they agreed to go along with other Democratic bills.

Later that same year, *The New York Times* noted that the legislative session had been harmonious and productive. Much of Lehman's program had been realized.[43] Steingut had shown himself to be a politician capable of taking a perspective broader than his Assembly District. He demonstrated his ability to work imaginatively with the power structure in constructive ways. It was Steingut who was largely credited with passing social security and unemployment benefits programs in New York State. To a degree, he outgrew the the old-style machine, with its parochial concerns, and expanded his visibility and influence by working through the state and national Democratic Party. By his efforts, the Madison Club, the people of his assembly district, as well as the rest of state benefitted. Of course, the members of the Madison Club also did extremely well at the same time.

Irwin Steingut was also a leader in the battle against the rise of anti-Semitism in the United States. In 1938, he spoke before the National Council of Young Israel at the Hotel Commodore and denounced the accusation that Jews were "communists" and therefore less worthy than other Americans.[44] Jews had cautiously entered the political arena open to them in American life. As immigrants from the tyrannies of Eastern Europe, they had brought with them little direct experience or confidence in politics. It took decades for them to feel at home with America's big city machines, which were being run by Gentiles.[45] Now, after having achieved middle-class status and having internalized American values and aspirations for a better life they were being tagged with pejorative and destructive ethnic labels.

At a dinner in Steingut's honor that same year, the Brooklyn Citizens Committee of the American Jewish Congress gave recognition to the Assemblyman's fifteen years of service to the people of the borough. Held at the

St. George Hotel in Brooklyn, the favored place for Madison Club events and the proceeds of the fund raiser went to the American Jewish Congress. Governor Lehman praised Steingut at the dinner because he had "consistently supported every Jewish activity in Brooklyn." Senator Robert Wagner also praised Steingut's efforts at fighting bigotry.[46] Steingut was an early contributor to what later became known as the liberal Jewish tradition in the United States which gave impetus to landmarks in social legislation and rights for all minorities.

When Irwin Steingut died in 1952. Rabbi Schenck noted in his eulogy that, "Mr. Steingut never forgot that he was a Jew."[47] Steingut, many times a delegate to the World Jewish Congress, had been active in Jewish affairs for many decades, mirroring the interests of his growing constituency, and his own values. Unlike his predecessor, John H. McCooey, Steingut was more issue-oriented and not totally confined by the concerns of the machine.

## Irwin Steingut's Dubious Dealings

Not everything about Irwin Steingut was exemplary. On May 22, 1941, the *Brooklyn Eagle* reported that a probe of the "Brooklyn Political Organization" was underway. Steingut complained to the press that although the accusations were made against his political home base at the Madison Club, the accusers had not made themselves known. The following day it was revealed that they were members of the club. The club was accused of misappropriating funds amounting to somewhere between $40,000 and $50,000. Steingut responded that the Madison Club never had $50,000 at any one time.[48]

At this time in the club's history, Samuel Herman was its financial secretary and a lawyer employed by Steingut's office. Samuel Herman has passed away but his wife

Sophie, an active club member since the 1920's, maintained that never to her knowledge or her husband's were any of the club's funds misused.[49] As a long-time friend of the Steingut's, Mrs. Herman strongly defended Irwin's honesty. A Kings County grand jury was instructed at the time to look into the charges. The club tried to set its house in order and its finances were scrutinized by its leaders and financial officers. Club leaders were upset that the complainants continued to hide their identity.[50]

In early June of 1941, County Judge Franklin Taylor, a member of the Madison Club, called for a speedy judgment by the grand jury because its' financial officers, and those others who handled funds in recent months, lay under a cloud of suspicion. Taylor also called for indictments or denunciations of the libellants.[51] By the end of the month, the grand jury exonerated the Madison Club of charges of misuse of funds. County Judge George W. Martin, who conducted the hearings, said a group of about fifteen citizens had made complaints. When the grand jury reported to Judge Martin, however, they said none of the witnesses whom Martin had named had made complaints to them. They also noted that the Madison Club officers were willing to have the club's books examined. As a result, the investigation ended and Steingut and the other club members were happy that the shadow of doubt had been lifted.[52] Nothing else ever came of the accusations.

The following year, Steingut and other club members found themselves in the middle of a new controversy. A note from Max Kalik, a well-known bookmaker of the time, reached the press. The note indicated that he owed $60,000 to Steingut. Steingut said it was a perfectly legitimate business deal, even though he charged no interest on the loan.[53] Steingut left himself open to justifiable criticism and suspicion. Wise public officials, one assumes, would not associate with notorious people. In reality, Brooklyn

Democratic politics had always had a close connection to the bookmaking enterprise. One of the most colorful examples was Abe Stark, a prominent Brownsville merchant and bookmaker who gave impressive sums to the Brooklyn Democratic Organization and, despite this common knowledge, was elected to the positions of Brooklyn Borough President and, in a city-wide contest, as President of the New York City Council. Such was the political culture and morality of Brooklyn.

Steingut's most serious confrontation with the law came in 1945 when he was briefly jailed for contempt of court for failing to explain $184,000 in excess spending over his reported income during the preceding ten years.[54] State Supreme Court Justice Daniel F. Imrie, who also fined Steingut $250, said his answers were "evasive." Special Prosecutor Hiram G. Todd put questions to Steingut dealing with his personal expenditures. *The New York Times* reported, "It was in reply to these questions by Mr. Todd that Mr. Steingut testified that he had found $96,000 in a safe belonging to his step-father after the latter's death."[55] Irwin Steingut was later cleared of the contempt charges by the State Appellate Division of the Third Department. A veteran club member and close friend of the Steinguts stated that she was present when the safe was opened and verified Steingut's story, noting that the while the money was not counted at the time, it was a very large sum.[56]

In 1954, a few years after Irwin Steingut's death, the state's Moreland Commission investigated horse racing. At the open hearings, one George Morton Levy, counsel to the Roosevelt Raceway in Westbury, Long Island, testified about "hidden stock ownership." He stated that he had obtained 500 shares in the Goshen Mile track Association for Mrs. Jeanne Weiss, daughter of Irwin Steingut. She had paid two hundred and fifty dollars for the stock, but when the Goshen track was absorbed by the Yonkers Trotting

Association, the stock soared to $45,000 in value.[57] Further investigation revealed more hidden ownership.

A Mr. Weisman, a large stockholder in the Old Country Trotting Association, said he invested money for Mr. Steingut and Jeanne Weiss but that the stock remained in Mrs. Weisman's name until it was transferred over to the Steinguts in 1948.[58] By having others purchase stock for him in these associations, Steingut was able to disguise, at least temporarily, his personal stakes. Inside knowledge of State decisions affecting the tracks enabled him to profit handsomely. George Plunkitt, as well as John McCooey, would have admired him and the many other political insiders who succeeded them and continued to enjoy the perquisites of their positions.

Later in 1954, more dirt was to hit the fan as the result of battling between Democrats and Republicans in the State. Republican Governor Thomas E. Dewey accused former Governor Lehman of corruption for signing a 1940 law authorizing pari-mutual betting at harness tracks. Under that arrangement those winners at the track divided the betting "handle," owners were allowed a regulated profit, and the state received taxes. Steingut, Lehman's close associate, stood to profit enormously from the law as he had acquired three-quarters ownership of a race track in Batavia, New York.[59] Under provisions of the law, race-track owners could take costs, profits and taxes from the pool wagered. This loose arrangement allowed corners to be cut when tax reports were filed with the state. Ironically, pari-mutual betting was designed to reduce corruption and cut into illegal book-making.

In contrast to the many rumors concerning the extent of Irwin Steingut's fortune, Irwin Steingut's will, filed in Brooklyn Surrogates Court, indicated that he had left an estate worth less than $50,000, along with $1,500 in liabilities. The estate his widow Rae Steingut received constituted entirely of stocks, bonds and cash. The will was dated 1939 and made no separate provisions for Mrs. Jeanne Weiss, his daughter, or his son Stanley, saying that the widow would provide for them.[60]

Despite all his failings, Irwin Steingut was in many ways superior to his predecessors. By addressing wider public issues he wisely shepherded the transition of power in the Brooklyn machine and his leadership brought new character to Kings County politics. He adjusted well to the changes and was always able to deliver the Brooklyn vote for the Democratic Party. During his many years in office, Governor Lehman came to rely on Steingut as a promoter and facilitator of his programs. Steingut skills matured and he remained Democratic Party Leader of the New York State Assembly for 22 of the 31 years he served in the Albany legislature.

As a new style machine politician, however, he cut corners and appeared to have used the knowledge and influence of his office for personal profit. Like his father Simon, Irwin was relatively unscathed by accusations and investigations into his political and personal dealings. But in the third generation, the political luck of the family was to run out. Ironically, it was Stanley Steingut, probably the most ethical of the three who was to suffer the consequences of decades of accumulated enmity.

## Footnotes

1. *New York Times,* January 23, 1934, p. 18:3.
2. *New York Times,* January 25, 1934, p. 18:4.
3. *New York Times,* June 9, 1913, p. 6:3.
4. *New York Times,* March 5, 1905, III, p. 6:1.
5. *Ibid.*
6. *New York Times,* January 23, 1901, p. 3.
7. *New York Times,* September 1, 1913, p. 2:8.
8. *New York Times,* October 20, 1915, p. 8:4.
9. *New York Times,* March 12, 1919, p. 11:4.

10. *Brooklyn Eagle*, January 21, 1930.
11. *New York Post*, February 20, 1969. Column by Paul Hoffman.
12. Interview with former Speaker of the Assembly, Stanley Steingut, March 22, 1981.
13. *New York Post*, October 20, 1965.
14. *New York Post*, October 20, 1965.
15. Interview with former Mayor of New York City Abraham Beame, May 19, 1981.
16. *Brooklyn Eagle*, October 28, 1946.
17. *Brooklyn Eagle*, January 3, 1934.
18. *Brooklyn Eagle*, January 5, 1935.
19. *Brooklyn Eagle*, January 30, 1934.
20. *New York Times*, August 30, 1934.
21. *New York Times*, August 30, 1934.
22. *Brooklyn Eagle*, February 25, 1934.
23. *Brooklyn Eagle*, February 25, 1934.
24. *New York Times*, May 30, 1929, p. 20:4.
25. *New York Times*, June 20, 1930, p. 20:4.
26. *New York Times*, June 15, 1933, p. 10:2.
27. *New York Times*, January 27, 1932.
28. *New York Times*, January 28, 1932, p. 2:4.
29. *New York Times*, February 28, 1932, p. 3:1.
30. *Brooklyn Eagle*, August 31, 1934.
31. *New York Times*, September 17, 1934, p.5:1.
32. *Brooklyn Eagle*, November 7, 1934.
33. *Brooklyn Eagle*, November 19, 1934.
34. *Brooklyn Eagle*, January 26, 1935.
35. *New York Times*, January 4, 1935.
36. *New York Times*, Janaury 10, 1935, p. 4:3.
37. *New York Times*, January 12, 1935, p. 3:3.
38. *Ibid.*
39. *New York Times*, January 20, 1934, p. 1:1.
40. *New York Times*, November 8, 1934, p. 4:5.
41. *New York Times*, November 19, 1934.
42. *New York Times*, March 3, 1937, p. 12:2.
43. *New York Times*, May 2, 1937, IV, p. 12:3.
44. *New York Times*, May 2, 1938.
45. Irving Howe, *World of Our Fathers*, p. 360.
46. *New York Times*, September 29, 1952.
47. *Ibid.*
48. *Brooklyn Eagle*, May 23, 1941.
49. Interview, March 3, 1980.
50. *Brooklyn Eagle*, May 24, 1941.
51. *Brooklyn Eagle*, June 3, 1941.
52. *New York Times*, June 28, 1941, p. 32:1, and *Brooklyn Eagle*, July 2, 1941.

53. *New York Times,* December 4, 1942, p. 27:6, and *Brooklyn Eagle,* December 3, 1942.
54. *Brooklyn Eagle,* August 21, 1945.
55. *New York Times,* September 27, 1952.
56. Interview with Sophie Herman, March 3, 1980.
57. *New York Times,* March 4, 1954.
58. *New York Times,* March 6, 1954.
59. *New York Times,* October 16, 1954, p. 1:4.
60. *New York Times,* October 8, 1952, p. 33:8.

# Political Change and Ethnic Succession

## Introduction

The drama of the rise, transformations, and fall of the urban political machine has occurred in the context of the great issues of the American "Melting Pot" and "Cultural Pluralism." Ethnicity and race have always been central issues in politics in America, and according to historian Richard Polenberg, the United States has long been divided by class, race and ethnicity.[1] In order for the nation to survive intact, it has sought through various mechanisms to reduce these divisions and has been more or less successful at different times in its history. The big city political machine, as argued by Robert K. Merton, Edward C. Banfield and James Q. Wilson, was well suited to take advantage of these societal divisions.

Social commentators in the 1960s revived, in a new guise, the "Americanization" issue which was of great concern in America during the period of mass immigration from 1880 to 1920. The re-emergence of racism as a major problem in America in the 1950s, the ensuing Civil Rights Movement and subsequent civil disorders especially increased the polarization between whites and nonwhite racial groups and awakened consciousness of the cultural and other differences among all ethnic groups. These differences had been for a time submerged during World War II and the Cold War confrontations in the 50s and 60s. Some called this phenomenon of heightened group interest among European-American groups "defensive ethnicity;" a white reaction to increasing black solidarity. For whatever reason, ethnic and subcultural diversity in American society came again to the attention of scholars and produced a debate over whether ethnicity in America was becoming more or less important. Conservative social critic Michael Novak referred to the issue of emerging white ethnic consciousness as "The Rise of the Unmeltable Ethnics."[2]

## The Melting Pot: Success or Failure?

Ethnicity, religion, nationality and race have always been important elements lubricating traditional urban political machine operations. In this chapter we will consider how the ideas presented in *Beyond the Melting Pot: The Negroes, Puerto Ricans, Jews, Italians, and Irish of New York City*,[3] contribute to our understanding of the Madison Club and Brooklyn's Democratic Party organization. In this provocative book, Nathan Glazer and Daniel P. Moynihan analysed historically, politically, and sociologically the conflict and competion among New York City's major ethnic groups; Catholics, Jews, white Protestants and Negroes. Its first edition, published in 1963, stressed the continued importance of ethnic identity in American society. However, Glazer and Moynihan predicted a decline in the importance of specific national identities and a rise in the value attached to religion in ethnic-interest group politics. They also expected that the newest groups in city politics, Blacks and Puerto Ricans, would follow in the pattern of accommodation-politics established by earlier white European immigrant groups. It was assumed, based on historical analogy, that Blacks and Hispanics would begin climbing up on the "ladder of ethnic succession" in New York City.[4]

The second edition of *Beyond the Melting Pot* published in 1970, began with a new preface in which Glazer and Moynihan attempted to explain the apparent refutation of their hypothesis that Blacks would use the same ladder for advancement as had the Europeans before them. They were forced to rethink their first assumption because of the unexpected appearance of the non-traditional, racial confrontation politics of the sixties and the development of what they saw as a "new" political form among Blacks-- namely racial separatism.

What they observed, and misinterpreted, was that, for many understandable reasons, some Blacks sought to gain political power outside of the traditionally gradualist mechanisms of the existing political machine. Addressing their miscalculation, Glazer and Moynihan, admitted that ethnicity and race had, momentarily overshadowed religion as a political organizational factor and added that their first calculations took place before the civil rights "revolution" and the Black ghetto riots.[5]

Although their analyses and discussion are of great value for our study of the Madison Club and Brooklyn politics, especially as "historical" data, it is obvious in "hindsight" that their first conclusions concerning Blacks and Hispanics were not so far off the mark. Were they to write a new preface they would have to note that in the 1980s in New York and other cities there has emerged a major and quite "traditional" Black and Hispanic ethnic political force. It would appear that the demonstrations, riots, and separatist flirtations in the sixties and early seventies have been overtaken by basic political organization-building and the development of viable Black and Hispanic political groups partners and competitors in urban electoral politics. Despite several other equally conspicuous errors of electoral prognosis, their ideas continue to be of great value in analysing contemporary political events. A case in point was their observation that the Democratic coalition in New York City of Irish, Italians, Jews, and Blacks "against the field," was shattered forever by the events of the sixties, which still holds true today.[6]

The most recent examples of this new fact of ethnic political life in America have been the suprisingly successful national campaign of Reverend Jesse Jackson for the Presidential nomination of the Democratic Party in 1984 and the mayoral victories of other Black politicians such as David Dinkins in New York City, William Goode in Philadelphia and Harold Washington in Chicago. These political accomplishments followed the earlier, less dramatic victories of Richard Hatcher in Gary, Indiana, Kenneth Gibson in Newark, New Jersey, and Tom Bradley in Los Angeles, California. Similarly, but less spectacularly, Hispanic political clout has spread in the Southwestern states and in Florida where the Spanish-speaking population has approached majority status.

More important for our purposes concerning the survival of the machine and its transitions has been the expanding visibility in American cities of Black and Hispanic urban machines which now face charges of corruption and patronage abuse. In what undoubtably will become a "classic" example in the history machine politics, Harold Washington, a Black candidate and leader of his own machine organization, defeated the remnants of Mayor Daley's powerful Democratic political juggernaut in Chicago with the support of the city's "white liberal," and the image-concious business communities. This is reminiscent of the reform movements in New York City which pitted liberals and business interests against the immigrant-based Democratic bosses of the past.

Especially valuable in the analysis of the Madison Club in its twilight years was Glazer and Moynihan's observation on the relevance of race as an underlying issue in New York City politics and the consequent racial polarization of communities. In fact, except for their considerable attention to the Puerto Rican and White-Anglo-Saxon-Protestant contingents in New York politics, Glazer and Moynihan's account of ethnic participants and their political histories reflects on a larger scale the historical evolution of the Madison Club. Briefly speaking; during the period 1905-1935 the club was led by Irish Catholic with Italian silent partners, and Jews on the periphery waiting in the wings. From 1935 to 1978 the club was led by Jews with Italian silent partners and Blacks biding their time in the wings.

## The Irish Slow Fall From Grace

For Glazer and Moynihan, the Irish era in New York City began in the early 1870s with Charles O'Connor's prosecution of William March Tweed and symbolically ended sixty years later when ex-Mayor James J. Walker sailed off into exile. Both these beginning and end points coincide well with the Irish Brooklyn Boss Hugh McLaughlin's arrival in the borough and the deposition and then death of the Madison Club's own County Leader John H. McCooey. During this period the Irish dominated both the police and the underworld- the good and the bad of the city. Because of the dominance of "Honest John" Kelly, Richard Crocker and Frank Murphy in Manhattan, McLaughlin, McCooey and Frank Kelly in Brooklyn, as well as Ed Flynn in The Bronx, one could say, in effect, that attacks on the "Boss" system in New York were attacks on the Irish Catholics.[7]

If the Irish in New York had any advantage in political competition other than innate tenacity, it was their attachment to the Roman Catholic Church, the largest religious organization in the country. Slowly over the decades Irish nationalism had reincarnated itself as American patriotism; and Irish radicalism became American Catholic conservatism. Discrimination against the Irish and Catholics in the United States and the battles of the labor movement initially gave the Irish a sense of solidarity and mission as they promulgated the machine image as the "Party of the People." The drive of the Irish for social acceptance and economic success in the city slowly changed them from humble "peasant tenants" to pretentious "noble landlords."

According to George Potter the Irish were well prepared to take over the machine when they came to New York. He noted that: "The great and the wealthy ran Ireland politically like Tammany Hall in its worst days. Had they not sold their own country for the money and titles in the Act of Union with England and, as one rogue said, thanked God they had a country to sell?...A gentleman was thought no less a gentleman because he dealt, like merchandise, with the votes of his tenants or purchased his parliamentary seat as he would a horse or a new wing for his big house."[8]

Conrad Arensberg in his study of the Irish Countryman had noted that "Irish familism is of the soil...It operates most strongly within allegiances to a definite small area."[9] According to Glazer and Moynihan this cultural predisposition made the Irish ideal candidates for the narrowness of local neighborhood political work. It must be added that this narrow local orientation is by no means a cultural characteristic exclusive to the Irish.

Although the Irish did not literally "invent" machine politics or Tammany Hall, they certainly left their mark on the institution. They did however, "invent" the Madison Club and the Brooklyn machine. The machine government established in New York and many other Northern cities was a merger of rural Irish custom and urban American politics.

The *paese* and villages of the Italians, the ghettos and *shtetls* of the Jews, and most recently, the informal groups based on previous southern residence called "homeboys," extended families, and church organizations of the Blacks would add their own cultural elements to machine's form and operation.

Although the Irish were extremely successful in politics, their success might be said to have caused their downfall as they were trapped by it. Ironically, it was at the height of their power during the campaign of Al Smith in the 1930s for President that they seemed to have fallen from grace in New York City politics. The eventual political failure of the Irish in the Democratic Party in New York, Glazer and Moynihan claim, runs parallel with their history of involvment in organized crime. They argued that although they were early leaders in the field: "Gambling and related activities are among the largest business activities in New York and certainly among the most profitable. With their political power, even if declining, the Irish ought to have a share of control in them, but the Southern Italians, with Jewish connections, have completely taken over. Bookmaking, policy, and drugs are complex, serious, exacting trades."[10]

Again with 1990 hindsight, we must somewhat modify the foregoing emphasis on Italian and Jewish hegemony in organized crime in New York by noting the increasing involvement of Blacks, Asians, Hispanics, recent Russian and other European immigrants, in New York City's still flourishing gambling, prostitution and drug trades. In some cases these new groups have already pushed themselves into the higher echelons of organized crime and have established competing ethnic based criminal enterprises.

*Beyond the Melting Pot* downplays the role of the Irish in organized crime. The American pattern of ethnic succession in organized crime is for groups to move upward to higher levels of criminal activity and leave the lower level "dirty" work for newer, more disadvantaged groups. Ideally, the process of ethnic succession leads to the abandonment of crime as a way of life once the participants have obtained social and economic mobility. Thus succession enables the third and subsequent generations to avoid it entirely.

In faint praise of the Irish, and without much supporting evidence, Glazer and Moynihan argued that, "The secret of the long tenure of many of the better known Irish politicians is that they were honest men by any standards, and certainly by the American standards of their time."[11] For social scientists to argue that one ethnic group is "more honest" than another is a bit presumptious. More likely it was the Irish dependence on the American Catholic Church for institutional support which seemed to tolerate political corruption and criminal involvement in very limited areas of activity.

The decline of the Irish in the Democratic machine can be viewed as reflecting their proportionate decrease in New York City's population, and their movement towards the conservative side of the political spectrum. Noting that, including Robert Wagner (half-Irish), seven of the last nine New York mayors were Irish, and since then two Jews and a WASP have occupied the office, Glazer and Moynihan erred in their overall assessment that "Al Smith was the last Irish officeholder who could command a large vote in

New York politics."[12] The later successes of Senator Robert Kennedy, Govenor Hugh Carey (both of whom had some connection to the old Irish Brooklyn machine) and Moynihan's own tenure as New York State's Democratic Senator belie their pronouncement.

But these more successful "liberals," as with the Italian-American Governor of New York Mario Cuomo, owed less to their own conservative-minded ethnic groups for votes than conventional wisdom would allow. For example, Cuomo in the 1982 Democratic Gubernatorial primary received overwhelming support from the Black and Hispanic communities as he ran against Mayor of New York City, Edward I. Koch. In that election, Jewish Mayor Koch, with significant previous liberal credentials, was viewed with great suspicion and hostility by minority voters because of his previous jockeying to garner support among more conservative Democrats in a field filled with liberal Democrats.

As with most other ethnic groups, as the Irish became more successful in America, they also became more conservative. Catholic Irish social and political conservativism was firmly established during the Franklin D. Roosevelt administration when Al Smith openly endorsed his Republican opponent in 1936, accusing F.D.R. of paving the way for communism. James Farley also broke with the President in 1940 after being denied an opportunity to succeed him, which Farley and the Irish seemed to have taken as a personal and "racial" insult.

For three decades the strident anti-communism of the Irish and the Catholic hierarchy in New York was to further distance the Irish from the Jews who were to replace them. This gulf widened from the 1920s, with the rise of the Soviet Union as an international power, through the "McCarthy" period of the 1950s. Anti-communism became political conservatism and Catholics, the Irish in particular, became increasingly alienated from the more liberal Democratic party. In local New York City politics the end of the Irish era came with the election of "reform" Democrat Robert Wagner in 1961.

It is strange that the end for the Irish on the national scene centers around the election of John Fitzgerald Kennedy in 1960. Glazer and Moynihan call it their "last hurrah" as, "On the day he died, the President of the United States, the Speaker of the House of Representatives, the Majority Leader of the United States Senate, the Chairman of the National Committee were all Irish, all Catholic, all Democrats."[13] Perhaps it can be said that the Irish controlled the crown but not the body underneath. The apparent Irish victory masked a wider and deeper failure in the Democratric Party machinery.

The trend toward conservatism among the Irish was well established by the 1960 Presidential campaign of Democratic candidate John F. Kennedy. Glazer and Moynihan note with some irony that Alfred E. Smith Jr. announced he was voting for Nixon and Madison Club Brooklyn boss John H. McCooey's grandson "turned up ringing doorbells for the straight Republican ticket." in Greenwich Connecticut.[14] The few Irish still left in the Madison Club's assembly district in the middle of Brooklyn, New York were more than likely registered as Republicans and planning to move out of the racially changing neighborhood.

In Brooklyn, Irish and Catholic areas became Republican Party domains, and later were led by a "half-Italian" Irish Catholic George Clark and Conservative Party leader Michael Long. By the 1970s issues such as support for the Vietnam War, abortion, the death penalty, aid to parochial schools, and affirmative action would further alienate this group from the increasingly liberal Democratic Party. In later years, during Stanley Steingut's fateful last general election in 1978, even local Jewish voters had become more conservative in Brooklyn. Steingut suffered greatly because of his liberal positions against the death penalty and for a woman's right to have an abortion.

## The Jews and the Machine

Central to the fall of the Irish was the concomitant rise of the Jews in the machine who took their place. "During the Averell Harriman administration in Albany, 1955-1958, for example, New York City Jews received two jobs for every one given the Irish."[15] Even while reclaiming some top positions as they inexorably declined in power, the Irish vacated those patronage slots underneath- the heart and soul of the party. Glazer and Moynihan noted that "None of the nineteen Congressman elected in New York City in 1962 were Irish, and only a fifth of the sixty-five Assemblymen were."[16] And, because religion was the major component of their definition of ethnicity, the collapse of the Irish in politics meant that New York was no longer "...a Catholic city as well."[17] "In 1962 James B. Donovan, the Democratic candidate for Senator, managed to lose even his home borough of Brooklyn to the Republican (and Jewish) Jacob K. Javits."[18] Coincidentally, the Madison Club's Irish Congresswoman Edna Kelly was "sacrificed" in reapportionment for the benefit of Black Congresswoman Shirley Chisholm and Jewish Congressman Emanuel Cellar.

Before 1950, Brooklyn's Jewish voters were divided among Democrats, Republicans and Fusion, Socialist, American Labor and Liberal Parties. Their gravitation into the Democratic Party signaled their changing life styles. It was during the LaGuardia mayoral administration that Jews first advanced in large numbers into positions of political influence in the city as a whole. Interestingly, the

Madison club, then with Jewish members poised for advancement in the wings, campaigned hard against LaGuardia's candidacy as they realized he was a real threat to what was left of the political *status quo* and its patronage benefits. City-wide, however Jews voted for LaGuardia in the 1930s and 1940s as they also voted for Roosevelt and Lehman. Helping to explain earlier Jewish allegiance to anti-machine candidates, James Q. Wilson found that New York City's reform mayors Low, Mitchell, LaGuardia and Wagner appointed a much larger proportion of Jews to their cabinets than did their regular organization predecessors.[19]

Glazer and Moynihan cite as an indication of the Jewish movement to the Democratic Party the elections to Congress of Sol Bloom, Nathaniel Dickstein and the Madison Club's own Emanual Cellar in 1922. Two years before that, six Jews were elected to Congress, all but one as Republicans and the sixth as a Socialist.[20] In the 1920s two of New York City's Republican county leaders for Brooklyn and Manhattan were Jewish--Meir Steinbrink and Samuel Koenig. Brooklyn had a Jewish Republican County leader before the end of the century and in the 1870s and 1880s Greenpoint had Jewish Republican leaders.

Catholics, on the other hand, had much earlier been tied almost exclusively to the Democratic party, and then only later moved toward the Republican and more conservative parties. Glazer and Moynihan emphasize that the Jews in New York rose more quickly in economic and political stature than the working class Irish and Italian Catholics. Their advancement in education also led them to later embrace more "liberal" positions on social issues. During the 1960s Jews and Protestants were found to be more favorable toward civil rights positions which moved the Catholic populace away from the liberalized Democratic party in New York City. In the seventies, Jews as well as Catholics moved quickly to the right of the political spectrum, in some cases taking the party with them, antagonizing the growing Black and Hispanic political leadership and splitting county organizations even further.

The replacement of Catholics by Jews in the New York political hierarchy is exemplified by the fact that in 1963 on the powerful Board of Estimate in New York City, consisting of the mayor, comptroller, city council president and the five borough presidents, there were five Catholics, two Jews and one black Protestant. In 1969 the numbers were five Jews, one white Protestant, one black Protestant and one Catholic. In that same year there was only one Catholic statewide officer; Lieutenant Governor Malcolm Wilson. Both Catholic officials were then, however, Republicans.[21] Arthur Klebanoff observed that "between 1950 and 1968, 51 of the 91 possible tenures in the New York State Senate and 82 of 229 available Assembly terms were served by Brooklyn Jews."[22]

## Italian Power Stalls

Despite its size, the relative impotence of the Italian electorate and their politicians is best exemplified by the debacle of Democratic Mayoral candidate Mario Procaccino in the 1969 race against Republican victor John V. Lindsay. The conservative Procaccino had won the factionalized Democratic Primary, but in the process the party was split apart. To use Procaccino's own term; the "Limousine Liberals" took over the city. Since then, no Italian has won city-wide office and only in the heavily populated Italian areas of the city have they achieved lower level elective offices.[23]

Lack of political organization was not the only problem afflicting Italian American politicians. Italians also suffered from bias and "stereotypes" when they sought city-wide office. One major stereotype they had to cope with was that of "organized crime." Glazer and Moynihan say that "The early Irish gangsters were succeeded by the Jews, and Arnold Rothstein, "Czar" of the New York underworld in the 1920s, was as closely linked to Democratic judges in Jimmy Walker's day as Frank Costello was 15 years later. After the mid-thirties, the most prominent gangsters in New York were of Italian origin, though their careers had begun in the 1920s."[24] Even today organized crime and "mafia" are seen as synonymous. The relative success of the Jews and Irish in more legitimate economic spheres, where political influence was equally desirable, made it possible for Italians to replace them in some lucrative organized crime activities. In some cases Italians and Jews involved in illicit businesses acquired respectable enterprises after the the Great Depression. By the 1950s, however, the Kefauver investigations and the New York State Crime Commission hearings on the links between politicians and organized crime figures focused almost exclusively on Italian-Americans.

According to Frank J. Cavaioli, in general, the way Italians adapted to America made normal political ascendency difficult. Most Italian immigrants were Southern Italian peasants with little or no education and a distrust of government in any form. Cultural values made extensive community and political organization impossible, and when Italians succeeded in politics, it was for the most part on a very local level.[25] Until the 1970s Italians were less educationally and socially mobile than the Irish and far less so than the Jews who leap-frogged over them to political power.[26] Fiorello LaGuardia, the City's first Italian-American Mayor, with a Jewish mother from Trieste and a Protestant father from Apulia, was raised and educated in the America's Far West. He was hardly representative of the vast majority of New York's Italians. In his election victory against O'Dwyer in 1941, LaGuardia did worse in Italian than non-Italian districts of the city. Italians were much more likely to vote for the second Italian-American Mayor, Catholic Vincent Impellitteri who ran as an Independent.

## Blacks and Racism Complicate the Political Equation

In the 1960s residents in many white neighborhoods felt threatened by a nonwhite invasion. Resentment among white-ethnic groups rose as they saw the inauguration of special programs for minorities. The media also contributed to the deepening "Black versus White" chasm. During the Civil Rights Movement, the prejudice of working-class European ethnics, especially Catholics and Italian Americans, like hard-line southern segregationists, were portrayed by the media as the root cause of the problems confronting minorities. Any thought, therefore, of a Black-Puerto Rican-White working-class political coalition became almost impossible.

As immigrants, Italians took slowly to American politics. The Irish were already well-established in the machine when Italians arrived in great numbers and their Jewish immigrant counterparts adapted and moved more quickly up the social ladder than both of them. In contrast to their Italian and Irish competitors Glazer and Moynihan also contended that Jews excelled in New York's intellectual life and raised the level of politics beyond the parochialism of the neighborhood. According to them, more socially liberal Jews promoted the interests of the poor and minorities in general, and therefore gained political support among Blacks and Hispanics which was of great value in later inter-ethnic political confrontations between themselves and the Irish and Italians.

But Jewish Americans also began drifting into more conservative political attitudes toward the end of the 1960s because of several factors, including the rise of Black militancy and Black anti-semitism. The Ocean-Hill Brownsville school district in Brooklyn could have easily been characterized as a poverty stricken ghetto. There, community leaders clashed with teachers over the issue of "community control" and deeply affected Blacks' relations with Jews who composed a major proportion of New York City teachers. Also, by not supporting the referendum on the Civilian Complaint Review Board, Jews lost their traditional liberal leadership. Although they became more conservative, they did not, as Italians and Irish had before them, defect in large numbers to the Republican Party. By 1978, however, Jewish voters and politicians had moved further to the right over the Allan Bakke Case which challenged in the U.S. Supreme Court the idea of minority preferences in medical school admissions, Affirmative Action, "excessive" military-spending, and related foreign policy issues regarding American support for the state of Israel.

According to Glazer and Moynihan, Blacks were politically "undercompetitive," which was a legacy of their past history of discrimination in the South.[27] They were not, like the Irish and Jews, quick to take on politics and were even slower than the Italians in getting their "fair share" of the patronage pie. For example, Klebanoff found that between 1950 and 1965 the proportion of Blacks and Puerto Ricans in Brooklyn rose from 9 per cent to 29 per cent of the total population.[28] Despite being 25 per cent of eligible voters, they were no more than 15 per cent of registered voters. During the 1960s Jews and Italians continued to represent districts that had become predominantly Black or Puerto Rican. The fall of the Madison Club in 1978, however, heralded a major change in this situation as minorities subsequently asserted their political muscle in Brooklyn with the help of Federally mandated redistricting policies.

Prior to the law suits which forced redistricting to reflect the relative size of minority populations, the major party organizations divided Black and Puerto Rican potential voting strength through gerrymandering. Despite a large number of Blacks in Brooklyn, Bertram Baker was the first, and only, Black Assemblyman from 1948 until 1962 when Thomas Russell Jones became the second. Baker and Jones represented almost entirely nonwhite areas in Bedford Stuyvesant, and, it must be noted, were very much in the mold and perhaps the "camp" of regular Democrats. They certainly were friends of the Madison Club and their own clubhouses served as ethnic satellites of the county organization. In 1964 William C. Thompson became the first Black State Senator. He won election within a district which appeared as Jewish and Italian politicians adjusted their own district boundaries and moved to areas with larger white populations in Brooklyn. These and other nonwhite leaders helped to build a minority organization in Brooklyn which filled the political vacuum as the Irish, Italians and Jews fled from their northern and central Brooklyn neighborhoods in the 1960s.

In many ways it can be said that Black political power in Brooklyn, historically slow in coming, might have come even later if it were not for Federal intervention. Granted, some few Blacks who worked for the machine received part of the spoils of the system as other "less powerful ethnic groups had in the past received the "leftovers." The Civil Rights Movement, however, did not respect the traditional rule that groups had to wait their turn in line for constitutional rights. In 1965, based on a suit that claimed that Black voters were denied equal rights, Brooklyn was carved into 5 Congressional Districts; including the first contiguous minority district. In 1968 New York State Assemblywoman, and very "regular" Democrat, Shirley Chisholm won the seat and served until 1982. Her fealty was noted by her support of Madison Clubber Abraham Beame in the Democratic Mayoral Primary against fellow Black politician Percy Sutton.

A later Federally-inspired redistricting in 1982 created two minority Congressional Districts. The seats in these districts were both won by African-American politicians. One was Ed Towns, an Assistant to the Brooklyn Borough President Howard Golden, and the other; State Senator Major Owens from Brownsville. In a classic "reform versus regular" battle, reform candidate Owens defeated regular Democrat, and State Senator, Vander Beatty. Beatty, also Black, ran under a cloud of charges and investigations into fraud in programs with which he was associated. He was later convicted of voting law violations which took place during his losing congressional campaign against Major Owens. In any case, after the fall of the Madison Club, Blacks emerged as a major power in Brooklyn politics assisted in part by the party disorganization created by the infighting. Until 1990, with few exceptions such as in the South Bronx, Black and Puerto Rican power in the rest of the city remained static or diminutive.

The continued frustrations of the Black electorate gave rise to more claims of discrimination and attempts to impose further changes on the operation of New York City politics which are seen to hamper minority participation. These issues included unduly complicated voter registration requirements, the run-off primary for Mayor, and proportional representation in city-wide legislative bodies such as the City Council and the Board of Estimate. The "one man-one vote" issue of proportional representation in New York City's legislative bodies was resolved by 1989 U.S. Supreme Court rulings and subsequent New York

City Charter Revisions.

The local context of Black political and neighborhood expansion in Brooklyn is highlighted in Jonathan Rieder's study of "Canarsie;" a white working class area on the southern fringe of the Madison Club's assembly district.[29] The growing fear in the community of a Black "invasion" and the role played by the local Democratic organizations which tried to prevent their encroachment is detailed in Riecker's study. The Canarsie neighborhood's local Democratic organization was well represented at the top of the Brooklyn machine during the 1960s and 1970s by Thomas Jefferson Club members County Leader Meade Esposito and the successor to Stanley Steingut as State Assembly Leader, Stanley Fink.

## Ethnic Changes at the Madison Club

Glazer and Moynihan claim that the victory of Robert Wagner in the 1961 Democratic Mayoral primary ended the Irish political system in New York City. Wagner's liberal coalition of middle and upper-middle class electorates, combined with modern political organization and techniques defeated the traditional working class party headed by Irish county leaders in Brooklyn and the Bronx. These leaders had sided with Tammany dinosaur Carmine DeSapio, displaying commendable but misplaced loyalty. "If Wagner wins," said one party leader, "you can close down every clubhouse in the city."[30] Wagner won handily and the city politic went through another metamorphosis. The club houses, of course, didn't close down, even for a moment.

Madison Club leader, Stanley Steingut had opposed Wagner in favor of his own candidate, Lawrence Gerosa, in both the primary and general elections. In retaliation, Wagner put his support behind Anthony Travia who defeated Steingut for the coveted post of Speaker of the Assembly in 1958. Travia served as Democratic Party Leader in the until 1969, when he was replaced by Steingut. Steingut had, in 1962, also defeated Travia for Democratic Party County Chairman in Brooklyn as their personal and intra-party rivalry continued.[31]

Later, the effect of John V. Lindsay's Mayoral victories, first as a Republican and then, incredibly, as a Liberal, destroyed any semblance of an all-powerful city-wide Democratic Party machine. While in office, Lindsay created his own "New Deal" and developed his own extensive organization built around city programs which circumvented the regular clubhouses. He increased the influence of the Liberal Party as well. The perception among working-class European-Americans that he and the other "liberals" catered to minorities added another demension to future political battles and undermined party loyalty.

The decline of the monolithic Democratic Party machine, as they knew it, was succinctly expressed by Glazer and Moynihan: "At the close of the 1960s the Democrats were more completely out of power in New York State and City government than almost any time in their history. The oldest organized political party in the world was reduced by way of offices to the Comptroller in Albany, Arthur Levitt, who had long since become a politically neutral figure, and the Comptroller in New York City, Abraham Beame, whose career would have to be judged to have passed its apogee."[32]

As noted by Salvatore LaGumina in his insightful study of New York State's 1970 elections, the failure of the Democratic Party had a great deal to do with breaking the age-old political traditon of ethnic ticket balancing. The Democratic Party that year ran Jewish candidates; Arthur J. Goldberg for governor, Adam Walinsky for attorney general, Arthur Levitt for comptroller, and Richard Ottinger for United States Senator. The only non-Jewish candidate for state-wide office was Basil Patterson, who is Black, for lieutenant governor. Additionally, while the Democrats virtually ignored Italian American voters, Nelson Rockefeller and the Republican Party courted them.[33]

Interestingly, after the Republican victories, both the remaining prominent Democratic figures, New York State Comptroller Arthur Levitt and New York City Controller Abraham Beame, were Madison Club members, and Beame's career was far from over as he became New York City Mayor in 1974. As the old party declined the Madisonians rose. While it was crumbling, Stanley Steingut became Kings County leader and then Democratic leader of the State Assembly and many other Madisonians also moved up the political scale in terms of power and patronage.

Like Tammany Hall and the Brooklyn machine, the Madison Club was once an Irish and Catholic organization, but by the 1950s it was the Jewish contingent which was firmly in control, predating the hegemony of Jews in New York City's Democratic Party in the 1980s. The Madison Club became essentially a Jewish organization. The Irish were a distant memory. A few Italians still hung around the club and the Blacks simply waited on the sidelines knowing their time would come.

## Footnotes

1. Richard Polenberg, *One Nation Divisible*. New York: Penguin Books, 1981.
2. *The Rise of the Unmeltable Ethnics.*, New York: MacMillan, 1972.
3. *Beyond the Melting Pot: The Negroes, Puerto Ricans, Jews, Italians and Irish of New York City.* Cambridge, Mass.: M.I.T. Press, 1970.
4. *Ibid.,* p. 314.
5. *Ibid.,* p. ix.
6. *Ibid.,* p. lxxii.
7. *Ibid.,* p. 226.
8. *Ibid.,* p. 224. Also see: George Potter, *To the Golden Door: The Story of the Irish in Ireland and America.* Boston: Little, Brown and Co., 1960, pp. 67-68.

9. Glazer and Moynihan, *op. cit.*, p. 228. See: Conrad Arensberg, *The Irish Countryman*. London: MacMillan Co., 1937, p. 107.

10. *Ibid.*, p. 258.

11. *Ibid.*, p. 259.

12. *Ibid.*, p. 263.

13. *Ibid.*, p. 287.

14. *Ibid.*, p. 272.

15. *Ibid.*, p. 263.

16. *Ibid.*, p. 263.

17. *Ibid.*, p. lxii.

18. *Ibid.*, p. 263.

19. James Q. Wilson, *The Amateur Democrat*, Chicago: University of Chicago Press, 1962, p. 304.

20. Glazer and Moynihan, *op. cit.*, p. 169.

21. *Ibid.*, p. lviii.

22. Arthur Klenbanoff, "The Demographics of Politics: Legislative Constituencies and the Borough of Brooklyn, 1950-1965." Unpublished senior honor's thesis. New Haven: Yale University, 1969.

23. Jerome Krase, "The Missed Step: Italian Americans and Brooklyn Politics," in *Italians and Irish in America*. Francis X. Femminella, ed., Staten Island, New York: American Italian Historical Association, 1985, pp. 187-98.

24. Glazer and Moynihan, *op. cit.*, p. 210.

25. Frank J. Cavaioli, "Italian American Political Behavior," *The ECCSSA Journal*. Vol. III, No. 1, Winter, 1988, pp. 47-62. See also Krase, *op. cit.*

26. William Egelman, "Italian American Educational Attainment: An Introductory Analysis Utilizing Recent Current Population Survey Data," in *The Italian Americans Through the Generations*. Rocco Caporale, ed. Staten Island, New York: American Italian Historical Association, 1986, pp. 197-211.

27. Glazer and Moynihan, *op. cit.*, p. lxiv.

28. Klebanoff, *op. cit.*

29. Jonathan Rieder, *Canarsie: The Jews and Italians of Brooklyn against Liberalism*. Cambridge, Mass.: Cambridge University Press, 1985.

30. Glazer and Moynihan, *op. cit.*, p. 273.

31. Klebanoff, *op. cit.*, p. 34.

32. Glazer and Moynihan, *op. cit.*, p. lxxi.

33. Salvatore J. LaGumina, "Ethnic Groups in New York Elections of 1970," *New York History*. Vol. 53, No.1, January, 1972, pp. 55-71.

# The Beginning of the End for the Madison Club

## Introduction

This chapter will set the stage for the end of the Madison Club. By the 1960s the Madison Club was like a giant tree whose crown had become too great for its roots. When the strong winds of change came it groaned and fell to the ground with a loud thud. As a political machine, it had taken advantage of the vulnerabilities of the populations which it had served. Despite handicaps and occasional setbacks, it grew steadily to become a state and national powerhouse in the Democratic Party. Its ascendancy paralleled the mobility of its original ethnic constituents; the Irish, Jews, and Italians. However, as the club reached for more power it lost contact with its local community base. While individual club leaders grew in stature, the neglected club was relegated to a mere competitor in a factionalized and often fractious county organization. In order to advance themselves, the "big shots" had distanced themselves from the parochial views of their constituents and in some cases they gravitated outside the limiting orbit of the Brooklyn machine.

By this time no individual domineering personality ruled the Brooklyn machine or the Madison Club as people like Boss John McCooey had done in the past. Now, more important to the welfare of the Madison Club than the particular people who ran it were the population changes which took place around them in the local neigborhood, and in the larger contexts of Brooklyn and New York City. These factors will be discussed in depth here as they created the treacherous stage upon which the Madison Club's last performance was to take place. Demography and geography determined the unfriendly audiences before which the Madison Club politicians would play.

## Rising and Falling Stars

Perhaps the best, and the most flattering example of the rise of a single Madison Club member to political prominence (and legend) was the career of Arthur Levitt- a product of the old-style machine who became one of its greatest enemies. Levitt was an attorney and prominent in Jewish community and civic affairs in Crown Heights and Brownsville in the 1940s. As President of Union Temple, the largest Jewish congregation in Brooklyn, he was noticed by Irwin Steingut who convinced him to join the club and become his campaign manager for his New York State Assembly race in 1946.[1] A few years later, Steingut's old friend Mayor Impelliteri appointed Levitt to the New York City Board of Education where he served three years, one of which as its President. At about the same time, Levitt's wife who was a teacher in Brownsville, was elevated to the position of School Community Coordinator.[2]

In 1954, two years after Irwin's death, the State Democratic Party arranged an "ethnically balanced" ticket of Averell Harriman for Governor, George Di Luca for Lieutenant Governor, and Aaron L. Jacoby for Controller. Jacoby was forced to withdraw because of a public contract scandal and this left a vacancy for the "Jewish" position on the slate.

Brooklyn's Democratic County Boss at that time, Joseph Sharkey urged Levitt to run for the job and he did.[3] Levitt, however, was never a typical political hack and when he became Controller he balanced his debts to the machine against his good government leanings by selecting qualified people for his staff and sprinkling less or un-qualified political appointees among them, such as William B. Volet a Madison Club stalwart who served for 24 years. In general, "ticket balancing" acts were part of the repetoire of successful Madison Clubbers.

In 1961, Levitt made the mistake of opposing Robert Wagner for Mayor as a "hand picked" candidate of Manhattan Tammany leader Carmine DeSapio. He eventually lost in the primary race and in the process also became estranged from the Brooklyn machine which had its own opponent to Wagner. When he returned to Albany to resume his duties as Controller, he quickly moved over toward the "good government" forces with whom he always appeared to feel more comfortable. As a consequence he slowly replaced many of the patronage holders with apolitical financial analysts. One of his major innovations was the introduction of New York State's first performance audits which made financial wheeling and dealing by political bosses more difficult, but not impossible.

Because of his fiscal objectivity as Controller, Levitt often presented political problems for the machine. As a result, in 1963 the party bosses tempted him with an offer of a position on the New York State Court of Appeals, the state's highest judicial body. He declined despite his earlier aspirations to the bench, citing his commitment to his new audit program. By this act of refusal he left the world of conventional machine politics and created a really nonpartisan office which kept him as Controller for 24 years.[4]

Another Madison Club "legend" was Abraham "Bunny" Lindenbaum who provides an excellent contrast to Levitt. For critics of the machine such as Newfield and DuBrul, Lindenbaum was the epitome of the "clubhouse lawyer" who entered politics in order to take advantage of opportunities for "legal graft." "Bunny" began his Madison Club career as a precinct captain in the early 1950s. At the time Abraham Beame was the Assistant Budget Director for New York City and Irwin Steingut was still alive.

Lindenbaum rose quickly to attain positions of importance and trust in New York City, such as New York City Planning Commissioner, and used them to benefit himself and his friends. According to Newfield and DuBrul, Lindenbaum was a master at collecting legal graft as evidenced by; patronage fees from the Surrogates Court, soliciting campaign contributions for Mayor Wagner from builders and landlords who did business with the city, negotiating zoning variances from the Board of Standards and Appeals, winning lower real estate assessments from the City Tax Commission, and receiving "consulting fees" from state and city construction projects. Abraham "Bunny" Lindenbaum died in 1980. He had outlived the Madison Club by two years.[5]

## Stanley Steingut: The Last of the "Big Shots"

In the 1960s and 70s, the Democratic Party became more "liberal" on social issues such as school integration, capital punishment and abortion. At the same time, the club's most active voters became more conservative, reflecting the rise in the nation during the Johnson and Nixon administrations of the so-called "silent majority." When the end came, the power of the Madison Club was based more on its past reputation than its current reality. The club and its leaders became the victims of their own success as important segments of the racially polarized community took out their frustrations on the most visible symbol of what they saw as liberal political oppression-- Speaker of the New York State Assembly Stanley Steingut.

Stanley Steingut was the last and perhaps the most powerful heir to the century-old legacy of the Madison Club. He personified the best and the worst products of urban machines. The grandchild of impoverished and oppressed immigrants, Steingut could wheel and deal with the most established American political aristocracies, such as the Kennedys and Rockefellers. By his own admission he had aspirations for a better reputation and sought out more "respectable images" and positions for himself and his family.[6] He probably would have characterized himself as a "reluctant Boss."

The fortunes of the Madison Club had always been tied directly to the successes and failures of its more or less illustrious leaders. Stanley Steingut was the last of the political "tsars" to be produced by the club. The accounts of his personal "Last Hurrah" have been heralded by some as the final pages in the history of the once monolithic Brooklyn Machine begun by Hugh McLaughlin over a century ago. As were other earlier pronouncements on the matter, such a prognosis on the end of the machine is likely to be judged premature. One thing, however, is certain; in 1978 Stanley Steingut lost both his position as State Committeeman and his State Assembly seat, shocking all the political "experts."

By the time Stanley Steingut inherited McCooey's throne, the Madison Club was not nearly the powerhouse of legend. Although not nearly as colorful as his grandfather Simon, nor as stereotypically earthy as Boss John McCooey, nor as polished and controversial as his father Irwin, some phases of his political history demand attention here. His political biography is marked by several controversial episodes, not the least of which was the "Nursing Home Scandal" which marred an otherwise distinguished career, and gave considerable impetus to his ouster. Ironically, if Steingut, the Madison Club, and the Brooklyn machine itself, had not become less tyrannical over time, there is no doubt he would have survived even the most damaging of investigations. As it was, even the rather innocuous findings of a state study, led by then Secretary of State, Mario M. Cuomo, into the use of political influence in the Medicaid and nursing home industries, was sufficient to cause him irreparable harm.[7]

Stanley Steingut was born on May 20, 1920 in Brooklyn's Crown Heights section. It was during the politically freewheeling "Roaring Twenties" that his political initiation was noted in an apocryphal remembrance by long-time Madison Club members. The oft-repeated story goes that Irwin Steingut was travelling around his district on election day with six year old Stanley. At one polling station in Crown Heights they stopped to chat with the precinct captain in charge of that election district. They spoke for a while and Irwin asked the captain when his son could vote for the first time. "Now," was the reply. Stanley proceeded to cast his ballot; undoubtedly for the Madison Club ticket. The precinct captain, it is said, was the future Mayor of the City of New York- Abraham Beame. Although the story might seem a bit far-fetched to the politically uninitiated, it must be remembered that those were days when almost anything could be done at the ballot box by those in power. Even in modern elections, stuffing the ballot box is not a totally extinct art.

Stanley Steingut's actual political career was even more dramatic and controversial than political folklore. At each step it seems his advancement was accompanied by disputes and resulted in a long trail of political enemies. Some of those who felt victimized by his rise to power openly participated in his downfall in 1978 while most others stood cheering silently on the sidelines as Steingut fell from power.

As related by some Madison Club oldtimers, Stanley Steingut was not particularly interested in a political career and also had not been especially active at the club when his father Irwin died in office in 1952. Although he recently completed his law school education at Saint John's University and was taking the bar exam, the decision to keep the seat "in the family" raised some hackles at the club. Several important club members balked at the choice of Stanley for the coveted position and eventually left in a fit of political pique. They felt that Stanley had not earned the position. After the dust of the arguments settled, those who supported Stanley were rewarded, as he quickly rose in stature. The political careers of those who went against him were, in some cases, ruined.

As always, the ethnicity and family ties of club members were crucial to understanding the political splits. Jewish members felt that in earlier days they had been short-changed by the Irish. Irish Catholics in particular were reluctant to accede to the rise of Jews to prominence in the Democratic Party machine after such a relatively short involvement. There was also competition between families in the club who were concerned about the prospects for themselves and their children. Stanley Steingut's succession to his father's seat in the assembly was viewed as the establishment of a political dynasty in Brooklyn and many were envious of the potential for power. In later years, Stanley's son Robert was given the nod by the County organization for Brooklyn's At-Large New York City Council seat, (tantamount to election) and another political family feud erupted.

The perception that Stanley was still trying to grab too much power for himself was not far off the mark. Several earlier incidents confirmed this suspicion. When, for example, Congresswoman, Stanley's co-District Leader, and otherwise prominent Madison Club member Edna Kelly demanded that he give up his party title if and when he gained the Minority Leader position in the Assembly, Stanley fought with her and won. It is said, he later used his power to redistrict her out of office. In another related enemy-making political battle with New York City Mayor Robert Wagner, Steingut lost out to Anthony Travia for the Minority Leader position in Albany after opposing Wagner for Mayor. He later gained the State Assembly leadership position but was forced to give up his county leader post to his sometimes friend and often business partner Meade Esposito.

During the 1970s, as Steingut's political power grew at the state level, his visibility in the local community faded. He made the fatal error of relying on others for his local operations. Insiders say that the real force in the club during part of his reign as Assembly Speaker was his co-district leader Beadie Markowitz who had earlier sided with Steingut against Wagner and Travia. Markowitz was a power in her own right and was one of the founders of the Kennedy Club, which had been established upon the assassination of John F. Kennedy in 1962. Years before that, she was a vigorous district captain with future Mayor Abe Beame and Nat Sobel, who later became a Justice of the Surrogate's Court. Her club admirers suggest that compared to her, Steingut was a political novice. When the Madison Club was forced to change its assembly boundaries, it moved into Markowitz's area and the district lines were carefully drawn so as to include her residence.

Although the move appeared to go smoothly, Steingut

and his entourage were perceived by the independently successful Kennedy Club members as unwanted intruders. However, with Beadie Markowitz at the club helm, still distributing favors, the friction was kept at a minimum and below the surface. Steingut made many enemies but they feared his power. The intra-club animosities grew slowly over the years and exploded upon Beadie's death when Steingut chose Pearl Anish, a local community activist, and relative newcomer to the club, to replace her. This generated a great deal of dissension between factions at the club as generations of insult and injury surfaced; in some cases in the form of political sabotage.

## The Club Separates from the Community

By developing within communities the capacity for self-government and problem solving, the community organization movement in the 1960s was perceived as the enemy of the remnants of the powerful political machines. At first, the machine saw developments such as Community Planning Boards, School Decentralization, and anti-poverty corporations, with their independent ties to city, state and federal agencies, as the last nail in the patronage coffin. But, eventually the regulars came to realize how easy it would be for them to take control of these new, and troublesome local entities. By the 1970s, in New York City, regular political organizations had solved the riddle of "maximum feasible local participation" and had incorporated these organizations as part of an expanded and modified new machine network.[8]

Stanley Steingut and others at the club were not as fearful of these kinds of activities as others might have been. They had quickly recognized the potential of the community organization movement and had already coopted some of its leaders. For example, as Speaker of the

Assembly, Steingut had a great deal of influence in the decisions about the distribution of state funds for local programs. When Abraham Beame was Mayor, club influence in city-funded programs is easily imagined. Also, the club and the Brooklyn machine itself, even during Republican Presidential administrations, had enough friends in Washington, D.C. to similarly effect local Federally supported programs.

The club, however, became too involved for its own good. The best example of this was the Community School Board 18 school integration controversy in 1972. Because of overcrowding and segregation in Ocean Hill-Brownsville, nonwhite children from that district were attending Meyer Levin Junior High School in a predominantly white, Jewish-Italian, section of the neighboring district. This East Flatbush/Canarsie District 18, made up a part of the Madison Club's new territory. The membership of the local school board was racially split with a 5-4 white majority. As Meyer Levin reached a 50% "tipping point" vocal members of the community demanded that the nonwhite pupils be distributed elsewhere, and intra-community conflict ensued. Local political organizations were caught in the middle as school boycotts, demonstrations, angry speeches, rallies, and violence marked the scene. The Madison Club took the mediator's position of compromise. And, regardless of the outcome, it was doomed to offend the most politically active constituents-the Jews and Italians in the new territory. Some of the anti-integration activists reemerged later in the movement to oust Steingut.[9]

As always, independent grass-roots community organizations presented dangers for the club. They created issues, leaders, forums and platforms from which to address the community. Some of the oldtimers at the club were fearful of these groups and cautioned against a too close involvement with them. They were afraid that independent-minded leaders would cause trouble and be difficult to control. Idealism and issues were always anathema to machines. Wisened political veterans feared that they might not receive credit for accomplishments in the community and might well be blamed for failures. They were right. Steingut believed he could rise above the crowd. He was wrong.

An old and sensible dictum in politics is; "nothing for nothing." You especially do not help your enemies to look good even if it's best for the community. But being against a community group is like being against a church or a synagogue. Political organizations remain powerful only to the extent that they can take credit for the good and avoid blame for the bad. Madison Club leaders were viewed as unconcerned about the community and responsible for its problems, such as "block busting," street crime, and urban blight. Locals knew that Steingut, Beame and others for years had maintained fictional addresses in the community and lived in "better" neighborhoods. In the last campaign, Stanley Steingut was successfully portrayed by his opponents as having "abandoned" the community and was therefore probably guilty of every evil attributed to him.

## The "Scandals"

The expansion of medical and social services by the federal government in the 1960's created new opportunities for political corruption. Historically leaders in the area of social services, New York State and New York City added to the welfare largess by adopting their own programs and funding services at even higher levels than Federally mandated. Social and medical services to the poor became a major industry. Given the enormous opportunity for corruption, it was inevitable that a political scandal would eventually break.

Demands for cutbacks in government spending for the "Great Society" of Lyndon Johnson during the ensuing Republican national administrations resulted in a close look at existing programs. What government investigators and journalists found was, in many cases, shocking. These revelations fueled further investigations by newly established public commissions. In New York State, much of the focus centered around the role of Stanley Steingut, Speaker of the New York State Assembly. Newspaper reports set the start of the "Scandal" in 1972, when Manhattan Assemblyman Andrew Stein claimed that Steingut had used "back room pressure politics" to snuff out a probe of Medicaid fraud and tried to interfere with Stein's own investigations into nursing home abuses in the state.[10]

Steingut had responded to the charges by saying that he was preparing to appoint his own committee to investigate, and that Stein, a junior Member of the Assembly, was merely attempting to take credit for its establishment and use it as a vehicle for his personal political advancement. In any case, Stein's Temporary State Commission on the Cost of Living, led to the creation by Governor Hugh L. Carey of a Moreland Act Commission and a Special Prosecutor to present evidence to Attorney General Louis Lefkowitz for possible Grand Jury proceedings. The Special Prosecutor appointed was Charles Joseph Hynes, then First Assistant to District Attorney Eugene Gold in Kings County.[11] The State investigations were matched by Federal grand juries and Congressional committee investigations.

In addition to the claim that Steingut tried to hinder Stein's investigations there were several more serious charges and allusions of corruption on the part of Steingut and other prominent New York City and State officials.

The principal insurer of Bernard Bergman's nursing home empire was Grand Brokerage; a company partly owned by Steingut and Meade Esposito.[12] An attorney for the Speaker, Daniel Chill, was also accused of representing Bergman before state agencies. Steingut claimed that Chill was not working for him at the time.[13] Stein also charged that Steingut had personally tried to stop his investigation of Bergman. Steingut, before a U.S. Senate Subcommittee looking into Bergman's activities, testified that he "could not recall" such a conversation with Stein.[14] At least one Madison Clubber, noted that Chill was close to Bergman and had at one time dated his daughter.

Eventually Bernard Bergman was convicted of both Federal and state crimes relating to fraud in his nursing home empire; but before it was over major politicians had been implicated or tainted in the press by any association with Bergman and fellow Medicaid fraud entrepreneur Eugene Hollander, such as Mayor Abraham Beame, State Comptroller Arthur Levitt, U.S. Senator Jacob Javits, State Court of Appeals Judge Jacob Fuchsberg, Republican Party fund raiser Samuel Hausman, Governor Nelson Rockefeller, Lieutenant Governor Malcolm Wilson, Attorney General of New York Louis Lefkowitz, State Senator John Marchi, Secretary to Governor Rockefeller; T. Norman Hurd, State Health Commissioner Dr. Hollis S. Ingraham, Mayor Robert Wagner, Deputy Mayor of New York City Stanley Lowell, and the New York Crime Family of Joseph Colombo.[15]

Although Steingut was publicly cleared, the scandal never faded far from public view and would reemerge in the 1978 campaign. The primary attracted even more press attention when, Andrew Stein, now Borough President of Manhattan, became personally involved as a major supporter of Steingut's opponents at the New Way Democratic Club. Naturally, the Nursing Home Scandal again received considerable media attention. Some insiders at the Madison Club said that the Stein-Steingut family feud predated the nursing home issue. They intimated that the animosity originated earlier when Stanley Steingut had a "falling out" with Andrew Stein's father Jerry Finkelstein. Steingut and Finkelstein had been close until about the time of Andrew Stein's entry into politics.

The Nursing Home Scandal called into question Steingut's integrity and made the "family dynasty" issue even more pertinent. The Steinguts were made to person- ify political evil. Allegations resurfaced concerning Steingut's father Irwin and his grandfather Simon. His son, City Councilman Robert Steingut also became an issue in the campaign because of another "incident."

Robert and his father were indicted in 1975 on charges they had promised to assist Hans Rubenfeld, a Bronx haberdasher in obtaining an honorary unpaid City ap- pointment in return for a $2,500 contribution for Roberts's City Council campaign. In a sense, the two got off on a technicality. The New York State Court of Appeals ruled later that they could not be tried on the election law violations. Judge Sol M. Wachtler, on the Steingut's appeal, ruled that District Attorney Eugene Gold had failed to put forth "evidence that there was materially harmful impact upon governmental processes."[16] The story of the "indict- ment" however was frequently replayed by the opposi- tion during the last campaign.

## Population and Power

The rifts in the Brooklyn machine and the Madison club in the 1970's were a microcosm of the conflicts taking place at the national level. The waxing and waning of the club's power can also be seen as a local and regional demo- graphic phenomenon. As detailed in the tables in the

Appendices, Brooklyn's population grew to 2,738,175 inhabitants in 1950 and then declined to 2,300,000 in 1980. New York City's and New York State's population growth also slowed and then declined at the same time. However, Brooklyn's proportion of the city population remained over a third of the city population until 1980. On the other hand, New York City contained over half of the state's population in 1950 but this dropped to 40% by 1970. These figures would lead one to expect, on a population basis alone, that the Madison Club was at its power apex between 1930 and 1950. That is, just about a decade before the transfer of power to Stanley Steingut.

The continued growth of other parts of the city, especially Queens and, more recently, Staten Island (Richmond County) in the 1970s further checked the power of the Madison Club and Brooklyn's Democratic organization. Then, not only did Brooklyn lose residents rapidly, but significant changes in its nativity, racial and class composition resulted in fewer voters. In the 1960's The Bronx and Brooklyn began to lead the city in loss of population. At the same time they led the city in the increase of minorities and low-income residents. The two once proud and boastful boroughs were fast becoming national symbols of urban blight.

## Brooklyn's Ethnic Composition Changes

Irish, Russian, and Italian immigrants, the backbone of the old machine of McCooey, Kelly, Sharkey and Stark, were a third of the borough's total population until 1930. Their children and grandchildren comprised the bulk of the borough's population until about 1970. Although large scale European immigration to Brooklyn halted, it did not mean the end of ethnic changes. By 1960, the numbers of Puerto Rican and other Hispanic and Black immigrants from the Western Hemisphere became significant, and then dominated the foreign-born scene in Brooklyn. They created new and equally vibrant immigrant ghettos as the earlier Brooklynites died off or moved away to "greener pastures."

The most important demographic factor in the decline of the Madison Club was the rise of the Black and other nonwhite populations in the borough. In 1900 there were only 19,673 Blacks in Brooklyn. In 1980, two years after the Madison Club disaster, the total was almost 700,000. The bulk of this growth took place after 1950 when the Black total stood at only 208,478. As Kings County's total population declined after 1950, the Black population increased until it was about 30% of all residents in 1980. If we add to Blacks, Other Nonwhites and Hispanics, in 1980 close to a majority of the people in the Borough of Brooklyn were non-European in origin. These remnants of Brooklyn's white European past were people the traditional-style Irish, Jewish, and Italian bosses could still try to exploit, but, ultimately they could not lead them. White voters in central Brooklyn often felt "betrayed" by the politicians who represented them.

Brooklyn was particularly well-suited for rapid growth and change because of its residential development patterns spreading out from the downtown Brooklyn "center." One finds younger neighborhoods as one moves away from this point. This pattern later provided for the classic "invasion-succession" syndrome of neighborhood change with minorities moving into center city areas as whites moved out toward the newer, and growing, fringe.[17]

Even when the Madison Club was a county-wide organization, the composition of its specific locale; the ward or assembly district, was an important consideration in its functioning and membership. In machine politics, close relationships between the organization and constituents are needed. Therefore the club members, and the club hierarchy, had to reflect (at least symbolically) the ethnic composition of the territory. Ethnicity influences attitudes toward various issues and in turn the strategies and stands of political organizations. Different ethnic groups have different feelings about participation in politics itself, making their concerns more or less important to political machines. The views and concerns of apathetic ethnic groups, for example, are seldom reflected in government policy.

## The Madison Club District Changes

Drastic changes for the Madison Club district occurred between 1960 and 1980 when the assembly district, despite at times frantic efforts at gerrymandering, increasingly became a "minority" area. There were not enough white Euro-ethnic voters in Broooklyn to satisfy the demands of the local white Euro-ethnic bosses. In 1950, Blacks and other nonwhites comprised less than one percent of the district's population. By 1960, this proportion had increased to about five percent. In 1970 the nonwhite population leaped to almost a quarter of the total and by 1980 over two-thirds of the residents in the Madison Club assembly district were nonwhite. An additional tenth of the district was made up of white Hispanics. This was the district that Stanley Steingut, Anthony Jordan Jr., Nathan Sobel, Abraham Beame and Beadie Markowitz tried to control.

Much of the increase in the Black population was due to nonwhite immigration. In 1970, of the 75,569 persons classified as "Foreign Stock" in the district, one fifth were Western Hemisphere immigrants. Another tenth of the foreign stock were from Asian, African and other less usual points of emigration. Eastern Europeans, still a majority in the district at the time, had slipped to slightly less than half of the foreign stock. Other Europeans totalled only a little more than a tenth of the foreign stock group. By 1980, of the 152,936 residents one third were foreign born. Of these, most were immigrants from the Western Hemisphere. For the most part, the district's immigrant population was Caribbean in origin. They came from Haiti, Jamaica, Barbados, Trinidad and other islands. Combined with native American Blacks, they made up the new majority and would shape the political future.

## Zoning for Power: Gerrymandering

What all this demographic shifting meant was that the Madison Club, as the seat of the Kings County Democratic Party, or as an important member of the ruling coalition, had to frequently adapt itself to major changes in the social and cultural make up of the borough. Sometimes the adaptation was successful, sometimes not. The population changes at the level of the assembly district parallel those for the county as a whole but had a greater and more direct bearing on the club and its operations. At the local level, the club had to deal more directly with constituents in order to remain in power. The most powerful check in an electoral system is that even the most powerful individuals and political organizations have to win elections to survive. One of the most common methods available to machines to deal with change that it is ultimately powerless to prevent, such as demographic shifts, is gerrymandering.

At the beginning of the twentieth century, party matters were restricted to the purview of county and ward "bosses." Therefore drawing political lines, or "gerrymandering," were limited to efforts of the party in power to insure majorities in state and city legislatures. Later, when party

primaries for candidates became state law, the importance
of local boundaries increased for political organizations of
both major parties but especially for the Democratic Party
which had a broader mass base. Competitors within the
party, regular factions, reformers, independents or other
"non-regulars" became more of a threat to the machine.
Political battles also became more sophisticated as coalition politics appeared on the scene. Keeping control meant
insuring that the district was "safe" for county and state
committee people as well as city and state officials. Increasingly, the study of population data and voting behavior was necessary to make the best decisions about where
new lines should be drawn.

The process of gerrymandering is relatively simple, and
for the most part legal, if not legitimate. Periodically, the
state legislature reconstructs electoral districts (the city
and Federal government also redistrict their own political
units). The reconstruction is based primarily on decennial
census information. A "nonpartisan" committee is appointed to redraw political lines. The stated intention of
the process is to insure that voters are proportionally
represented. Naturally, those political groups with the
greatest power have the greatest influence in effecting new
boundaries.

Behind the scenes, a great deal of argument and eventual compromise takes place. The end result is that the
most powerful have districts that they find "easy to live
with," most often at the expense of the less powerful and,
occasionally, those that the leadership have determined
should be given a difficult time during elections. Until the
1970s, the Madison Club had always had sufficient influence and foresight to benefit from "safe" district lines.

Gerrymandering had helped maintain the supremacy
of the club and its senior politicians, but in the 1970s
uncontrollable demography and some important public

issues had finally caught up with the organization. Competition from other regular clubs in the county had also limited its ability to "raid" new territory for safe havens. In particular, the club, in its attempt to flee from the growing Black population in central Brooklyn, ran into political organizations in southern Brooklyn who were unwilling to give up their own comfortable situations. These predominately white districts were literally prevented from further movement away from the growing Black population by the Atlantic Ocean which formed the southern boundary. Equally important was the impact of the 1960's Federal Civil Rights and Voting Rights regulations which severely limited the free hand of political district architects to effectively disenfranchise minority voters.

This was done not out of simple prejudice, but in order to maintain the power of particular leaders and voting blocks. Controlling the shape and therefore the population of districts has many benefits for state legislative encumbents. Staying in office increases seniority and that means more power as individuals gain membership on and sometimes the chairmanships of important committees. Discussing the fruits of Brooklyn gerrymandering, Arthur Klebanoff cites the political dominance over two decades of State Senators Samuel Greenberg and William Rosenblatt, and Assemblymen Max Turshen, Stanley Steingut (and his father Irwin), Anthony Travia, Lawrence Murphy, Alfred Lama, Louis Kalish, Joseph Corso and Bertram Baker.[18]

During the 1950s and 1960s these men, because of their guaranteed seniority, chaired or served on the most powerful of legislative committees. They also exercised great influence even when the Democratic Party was out of power in Albany. Max Turshen, a Madison Club neighbor and rival from Brownsville, was especially powerful with 30 years seniority. In 1966 he chaired the Judiciary Committee, which among other things handed out judgeships, an important political inducement. In general, it was the powerful committees that were able to distribute the state's largess. Just as Steingut was to do, Turshen eventually moved his own district southward in Brooklyn in search of "safe" Jewish areas as Brownsville became Black.[19] As the Madison Club was also seeking a refuge from the growing Black population, Turshen was forced into a new district and lost his seat to a young rising star of Brooklyn politics, Steven Solarz. This move against Turshen generated considerable resentment toward the Madison Club from his supporters both in, and out of, the club.

Klebanoff notes that the New York State Constitution gives the authority for drawing state senate lines to Albany and assembly district lines, which must fit senate lines, to the New York City Council. Therefore the party or faction in power in these bodies was relatively free to construct boundaries advantageous to their own interests. It should also be noted that the judges who might review the district boundaries are usually products of the various party machines. Assembly district lines are the major focus of attention by political party geographers. These are the units from which the party's District Leaders (State Committeepersons) are elected who are closest to constituents. The assembly district is also the normal basis for political clubs. In turn the a.d. is composed of smaller election districts (e.d.s) from which members of the political parties' County Committee are elected. These persons, theoretically, elect the county leader. The public, and news commentators, however, tend to focus on gerrymandering as it pertains to the election of public and not party officials. Such a view has resulted in misplaced emphasis by political analysts, for in Brooklyn, where for almost a century Democratic candidates cannot help but win in general elections, it has been the party convention or primary that determined the ultimate victor.

Because of a combination of Republican power and bias against the city, despite its containing most of the population in New York State, until 1964 New York City had less than 45% of total seats in the legislature. Proportionately, in 1953 the 38 upstate counties had one assembly district for every 51,203 persons while New York City had one for every 135,511. Although Democrats suffered because of this bias, Klebanoff's research, focusing on the 1944, 1953 and 1969 reapportionments showed Brooklyn was the source of Democratic power in the State Legislature and the Madison Club was a major center of the county's influence.[20] With the exception of the period 1958-1968, between 1930 and 1978 either Irwin Steingut or his son Stanley served as Democratic leader of the state assembly. And Stanley served as Democratic county leader from 1962 until his ascension to assembly leader in 1969. Throughout most of this period district lines were almost freely drawn to satisfy the organizations wonts resulting in oddly shaped districts that made only "political sense." Party politics has always been the paramount activity of machine organizations, and the Madison Club had to be concerned with being situated in a district which was easily controlled. Control meant a constant base existed for building strength through seniority and consistency of loyal voter turnout. Knowing the neighborhoods served by the club tells one about the ethnic and other important characteristics of voters, and potential voters.

Although ethnic political considerations have tended to be the most salient, there are other local interests which may be formally, as well as informally, organized. For example, whether the major constituents are tenants or homeowners will influence political positions on issues such as real estate taxes and rent laws. The availability and quality of public transportation is another issue which is geographically based. Issues and interests such as these

also changed with the boundary line shifts over the decades.

Despite not often being expressed outside of campaign
headquarters, probably the most important geographic
aspect of the political machine process in cities is concentration of population. Large scale apartment houses and
complexes provide easy access for political organizations
to large numbers of potential voters. Dense populations
present both opportunity and danger. If they are with you,
small geographic areas composed of large numbers of
apartment dwellers can swing a whole district. If they are
against you, they pose a great problem. Another characteristic of these "choice" areas is their class, and, usually,
ethnic homogeneity which make them somewhat more
"predictable" voters. On the other hand, their accessibility
and concentration holds potential for successful opposition. This helps to explain why areas with large concentrations of registered voters receive overwhelming political
attention in cities during election years. It also explains
why almost every political aspirant in New York City is for
"rent controls" and is publicly pro-tenant.

In 1950, except for the old Italian section of Wingate, or
"Pigtown," as it was called, the assembly district area was
highly urbanized and densely populated. Concentrations
of large apartment buildings dominated the northern
section. These concentrated voters, in essence, determined
the outcomes of most elections. More homogeneous ethnic
neighborhoods of one and two-family homes spread over
the rest of the community, interspersed with apartment
complexes. In a pattern that was to become crucial. Jews
tended to predominate in apartment house areas, and Irish
and Italians in less dense community settings. The elderly
were, during this time, almost numerically inconsequen-
tial as voters in the district. In later decades, however,
elderly apartment house dwellers became crucial as

younger Blacks absented themselves from electoral politics and younger Jews, Italians and others left the changing neighborhoods. 1950 also saw the introduction of a semblance of proportional representation in the state which caused a significant shrinkage in the geographic size of the assembly district. As shown in the assembly district maps collected in the Appendices, the area of the district was cut in half. The East New York and the Flatlands-Canarsie portions of the district were eliminated, thereby increasing the power of the densely populated Crown Heights section and subsequently the Jewish vote. This was especially true of the growing Hassidic and Orthodox Jewish congregations whose political participation was virtually monolithic. The central section of the 41st Assembly District, containing Italian and Irish Catholic voters, changed very little. The Madison Club headquarters was now located at 4016 Church Avenue, after having moved from St. Marks Avenue, far to the north, and then to Eastern Parkway as the district's boundaries shifted southward.

In the 1950s, Bedford-Stuyvesant and Brownsville rapidly deteriorated and nonwhite minority populations became the majority. It must be stated here that, despite nostalgic protestations to the contrary, these areas were already physically blighted prior to the nonwhite settlement. Brownsville and East New York had also already gained quite unsavory reputations in the 1930s and 1940s. These neighborhoods were the settings for teenage gangs and the notorious "Murder Incoporated" organized crime groups. The areas became slowly depopulated as the Irish, Jews and Italians became economically and therefore geographically mobile. The portions of the original 18th Assembly District to the west (Flatbush) and south (Flatlands/Canarsie) had become politically powerful neighborhoods in their own right, but were still aligned with the Madison Club. The political map, however, in Brooklyn was now much more complicated as factions in the county competed with one another for hegemony through ethnic and coalition politics.

The 1960 map for the Madison Club's district showed slight but important boundary changes as the club gave up small parts of its western section to the neighboring Andrew Jackson Club, which was a powerful ally led by district "Boss" Bernard Bloom, his brother State Senator Jeremiah Bloom, and Assemblyman George Cincotta. Due to these line changes, the club also came to represent some East Flatbush territory recently populated by Democratically loyal Jewish voters who had fled other sections of Brooklyn.

Gerrymandering by powerful political organizations such as the Madison Club is not limited to larger scale concerns such as potentially helpful or dangerous voting blocs. It also can be an expression of smaller scale, sometimes personal, concerns. If one looks closely at the varied boundaries of the Madison Club district over the years unusual deviations from what could have been straight lines appear. In some cases, these anomalies represent the inclusion of families or individuals important to the club. In other cases, they may be attempts to exclude potentially dangerous individuals such as expressed candidates for office. Simple demographic analysis can never provide a logical explanation for what are at times incredible intricately shaped political districts.

Between 1970 and 1980, the boundaries for the 41st Assembly District were greatly expanded and ensnared some of the club's earlier territory. These areas had changed considerably over the decades and were then by no means politically "virgin." The Madison Club boundaries now stretched from the edge of Black Bedford-Stuyvesant just beyond then predominantly Jewish Crown Heights, carefully skirting around the severely blighted Black Brownsville ghetto, and into the white working and middle-class Canarsie and Flatlands neighborhoods. The racial turmoil, urban riots, New York City school strike over decentralization, and the heated debate over the Police Civilian Review Board were issues which placed these diverse communities on a political collision course. The Madison Club was figuratively and geographically right in the middle of the conflict.

Political analysts and club members had suggested that the organization move its boundaries even further south and cut off the dense Crown Heights section, which was populated by well organized Hasidic Jewish congregations who were traditionally loyal to the club. The club officers, however, were constrained by a promise to the community leadership not to abandon them to the changed Central Brooklyn population of Blacks and Hispanics. As described by Klebanoff:

"Meanwhile Steingut's district drawing efforts were constrained by an immobile clubhouse--the Madison Club--which his father had overlorded in the 1930's and 1940's after ending John McCooey's twenty-five year reign as Brooklyn Democratic chieftain. The political footings of the Jewish immigrant who had come to Crown Heights from the slums of the Lower East Side of Manhattan could not be easily abandoned by his son."[21]

In interviews with Madison Club members the reason for the constraint was more political than sentimental. Irwin had made a promise in exchange for political support which never faltered. The 43rd A. D. to the west of the Madison Club had begun to change quickly from white to nonwhite, and their neighborhood counterparts in the 41st looked with fear at the possibility of neighborhood change. These fears were heightened during the decade as minority politics and politicians became more visible and local conflicts arose in the borough over school ("busing") and residential integration ("block-busting") issues.

The Madison Club officers, in cautious attempts to bring the growing numbers of minority voters into the fold, increased their contacts with the minority community. As a consequence, the club headquarters became more and more integrated itself. As the 1978 voting returns of the "Last Campaign" were to show, new Black voters were more loyal to the organization than older white-ethnic constituents. They did not vote, however, in sufficient numbers to prevent the defeat, as the traditional voting loyalty of the district dissipated over the conflict filled decade. In many ways the 1978 campaign was really a battle between the "North" and "South."

## Counting the Voters

Special attention must be paid to the proportion of total New York City voters living in Kings County as an indicator of the club's waxing and waning power. This simple proportional indicator of political power can also be converted to power rankings for the respective county organizations. The proportion of the county's voters living in the club's assembly district is an index of power within the county itself.

As the tables on "Democratic and Republican Registration and Voting by County and New York City-wide" located in the Appendix prophetically demonstrate, the proportion of New York City's Democrats living in Brooklyn reached its peak in 1950 and slowly declined from a third in 1950 to thirty percent by 1978 when the Madison Club was voted out of existence. Although Kings County retained its number one ranking of Democrats in the city from 1925 until 1980, the figures show other important changes in the ranking of counties. Kings County reached its voter registration peak in 1950. In 1955 a new trend was discernible; the growth of Queens County's voting strength and the decline of the Bronx's. The combination of the Brooklyn-Bronx voting strength had meant control of the city in that it equalled or surpassed half of the city total until 1975. Queens County moved into the second place rank in 1955 and increased from almost twenty-two percent of all Democratic voters to over twenty-seven percent in 1980, while Kings and Bronx Counties were declining. In fact, in 1980, Queens County's *total* registration was the greatest for all New York Counties, surpassing Kings in that category. The battle for control of New York City was no longer a simple matter of putting together a two-county machine coalition. Internal county divisions had also become acute in the 1950s and even putting together effective coalitions within the county was no easy matter.

In many ways, a Brooklyn-Bronx political connection was a natural. The two counties had similar development patterns and ethnic histories of Irish, Jews, and Italians. This connection served the Madison Club well until its defeat in 1978. The rise of Queens County might also be seen as related to the ascension of Queens' own Mario Cuomo as Democratic Governor to replace Brooklyn's Hugh Carey in 1982. Cuomo defeated New York County's one time reform leader, Mayor Edward I. Koch. Seen in this light, New York City has long been an inter-county political battleground.

Another indicator of the Madison Club's strength was the proportion of the county's total Democratic vote which it directly controlled within its own assembly district. As noted in previous discussions, the size of the electorate is influenced by demographic factors and geographical factors and the ability of the organization to operate successfully within its own boundaries. In other words, the fact that voters live within the district does not automatically commit them to support club candidates. Until 1978, however there was very little, if any, opposition to the will of the club.

Although the Madison Club assembly district itself was never the first ranked in Democratic registration in Kings County, it contained, until 1960, one of the largest concentrations of loyal voters. This provided club politicians with seniority and stablity. In coalition with Irish and Italian clubs in South Brooklyn, Greenpoint, Williamsburgh and Bushwick and Jewish organizations in Brownsville and East New York and other more diverse neighbors or partners in Flatbush, they were able to maintain their disproportionate strength for a time despite increasingly disappointing voter turnout and registration. Ultimately the numbers and the more difficult coalition politics put the club to rest.

Oddly enough, for the political machine, having large numbers of registered voters is not necessarily a good thing. Voters must be controlled and manageable. Because of the ethno-religious basis of most traditional urban machines, the political participation of some ethnic groups is not desirable. In earlier years it was in the best interests of Anglo-Saxon or Germanic Protestant groups to diminish Catholic and Irish political participation. Later, for the Irish bosses, the Jews and Italians were equally threatening.

The minorities in American cities which suffered most from being shut out were, of course, Blacks and Hispanics. For decades the Irish, Jews, and Italians in Brooklyn effectively denied the new minorities their fair share of political representation and political power by gerrymandering, but the process and procedure of voter registration and the exercise of the voting franchise was also a significant barrier. Therefore the machine both directly and indirectly controlled access to the polls.

Although not nearly as blatantly discriminatory as

"Grandfather Clauses," "poll taxes," intimidation and other overt mechanisms of discrimination practiced in the American "Jim Crow" South, Brooklyn political clubs accomplished similar disenfranchisement by taking advantage of existing voting laws and, in general, consciously ignoring the plight of the un- and under-represented minorities. Additionally, in many ways the ethnic satellite political organizations of Blacks and Hispanics played a major role role in preventing the growth of effective opposition. As in the past, minority group leaders were cultivated by the machine to serve its interests and not those of the minority groups. For this obeisance, local ethnic leaders were personally rewarded, for example by being appointed to the bench or given high level government posts.

Changes in Federal and state laws, however, eventually made such control more difficult and created the potential not only for increased minority group participation in politics but minority power. For example, administrative changes which speeded the process of citizenship more quickly moved European immigrants into political prominence. Laws regarding immigration also had major effects on the potential composition and issues of the electorate. Even more basic were changes which simplified voter registration requirements, spurred in major part by the Civil Rights Movement.

Prior to 1957, in New York State, qualified voters had to register every year in order to be eligible to vote. After 1957, voters were given permanent registration, and it was maintained if they voted every two years. Of course, if a voter changed residence, he or she was required to change their registration address in order to vote in their new area. Even this process was a disadvantage for minority politics as nonwhites tended to move their place of residence more frequently than whites. Greater opportunity for enfranchisement was given to Hispanics in 1965 with the elimination of the English language literacy requirement for voting. When the voting age was lowered to eighteen, the number of eligible minority group members increased dramatically. Demographically speaking, nonwhites in Brooklyn tended to be younger than white citizens. All these voter registration modifications created an "opportunity" for increased electoral participation but did not guarantee it. Despite these changes, in the 1970s, minorities were still twice as likely not to be registered as whites. One part of the reason for the low level of political participation was discrimination by the white-dominated machine, but another part was cultural. Especially for American-born Blacks, the long history of past discrimination had resulted in negative political habits which were equally important and very hard to break. In effect minorities in cities became a major potential force who, as expressed by Klebanoff; "...waited for someone to organize them."[22] After the Madison Club's fall those "someones" quickly appeared on the scene.

In 1900, less than five percent of all Democratic voters in Kings County lived in the 18th Assembly district. This proportion rose to over seven percent by 1925. In 1930, due primarily to the increased geographic size of the district itself, the proportion rose to about ten percent. The proportion remained that high until redistricting in the 1940s when it was cut in half. The district's share of total Democratic voters continued to decrease over the years, to less than three percent of the county registration in 1980. These figures represent both changes in the size of the district, and more importantly, changes in the characteristics of the district's population. As minority groups began to heavily populate the Madison Club territory, political operators not only had difficulty controlling voters but the number of voters themselves fell drastically.

## Footnotes

1.  *The New York Times*, January 5, 1965.
2.  *The New York Times*, December 15, 1958.
3.  *Ibid.*
4.  *The Village Voice*, Article by Geoffrey Stokes, n.d..
5.  Characters such as "Bunny" and others were often mentioned at the Madison Club by minor members with some degree of pride because of their notoriety. His story is given extensive treatment in Jack Newfield and Paul DuBrul, *The Permanent Government*. New York: The Pilgrim Press, 1983, pp. 103, 110-11, 141, and 182.
6.  nterview with Stanley Steingut, March 21, 1981.
7.  See especially: "Summary of Preliminary Written and Oral Report to Governor Hugh L. Carey, Re: "Nursing Homes" from Mario M. Cuomo," Albany: State of New York Department of State, 270 Broadway, New York, New York, Mario M. Cuomo, Secretary of State, January 16, 1975.
8.  "Maximum feasible local participation" became the by-word of federal support for many local programs. Local political organizations responded by taking over or creating their own "local" conduits for funds. This phenomenon was noted earlier by Ira Katznelson in respect to Mayor John V. Lindsay's development of local clubs which were supported by program funds. See: Katznelson, "Urban Counterrevolution," in *1984 Revisited: Prospects for American Politics.*, Robert P. Wolf (ed.), New York: Alfred A. Knopf, 1973, pp. 139-64.
9.  For a full discussion of this and other related issues see: Jonathan Rieder, *Canarsie: The Jews and Italians of Brooklyn Against Liberalism.*, Cambridge, Mass.: Cambridge University Press, 1985.
10. "Steingut Tells of a Task Force that Didn't Exist," *The Long Island Press*, September 23, 1975.
11. "Summary of Written and Oral Report to Governor Hugh L. Carey," M.M. Cuomo, *op. cit.*
12. *The New York Times.* September 25, 1975, p. 36.
13. *Albany Times Union*, February 2, 1975, p. 1.
14. *Albany Times Union*, February 2, 1975, p. 9.
15. *New York Daily News*, February 7, 1975, p. 3, *New York Post*, January 1, 1975, p. 1., *Albany Times Union*, February 5, 1975, p. 1., *The New York Times*, January 6, 1975, p. 30., *Albany Knickerbocker*, February 7, 1975, p. 2b., *Staten Island Advance*, July 31, 1975, p. 1.
16. *The New York Times*, July 15, 1977, II, 3:3.
17. Jerome Krase, *Self and Community in the City.* Washington, D.C.: University Press of America, 1982.
18. Arthur Klebanoff, "The Demographics of Politics: Legislative Constituencies in Brooklyn, 1950-1965." Unpublished senior honor's thesis. New Haven: Yale University, 1969, pp. 33-36.

19.  *Ibid.,* pp. 26-34.
20.  *Ibid.,* p.17.
21.  *Ibid.,* p.46. See also: *The New York Post,* December 8, 1959, October 20, 1965 and February 20,1969.
22.  *Ibid.,* p.85.

# The Madison Club and the Permanent Government

## Introduction

At one time or another during the 1970's a Madison Club Congressman, Emmanuel "Manny" Cellar had the greatest seniority in the U.S. House of Representatives. The Governor of the State was a Brooklyn machine-born and raised product-- Hugh Carey. The Mayor of New York City was the club's own Abe Beame. The New York State Controller was one-time club member Arthur Levitt, and the Speaker of the New York State Assembly was Madison scion Stanley Steingut.

To the casual observer, the Madison Club was "sitting on top of the world." At the time of the United States Bi-Centennial Celebration in 1976, New York City was the center of world attention, and more than fifty members of the club had city or state jobs.[1] Like the Madison Club, however, it too was about to collapse. The cause of the city's collapse was the "Fiscal Crisis" and the Madison Club was a major character in this long and drawn out political drama.

Most conventional studies of urban ethnics and machine politics such as those by Merton, Banfield and Wilson, and Moynihan and Glazer are ideologically conservative, or neo-conservative.[2] They tend to view the urban political system as one in which ethnic groups "naturally" compete with one another for control of the city-wide or county-wide party organization. In turn, the party machine is seen as locked in mortal combat with "The Establishment," "reformers," "progressives" and/or other "good government (goo goo's)" types who represent political idealists as well as local business elites. This competition for the ultimate control of cities has also been seen in a ethno-cultural context as the established "Americans" attempt to stem the rising tide of the "Un-Americanized." More recently, urban politics has been described as a form of racial confrontation, as central cities have become increasingly divided between various white and nonwhite groups.

To over-simplify the position of the opposite ideological camp, "Radical" or "Conflict" studies of American urban politics see local political struggles as part of the never ending battle of the "haves" versus the "have nots," or as Marxian "class warfare." From this perspective, the political parties and the machine are viewed as "tools" of the ruling class (bourgeoisie) which serve to help control the masses (proletariat) and not to advance their interests. For most Marxists, and neo-Marxists, ethnicity, race and religion are at most secondary factors in political analyses. Indeed, some have argued that scholarly interest in ethnicity is counterproductive (and perhaps counter-revolutionary) because it distracts attention from the "real" structure of power in America. Even the most radical of social scientists do admit, however, that elite groups can use ethnicity, race and religion as "political formulae" and employ them in strategies for gaining and maintaining political power.[3]

## A Radical View of the Machine and the Club

In the style of Lincoln Steffens and other early 20th Century "Muckrakers,"[4] Jack Newfield and Paul DuBrul argued that the New York City "Fiscal Crisis" provided the opportunity to identify who are the "Real Powers" in the city. *A la* C. Wright Mills,[5] they employed a radical, or Marxist, perspective in their research and demonstrated that New York City is run by a "Permanent Government" or "Power Elite." This loose network of approximately 2,000 people, according to them, maintain their power through control of the financial, real estate and governmental processes.[6]

Before we begin to discuss how the Madison Club and the Brooklyn machine fit into Newfield and DuBrul's description and analysis, it must be emphasized that the authors realize that their view is neither less nor more "objective" than the other, more conservative perspectives previously presented. The tone, however, of their work, because of its journalistic nature, does connote a sense of judgement not typical of social scientific analysis. Therefore we have included this caveat for the reader.

The tone of their writing, however, does not reduce the value of their work in helping us to assess the role of ethnicity in machine politics and the place of the Madison Club in New York City politics during its last decade of existence, which was dominated by attention to New York City Fiscal Crisis.

## What was the "Fiscal Crisis?"

Newfield and DuBrul cite many factors which led New York City to the brink of bankruptcy in 1975 and to the taking over of the city's financial affairs (and therefore its political power) by the Municipal Assistance Corporation and the Emergency Financial Control Board. Although they had helped to create these problems, most of the subsequent events were far beyond the ability of the city's sputtering machines to control. Double-digit inflation, devaluation of the dollar and a Republican Presidency were clearly beyond its purview. Closer to home were the creation, by machine-supported politicians, of semi-autonomous public agencies like the Metropolitan Transportation Authority, Battery Park City Authority, Urban Development Corporation, Tri-Borough Bridge and Tunnel Authority, and the Port Authority. These powerful agencies were led by men as well known as the "Power Broker" Robert Moses and as obscure as one of Brooklyn's own members of the Permanent Government, one-time MTA Chairman Harold Fisher, who rose out of the Brooklyn working-class. Lacking public accountability, these quasi-public agencies spent and borrowed billions of dollars to finance grandiose projects and development schemes.

The major beneficiaries of these efforts were the politically connected developers, banks, and other financial institutions which were part of the "Golden Triangle" of politics, real estate and banking. This configuration of interest groups was the "cornerstone" of the Permanent Government, at least through the decades of the 1960s and 1970s.[7] In earlier decades dominant industries may have been shipping, manufacturing, entertainment, retailing, etc., but since the gradual "de-industrialization" of the city after World War II, most economic and political issues in New York City have revolved around the value of land. When it came time to account for decades of mismanagement by the profligate Golden Triangle however "the poor and the powerless" would be the ones to suffer.[8]

In simple terms; New York City had over-borrowed and, when the debt was called, it was unable to pay. Especially during the Mayoralties of Robert Wagner, John

Lindsay, and Abraham Beame, the city had resorted to "bookkeeping gimmicks" to mask mounting budget deficits. These were deficits that the city, according to its Charter, was not permitted to create.[9] The Madison Club had a greater direct involvement in this problem because Mayor Beame had also served as City Controller to both Wagner and Lindsay. In a more positive vein for the club's alumni, State Comptroller Arthur Levitt had vigorously warned of the impending crisis and against risky financial schemes.[10]

## The Place of the Club in The Structure of the Permanent Government: Controlling the Law-Making Process

Newfield and DuBrul give the Permanent Government a pyramidical shape with the institutions of banking and finance at the apex and clubhouse politics and politicians near the base, just above unions. No politicians compared in power to the major bankers, brokers, and developers. It can be deduced from their description that the clubhouse system is a "service" provider to the higher levels of the Permanent Government. The political club and local politics become merely places for transactions and the use of electoral power for personal gain. Understanding the role of the clubs helps to explain how individual politicians could have advanced themselves to positions of power while the fortunes of the neighborhood communities they represented declined. For example, powerful Assemblymen Stanley Steingut and George Cincotta, represented racially "changing neighborhoods" which geographically paralleled each other. In these struggling Brooklyn communities, residents had great difficulty obtaining mortgage loans and insurance for their homes and businesses. Banks and insurance companies had "red-lined" these areas, placing them off-limits for loans and coverage because, as minority neighborhoods, they were seen as bad risks. Despite the problems of their new constituents these men, who also had close ties to the banking and insurance industries, fought against anti-redlining legislation.[11] Cincotta, in fact, chaired the Assembly Banking Committee while his own "changing" neighborood was red-lined.

According to Newfield and DuBrul, decisions about who gets contracts for public-works projects, zoning variances, and the distribution of government funds take place in settings where it is easy for public accountability to dissappear from political discourse.[12] But, oddly enough, they note that the Permanent Government is bipartisan despite the dominance of the Democrats in New York City. For example, Alton Marshall, a prominent Republican and Democrat Stanley Steingut sat on the same board of directors at the City Title Insurance Company. The writers also curiously note that when New York State Republican Party leader Perry Duryea was indicted for violating state election laws, his attorney was Harold Fisher who had long been involved in Kings County Democratic affairs as an election law expert and fund raiser, having served also at one time as King's County Boss Meade Esposito's personal lawyer.[13]

Newfield and DuBrul note the ease with which city or party officials move between government and the businesses which depend on city funds or favors for their welfare. To them, this symbiotic relationship helps to explain why the machine didn't challenge the banks and financial institutions to whom the city owed the bulk of its debt during the fiscal crisis. Instead of fighting the banks, the machine helped to transfer the debt burden to the shoulders of the public at large. Their efforts were especially useful in allowing for the pensions, benefits and salaries of unionized city workers to be tapped to salvage the banks exposed financial positions.

The contempt of machine politicians for constituents is not difficult to understand. For over a hundred years, local political organizations like the Madison Club had served members as springboards for careers or as way-stations on their journeys from the neighborhood to corporate board rooms, or from elected to non-elected members of the Permanent Government. Geographically speaking, ethnic politics enabled people to escape from the poor and working class ethnic ghettoes of Brooklyn to the "gilded ghettoes" of the suburbs.

Although Newfield and DubBrul's comprehensive study of the New York City fiscal crisis is fascinating and worthy of a great deal more attention, for our purposes one particular aspect of their analysis is more important; how the "Clubhouse System" is intrinsically connected to "Legal Graft" and "The Political Economy of Organized Crime." Their discussions are invaluable in helping to explain the role of the Madison Club in its last decade as a connection as well as a buffer, perhaps even a "Flak Catcher," between the Permanent Government and the ethnically and racially changing city electorate.[14]

## Legal Graft

The tie that binds the various epochs of the Madison Club and the Brooklyn machine together is legal graft, or as George Washington Plunkitt has put it earlier, "honest graft." This is because "Politics is business. And legal graft is the currency of the Permanent Goverment."[15] In their book, Newfield and DuBrul provide numerous and varied examples of legal graft from bond sale commissions to zoning variances.[16] They report as major recipients of legal graft City Title Insurance Company and Grand Brokerage. Both had been long connected to the Brooklyn machine and, during their time of power, to Stanley Steingut and Meade Esposito.[17] As a result, clubhouses like Steingut's James Madison and Esposito's Thomas Jefferson, were crowded with both active members and political loiterers whose livelihood was dependent on one or more of these "services."

As might be expected, many of the incidents they describe involve Madison Club characters and other Brooklyn political figures. For understanding the history of the Madison Club, three of their examples are especially insightful. The first involves the "farce" of judicial nominating conventions and elections. Newfield and DuBrul noted in 1981 that 126 of 150 New York State Supreme Court judges elected in New York City were endorsed by both the Democrats and Republicans.[18] As you may recall from previous chapters, this venerable practice by which party leaders make nonpartisan "deals" for judgeships goes back at least to John McCooey's time.

The second example also can be traced back to Boss McCooey; the practice of lowering real estate tax assessments for property owners who have made contributions to the "right" candidates and who hire the "right" lawyers. This specific type of grafting is not only profitable to all involved, it is also hard to prove because there are no precise standards and guidelines for making property value judgements. What is the incentive for politicians to remove the opportunity for legal graft?[19]

A third practice highlighted in *The Permanent Government* involves depositing millions of dollars of government funds in non-interest bearing accounts in politically favored banks. Here they cite another family name from Brooklyn's political history- James Farley. Newfield and DuBrul note that James Farley, Jr., the son of F.D.R.'s Postmaster General, was a director of Central State Bank which received interest free deposits of City funds.[20]

## The Clubhouse System

Although many scholars and social commentators such as Banfield and Wilson, and Glazer and Moynihan, have argued that the era of big-city political machines, with a few exceptions, ended decades ago, Newfield and DuBrul strongly disagreed. They contended that those who pronounced the demise of the machine were tied to "outdated stereotypes" of the big-city machine and the actors who participated in it. For them, the modern machine should be viewed as a corporation designed to profit its "Class A shareholders."[21] According to them, Abraham Beame was the epitome of the machine politician who saw as his mission the rebuilding of the clubhouse after it was damaged during the Lindsay's somewhat reform-minded mayoralty.[22]

Because of Beame's long service to the Madison Club (since 1929) and the Brooklyn organization, he was appointed by Mayor Willliam O'Dwyer in 1946 to Assistant Budget Director. In 1952 Mayor Vincent R. Impellitteri promoted him to Budget Director. While in the Budget Bureau, Beame had four Irish Catholic advisors who were the caretakers of what was left of John McCooey's organization; John Carty, William S. Shea, James Carroll, and James Cavanagh. When he became mayor, he made Cavanagh his first deputy, John Carty's son was given the job of running the Office of Neighborhood Services, and James Carroll's brother John was made Municipal Service Administrator. Many other appointments from the Madison Club's "back rooms" were made, such as Irving Goldman as Commissioner of Cultural Affairs, and Sam Berman as lobbyist for the Off-Track Betting Corporation. More party regulars were appointed at the behest of the other county bosses with whom Beame cooperated: Pat Cunningham of the Bronx, Matthew Troy and Donald

Manes of Queens (Manes was a Crown Heights, Brooklyn native.), and, of course, the club's political neighbor Meade Esposito of Brooklyn. The success of the machine in re-grouping itself during Beame's mayoralty increased the severity of the fiscal crisis which brought the city to its knees. Three years after Beame's election as mayor, "The City Club... estimated in 1976 that '5,000-7,000' unneces-sary patronage jobs on the city payroll remain filled...which cost the taxpayer between $100 million and $150 million a year."[23]

Clubhouse politicians are interested in positions or issues which have profit potential. They are willing to do anything to win them. For example, City Marshalls, Public Administrators, and Surrogates Courts control millions of dollars worth of property and can dispense enormous amounts of patronage.[24] These are some of the lower level political institutions and mundane concerns that ordinary citizens, and social scientists, ignore when trying to ex-plain politics. They overlook this level of politics in favor of "larger" issues and positions, whereas these pecuniary factors are the nitty gritty of the machine. Self interest and the hope for personal reward fuels involvement at the local club level. According to Newfield and DuBrul most of those involved in Abe Beame's mayoral campaign wanted jobs and when he got in office he gave them positions "regardless of qualifications."[25]

## "Organized" Crime

In bitting journalistic style, Newfield and Dubrul ex-pose the underside of machine politics and allude to connections between the Brooklyn machine and various quasi-legal and blatantly illegal activities. This is best illustrated by their litany of the past and future offenses of some of the "guests" at the 1974 Kings County Democratic

Party's Annual Dinner such as: Congressman Frank Brasco-imprisoned for conspiracy to accept a bribe; Congressman Bertram Podell-imprisoned for accepting a bribe; Eugene Hollander-guilty of Medicaid fraud; Queens County "boss" Matthew Troy-guilty of income tax evasion; Carmine DeSapio-imprisoned for bribery; Congressman John Murphy-guilty of conspiracy and conflict of interest in the FBI's Abscam undercover sting; Councilman Sam Wright-guilty of accepting a pay-off; Anthony Scotto, president of ILA Local 1814-convicted of of racketeering, conspiracy, bribe-taking, and tax evasion; Congressman Mario Biaggi-convicted in 1981 of Federal racketeering and obstruction of justice charges related to "Wedtech"- a Bronx military contractor; Joe Pape, former Manhattan district leader and business associate of Stanley Steingut-indicted for falsifying records to conceal bribes; Assemblyman Harvey Strelzin-partner in a garbage-disposal business with mobster Anthony Ricci; Milton Kessler (an aid to Councilman Howard Golden)-managing agent for a Crown Heights slum building cited for 130 violations; Frank Vaccaro-suspended by the Commission on Judicial Conduct for accepting gifts from a lawyer who appeared before him; Roy Cohn-indicted and acquitted three times; District Leader George Meissner-convicted slumlord; Bernard Deutsch-convicted of stock fraud; Judge Jerome Steinberg-indicted for perjury and contempt; Bay Ridge District leader Frankie Folan-caught selling airline tickets for non-existent flights; American Bank and Trust Company directors Arthur Vare, Stanley Kreitman, and Saul Kagan-bank charter revoked for violations of law; restaurateur Larry Gurino-denied a liquor license because of business connections with individuals who have "close connections" with organized crime; builder Vincent Caristo-banned from Board of Education construction because of past bid-rigging; Sidney Lipkins, chairman of Broadway

Maintenance Corporation-his company accused of "extensive irregularities" and "excessive pofits" in servicing traffic lights and parking meters, also accused of overbilling; Fortune Pope, president of Colonial Sand and Stone Company and owner of *Il Progresso* - guilty of filing false proxy statements with the American Stock Exchange; builders Donald and Fred Trump-accused of Fair Housing Act violations against Blacks in their rental policies; Louis Friedman-removed from the State Supreme Court for abusing his office and obstructing an investigation; former Taxi Commission chairman Norman Levy-convicted of fixing parking tickets (later reversed); Brooklyn Supreme Court Clerk Joseph Parisi-indicted for illegally using pension funds.

Finally, as perhaps the greatest of all ironies, among the hundreds of guests at the dinner were Brooklyn Supreme Court law secretaries George Kerner and Frank Gilligan. Gilligan was also the treasurer of the Kings County Democratic Party. Two years later, both of them pleaded guilty to stealing the receipts of this dinner and three previous ones, for a total of $100,000!!!! The guest speaker at the dinner, held at the Waldorf Astoria was Mayor Abraham D. Beame.[26]

For insight into the mentality of machine politicians, Newfield and DuBrul cite an 1974 interview with then Councilman Howard Golden, who they called an "unconcious Plunkett." Golden was asked why, despite the indictment of Bertram Podell for bribery, he and his political club were working so hard to re-elect him. "We're for Bert only because we have inside information that he's guilty and will be convicted," Golden answered. When Newfield and Dubrul expressed puzzlement, Golden continued: "Schmuck. If we help Podell win the primary and then he is convicted, that way we get to pick his replacement, and stop that kid Steven Solarz. We want to save this seat for our guy, Leonard Silverman."[27]

Howard Golden has since then been elected Brooklyn Borough President and in 1990 was concurrently holding the position of Kings County Democratic Boss after the "forced" retirement of Boss Esposito. Esposito was convicted of giving an illegal gratuity to Mario Biaggi in 1987. In the following year Esposito was convicted of bribery in a kickback, money laundering, tax fraud, commercial bribery and conspiracy case.

It has been argued by many, but never proven, that the influence of stereotypical organized criminals on city governance has declined. It is more likely that new organized criminals have replaced the older cohorts. According to *The Permanent Government's* authors, organized crime developed as a major influence on city politics during Prohibition, hitting its height in the 1940s and 50s when mob bosses Frank Costello, Thomas Luchese, and Joe Adonis "cemented" their alliance with the clubhouses. By that time, Costello had become so powerful that he arranged for Tammany's backing of Brooklyn District Attorney William O'Dwyer in the 1945 election for mayor. Under O"Dwyer it was a "golden age" for the mob.[28] Their direct influence on political decision-making continued until the televised hearings of Senator Estes Kefauver whose U.S. Senate committee concluded that there were "deep systemic" influences of the Mafia in the Democratic Party of New York.

There has always been symbiotic connections between one or another form of organized crime and political machines. The record of corruption and the heralded "clean ups" is like a long-running television series where the major script changes refer only to the ethnicity, race and religions of the characters who are cast as villains or victims. In many cases the same individuals who are cast as crusaders are later revealed as criminals. The history of organized crime and politics in New York City leads one to agree with radical criminologist William J. Chambliss that the close relationship between organized crime and urban political systems is endemic in capitalist societies.[29] Unfortunately for socialist countries, organized criminals find ideology no barrier to their activities as witnessed by extensive organized crime activities in Eastern Bloc nations such as Russia and Poland.[30]

William O'Dwyer was a good example of the political "split personality" syndrome of reformer-corrupter. As a Brooklyn District Attorney he made a reputation for himself by crusading against organized crime; especially in the non-Irish Catholic neighborhoods of East New York and Brownsville, the site for the notorious "Murder Incorporated" gang. Formerly a policeman, and a judge, O'Dwyer vowed to clean up Brownsville which he declared had "spawned more gangsters and criminals than any other section of the city."[31] At the time the neighborhood was composed primarily of working-class and foreign-born Jews. O'Dwyer, running for Mayor against Fiorella LaGuardia, was competing for headlines with State Special Prosecutor Thomas E. Dewey. Dewey was crusading against the evils of Tammany Hall and ultimately aiming his anti-crime campaign for the governorship. Dewey had been appointed as Special Prosecutor to go after organized crime and corruption by Governor Herbert Lehman, a member of one of America's most accomplished Jewish families, who established the Special Prosecutor's office in 1935.[32] It is possible that Lehman, because of his own Jewish identity, was especially sensitive to showing concern about organized crime in the essentially lower and working class Eastern European Jewish community.

According to Jenna Weissman Joselit, author of *Our Gang: Jewish Crime and the New York Jewish Community,*

*1900-1940*, it was about that time, toward the end of the Depression, that Jews in large part began to leave the lower levels of organized crime and labor racketeering in New York while maintaining their hold on higher eschelon positions. Slowly Italian Americans like Albert Anastasia and Charles "Lucky" Luciano formed alliances with the likes of Louis "Lepke" Buchalter and Meyer Lansky.[33] By the 1950s, Italian gangsters were to dominate at least the "public" view of organized crime in New York. This meant that Jewish and Irish organized criminals had socially and politically "arrived."

As far as the actual business of organized crime was concerned nothing was really changed very much by the highly publicized serial crusades of politically ambitious prosecutors or the succession of different ethnic groups. For example, in 1972 the Knapp Commission report on the New York City Police Department, which gave special attention to the Brooklyn scene, concluded that corruption was "an extensive, department-wide phenomenon."[34] These connections between the police and gambling, prostitution and drug trafficking flourished during the consecutive terms of office of "reform minded " Mayors Robert F. Wagner and John V. Lindsay. Also in 1972 Kings County District Attorney Eugene Gold and his Assistant District Attorney Charles J. Hynes "went after" Italian-American organized criminals in Brooklyn again. After sixteen months of dangerous work they were able to get indictments of fifty-four carting companies and the officers of the Trade Waste Association for conspiracy, restraint of trade, and perjury before a grand jury. These indictments were followed by several convictions and court orders. Newfield and DuBrul noted that despite these efforts, Brooklyn's carting industry is still run by the mob.[35] The influence of organized criminals is still so pervasive that it has become "accepted" by many industries and even by public officials. Garment industry businessmen have come to see extortion as "merely another tax or licensing fee."[36]

In Brooklyn, organized crime and political machines have been around so long that history even appears to be circular. For example, at the same time as the Knapp Commission was conducting its investigations into New York City Police Department corruption, in "The Impact of Organized Crime on an Inner City Community," Harold Lasswell and Jeremiah McKenna concluded that "Organized crime was the single most powerful force in the community."[37] The particular neighborhood community they had studied was Brooklyn's Bedford Stuyvesant- the largest black community in New York City where seventy years earlier John McCooey had first established the Madison Club. Throughout the 1950's and 1960's, these neighborhoods were controlled by machine politicians, both white and nonwhite, with long ties to the club.

## The Fiscal Crisis Divides the City

The combined mayoralties of Wagner, Lindsay and Beame which lasted from 1954 until 1977 were described in *The Permanent Government* as a "Temporary" one. Actually, according to the authors, this particular string of mayors was merely one segment of a long line of other, equally temporary, governments. During the Wagner-Lindsay-Beame years, the sovereignty of the city was "given away" to the likes of power broker Robert Moses and political boss Carmine DeSapio as a prelude to abdication to the banks and the Municipal Assistance Corporation.[38] Perhaps more importantly, it was also a time when the city's ethnically-based local political organizations fought openly with one another for the decreasing amount of spoils available to them due to deepening economic recessions.

In addition, new ethnic factions arose in New York and contested the traditional "splits of the take." While the county-wide and neighborhood machines fought with each other, semi-independent "reformer" Mayors Wagner and Lindsay were able to capture City Hall. They did this, however, without completely vanguishing the traditional bosses. Decades later when the machines regained power with Beame as Mayor, the free-wheeling New York political game was over. The city had been figuratively leveled by strikes, massive urban decay, blackout looting, drug addiction of epidemic proportion, ghetto riots, the Knapp Commission findings of widespread police corruption, and several municipal government scandals. During these turbulent times the formula for political success became more than ever before- "divide and conquer."

As common political ground was hard to find, interest groups were described in ethnic, racial and religious terms. It was difficult to distinguish political discourse from ethno-religious debates on homosexuality, abortion, affirmative action and the death penalty. Throughout most of this period the Madison Club was represented at the city-wide decision-making level by Abraham Beame. Beame was Controller of New York City under Mayor Wagner from 1961 to 1965, when he gave up the seat and ran against John Lindsay for Mayor and lost. He regained the Controller's job in 1969 and served there under Lindsay until 1973 when he ran for, and won, the mayoralty. In 1977 Beame ran and lost a bid for re-election in an extremely racially polarized contest.

In their mayoral campaigns, Robert F. Wagner, Jr. and John V. Lindsay, at least on the surface, ran against the machine, but once in office they slowly became ensnared in its web as they sought personal political success and higher office. In order to guarantee success in New York City politics, "deals" have to made with the bosses. For example; if as a candidate you don't make deals, you can't count on easy primary victories which allow you to save energy and cash for the general elections. Beame on the other hand always ran as a machine candidate. In all of these campaigns, regardless of the different mayors' reform or machine images and rhetoric, the real issues at the grass roots level were race, ethnicity and religion.

Madison Club veteran Abe Beame, the city official Newfield and Dubrul cite as the most connected to the fiscal crisis, ran for Mayor in 1973 in the thick of rumors of city bankruptcy with the slogan, "If you don't know the buck, you don't know the job."[39] In New York City and State politics, having a Jewish candidate for Comptroller (controller of the revenue) has been an innovative, but still insidious use of anti-Semitism which portrays Jews as especially good at "knowing the buck." The gut concerns of most of the people were different and they had little to do with fiscal matters. Still in the majority, white New Yorkers were alarmed by the growing visibility of minorities in "their" city and "their" neighborhoods.

In June of 1973, Beame was running in a mayoral primary against Herman Badillo, an anti-clubhouse, Bronx politician who was also Puerto Rican. According to Newfield and DuBrul, Pat Cunningham, Boss of the Bronx, Brooklyn Boss Meade Esposito, and the Permanent Government were against Badillo because of his independence. It is clear that many of the "people" on the other hand were to vote against him because of his ethnicity. The 1973 Democratic mayoral primary echoed with racial and ethnic appeals. Unexpected by most political observers, even the Black Democratic party machine in Harlem lined up against Badillo as Manhattan's Black Borough President Percy Sutton ordered 150,000 flyers printed and distributed in an attempt to distance Badillo from the Black electorate. Making an appeal for Black voters in his own campaign literature, Badillo's media advisers favorably compared him to the highly touted Black Mayor of Los Angeles, Thomas Bradley. The Harlem organization's flyer, on the other hand, simply said: "BADILLO IS NOT BRADLEY, BRADLEY IS HONEST."[40] The Harlem organization's opposition to Badillo reflected a long-standing rift between Black and Puerto Rican politicians in the city. They were also indirectly, and not so subtly, stating that Badillo was not Black.

Across the East River in middle-class Jewish neighborhoods in Brooklyn, anti-Badillo campaign workers handed out copies of what appeared to be a "newspaper" falsely claiming that Badillo was in favor of siting "Forest Hills type projects" around the city. At the time, the Jewish middle-class neighborhood of Forest Hills, Queens was vigorously opposing an attempt to construct a low-income housing project there.

These clubhouse workers also distributed an apparent "reprint" for the *Daily News* saying that it had endorsed Beame in the run-off primary. This was also false. Sheldon Katz, at the time Vice-President of a landlord association and brother of Leon Katz a landlord and Flatbush City Councilman, admitted responsibility for the literature.[41]

In the Bensonhurst, Canarsie and Bay Ridge neighborhoods of Brooklyn which are described as "conservative, ethnic and regular" another anonymous illegal leaflet was distributed. It was written half in English and half in Italian and appealed to even baser instincts and fears. "Abe Beame's opponent is in favor of quotas in hiring and education." "Abe Beame's opponent is supported by the Black Panthers and Young Lords." At the time the Black Panther and the Puerto Rican Young Lords were highly publicized radical organizations associated with "terrorist" activities.

Newfield and DuBrul traced the leaflet to Ropp Press in

Brooklyn. It was paid for by the Beame committee whose chair, Joseph Slavin, later became a judge. They also found Arthur Brasco in charge at Beame's campaign headquarters. Brasco was the brother-in-law of Meade Esposito's chauffer and the cousin of Brooklyn Congressman Frank Brasco who was later convicted of conspiring to take a bribe from a mobster. Lineage aside, Brasco told Newfield and DuBrul that the literature had been sent into the "Italian districts" where kids were given a "few bucks" to distribute them.[42]

While the residents of New York City fought amongst themselves for jobs and housing the various county-wide machines split up the municipal budgetary pie as the city drifted toward default. When it came time to settle accounts the people of New York City, especially the poor, working class and minorities would foot the bill of increased taxes and decreased services. The institutions and programs which provided the figurative "rungs on the ladder" for the advancement of the Irish, Jews and Italians were sacrificed in the interest of the banks and the other economic elites of the city who, along with organized criminals and corrupt politicians congregated at the 1974 Democratic Party dinner.[43]

Perhaps, the most tragic and ironic example of the Brooklyn machine "selling out" its most disadvantaged constituents was the elimination of free tuition at the City University of New York in 1976. There had been no tuition charged at CUNY since its founding in 1847. This change was also ironic in that the University had provided opportunity for the mobility of New York's older minorities; the Irish, Jews and Italians, into respectable white-collar and professional middle-class positions. Among the beneficiaries of free tuition was Abraham Beame, a graduate of City College and the first CUNY alumnus to become Mayor of New York City.

It was the Board of Higher Education which governed CUNY who made the fateful decision. The members appointed by Brooklyn's own Governor Hugh L. Carey and Mayor Abraham Beame swung the vote in favor of the imposition of tuition led by BHE Chairman Harold Jacobs. The majority in favor of tuition was created when former Chairman Alfred Giardino, Vincent Fitzpatrick, Sandra Lopez de Bird, Rita Hauser and Francis Kilcoyne resigned in protest of the pressure directed toward them to approve the end of free tuition. Only Vinia Quinones, the sole Black member of the board, was left to vote against it.[44]

As might be expected, the Brooklyn influence on the two newly created organizations which took control of New York City's finances was overwhelming. The Municipal Assistance Corporation (MAC) was established in 1975. It was responsible for converting New York City debt to long-term bonds. Of the nine original members, five were picked by Governor Carey and four were chosen by Mayor Beame. The Emergency Financial Control Board (EFCB) which was empowered to oversee the finances of the city consisted of the Governor, the Mayor, the State Controller Arthur Levitt (originally from the Madison Club), the City Comptroller and three business members.[45] MAC and EFCB controlled the budget of the city and in effect took over decision making powers from the Mayor and the New York City Board of Estimate. Political control of New York City was transferred from an elected to an appointed body.

Not surprisingly, the results of this shift in power were wage freezes and layoffs for city workers, service cuts, higher transit fares, and tuition at the City University for everyone. Even more ominous for the city's future fiscal health was the shifting of a substantial part of the city's bonds from the banks into the municipal employees pension portfolios. No attempt was made to raise revenues from the Permanent Government, for example by collecting the millions of dollars owed the city in unpaid real estate and other taxes. Another possible route to solving the crisis would have been making banks forgive part of the interest on the debt. The major portion of the debt was owed to banks and financial institutions which bought the bonds to finance the favorite projects of the Permanent Government such as the Urban Development Corporation extravaganzas.

## From Beame to Koch

During the time of the fiscal crisis, the quality of life in New York neighborhoods suffered greatly. As resentment rose, intergroup hostility also increased. Brooklyn neighborhoods and Brooklyn politics were even more racially and ethnically divided. At the city-wide level these ethnic divisions were apparent during the unsuccessful campaign of Abraham Beame as he ran for reelection in 1977. Because of a New York State election law designed to prevent "minorities" from winning the nomination, the important action in that campaign was in two Democratic party mayoral primaries. The law required that, for city-wide offices, a winning candidate receive at least forty percent of the primary vote in order to avoid a run-off primary with the opponent who received the second highest highest vote count. The candidate list for the initial primary was racially, religiously and ethnically diverse with Jewish candidates Koch, Beame and female candidate Bella Abzug, Italian Catholic Cuomo, Black Percy Sutton and Puerto Rican Herman Badillo. Koch's campaign was the most effective and divisive, leaving him only politically liberal candidate Cuomo to deal with in the run-off. The tactics and outcome of the campaign were precursors of Stanley Steingut's and the Madison Club's losses a year later in 1978. The results of the first primary were as follows: Edward Koch-180,248; Mario Cuomo-170,560; Abraham Beame-163,610; Bella Abzug-150,719; Percy Sutton-131,197; Herman Badillo-99,808; and Joel Hartnett-13,927.

Although top vote-getter Koch had presented himself as a liberal-minded "reformer" who earlier in his political career had made a name for himself by battling against Tammany Boss Carmine De Sapio in lower Manhattan, he campaigned as a conservative and for a time became the most popular mayor since LaGuardia.[46] His astute 1977 campaign strategy emphasized fear of crime and took advantage of white-working-class hostility toward minorities. It promised more cops and the reinstatement of the death penalty. He publically referred to some prominent Black leaders as "demagogues," and frequently railed against "quotas," "reverse discrimination," "welfare programs," "soft judges," black anti-Semitism, and "welfare empires." Newfield and DuBrul characterized his campaign strategy thusly: "Through code words, symbolism and rhetoric, Koch communicates an attitude of hostility to blacks, and this is a dirty little secret of his vast popularity with the white majority that votes."[47]

Assisting Koch in his campaign strategy was the social reality of New York City life at the time. 1977 was the year of the "Son of Sam" serial murder spree of young women, the summer black-out riots in minority neighborhoods, and bombings by Puerto Rican terrorists. It is no wonder he made the death penalty an integral part of his campaign rhetoric.

While campaigning in Brooklyn, "Ed Koch stopped a woman on the corner of 48th Street and 18th Avenue. 'I'm for capital punishment, are you?' he asked her. The woman's disinterested face became animated. She furrowed her brows and nodded...'Did you know that Beame was against capital punishment until three weeks ago when he saw the polls?,' Koch told her."[48] A *New York Times* poll had shown that 75% of registered Democratic voters favored capital punishment. In literature distributed in Brooklyn and Queens the "death penalty" was one of the "5 reasons to vote for Koch." In Koch's literature given out in liberal Manhattan, mention of the death penalty was omitted.

Koch survived the initial primary along with more liberally-minded New York State Lieutenant Governor Mario Cuomo who tried to run a campaign based on a theme of "bringing people together." Cuomo was best known then for his role in arranging a compromise in the Forest Hills low-income housing dispute. Koch then defeated Cuomo in the run-off Democratic Party primary election in September by a vote of 431,849 to 354,222. But their battle did not end there because Cuomo had been given the Liberal Party designation he faced Koch again in the general election in November but lost to him for the third time 712,976 to 587,257.

By the time Koch faced Cuomo in the second primary he had gained the support of the party bosses including Brooklyn's Meade Esposito, Abraham Beame and Harold Fisher.

Unfortunately for the members of Beame's Madison Club, despite his upsetting experience in the election as an entrenched politician losing in an ethnically charge race by a conservative "reformer," they did not see the handwriting on the wall which foretold of their own political future. They also didn't learn from Mario Cuomo's two defeats by Koch that white, working-class voters in New York City had become disenchanted with liberal politicians and their positions on issues like capital punishment and the provision of services to the poor. Only a year later, Stanley Steingut and the rest of the Madison Club would suffer the same fate as Beame and Cuomo- losing to virtually unknown candidates in a highly charged local campaign which attracted national attention.

## Footnotes

1. Jack Newfield and Paul DuBrul, *The Permanent Government*. New York: The Pilgrim Press, 1981, pp. 111-12.
2. See: Robert K. Merton, *Social Theory and Social Structure*. Glencoe: The Free Press, 1967; Edward Banfield and James Q. Wilson, *City Politics*. New York: Vintage Books, 1966; and Daniel P. Moynihan and Nathan Glazer, *Beyond the Melting Pot*. Cambridge, Mass.: M.I.T. Press, 1970.
3. For readings on "radical" or "conflict" perspectives and the "ethnicity vs class" debate see: William J. Chambliss (Ed.), *Sociological Readings in the Conflict Perspective*. Reading, Mass.: Addison-Wesley Publishing Co., 1973; Ira Katznelson, *City Trenches: Urban Politics and the Patterning of Class in the United States*. New York: Pantheon Books, 1981; Herbert Gans, *The Urban Villagers*. New York: The Free Press of Glencoe, 1982; and Gaetano Mosca, *The Ruling Class*. New York: McGraw-Hill, 1939.
4. For examples of "Muckrakers," see: John Spargo, *The Bitter Cry of the Children*. Chicago: Quadrangle Books, 1968; and Lincoln Steffens, *The Shame of Cities*. New York: Hill and Wang, 1957.
5. C. Wright Mills, *The Power Elite*. New York: Oxford University Press, 1956.
6. Jack Newfield and Paul DuBrul, *op.cit.*, p. 63. Also see pp. 64-99 for references and discussions concerning many persons prominent in Brooklyn politics and the Madison Club.
7. *Ibid.*, p. 76.
8. *Ibid.*, p. 31.
9. *Ibid.*, p. 15.
10. *Ibid.*, pp. 18, 88.
11. *Ibid.*, pp. 88-89. See also Jerome Krase, *Self and Community in the City*. Washington, D.C.: University Press of America, 1982 for a study of Brooklyn's changing neighborhoods in the 1970's.
12. *Ibid.*, p. 64.
13. *Ibid.*, p. 75.
14. *The Permanent Government* is especially valuable for a study of the Brooklyn Machine and the Madison Club because of the dissappearance of Brooklyn newspapers such as the *Eagle* and the paucity of coverage in citywide papers of "local" politics. Most neighborhood papers serve more as organs of local clubs than objective reportage. Newfield and DuBrul's journalistic orientations and experience with New York's *Village Voice*, although ideological

biased toward the left, makes their book as much a repository of recent political history as an interesting interpretation of those events.

15. *Ibid.*, p.100.
16. *Ibid.*, p.100.
17. *Ibid.*, p.103.
18. *Ibid.*, p.117.
19. *Ibid.*, p.119.
20. *Ibid.*, p.123.
21. *Ibid.*, p.180.
22. *Ibid.*, p.111.
23. *Ibid.*, p.111.
24. *Ibid.*, see pp. 180-95 for a detailed description.
25. *Ibid.*, p.111.
26. *Ibid.*, pp. 175-78.
27. *Ibid.*, p.179.
28. *Ibid.*, p.215.
29. Chambliss, William J. *On the Take: From Petty Crooks to Presidents.*, 2nd Edition. Bloomington, Indiana: Indiana University Press, 1988.
30. For organized crime in a variety of settings see: Robert J. Kelly (Ed.), *Organized Crime: A Global Perspective.* Totowa, N.J.: Rowman Littlefield, 1986.
31. Jenna Weissman Joselit, *Our Gang: Jewish Crime and the New York City Jewish Community, 1900-1940.* Bloomington, Ind.: Indiana University Press, p. 150.
32. *Ibid.*, p.107.
33. *Ibid.*, p.157.
34. Newfield and DuBrul, 1981. p. 144.
35. *Ibid.*, p. 220-21.
36. *Ibid.*, p.223.
37. Harold Lasswell and Jeremiah McKenna, "The Impact of Organized Crime on an Inner City Community," New York: The Policy Center Inc., Mimeo, 1970.
38. Newfield and DuBrul, *op. cit.*, pp. 128-157.
39. *Ibid.*, p.157.
40. *Ibid.*, p.149.
41. *Ibid.*, p.150.
42. *Ibid.*, p. 150-51.
43. *Ibid.*, p. 175-79.
44. *Ibid.*, p. 173-74.
45. *Ibid.*, p.162.
46. *Ibid.*, p.248.
47. *Ibid.*, p.257.
48. *Ibid.*, p.262.

# An Insider's View of the Last Campaign

## Introduction

This chapter is presented as a personal narrative of how the Madison Club of Brooklyn ended its seventy-five year reign over politics and patronage. In the years to come political historians will probably argue that the once invincible Madison Club candidates lost to a rag-tag group of political novices because of issues such as corruption and capital punishment. This insider's view reveals something very different. It shows individuals and groups wrestling with each other over personal needs and aspirations which were tinged with racial, religious and ethnic undertones. In other words, this chapter demonstrates that politics is a very human game.

Most studies of political organizations claim to be "completely objective." There are, however, important advantages to subjectivity which allows scholars to make connections from the theoretical world of urban politics to the actual experiences of real people. One often forgets that the subjects of historical political studies are, at base, quite ordinary. Politicians, workers, "Bosses," "Ward Heelers," and voters, are, after all, not genetically different from sociologists, historians and college students who study them. People involved in politics ought not be looked at in the same way that a chemist studies compounds or an entymologist studies ants. By providing a glimpse of politics through a personal lens, the clubhouse phenomenon becomes more understandable; not as a deviant or esoteric form of human activity but, as Erving Goffman or Alfred Schutz might say, as a part of everyday life which is taken for granted by participants and observers alike.[1]

The methods for describing this down-to-earth, personal context in social science have been variously called, "participant-observation" at one extreme and "ethnomethodology" at the other.[2] Such terms, however, tend to give these sensitive perspecitives too great an air of stuffy scientific respectability. In contrast to the rarefied atmosphere of most academic products, let us think of this narrative as simply the story of the Madison Club and the practice of urban political machines, told from the point of view of a sociologist who was at the same time a club member and deeply involved in the final, and fatal, last campaign.

## The Personal Bases of Political Involvement

A number of important underlying questions of general interest will be implicitly addressed in this final chapter such as: What makes people join and participate in political organizations? How does the seemingly mysterious social interaction in "smoke-filled" rooms take place? What are the personal rewards and punishments for political activism? And, as the great German sociologist of the mundane, Georg Simmel, might ask; "Why are people so 'fascinated' with the symbols of power in closed political organizations?"[3] I emphasize these sorts of theoretical points now because, as the narrative progresses, they will become submerged, and perhaps also forgotten, in the descriptions of practical historical events.

The reasons why people get involved in local political organizations vary greatly. In most cases, the long term members of the Madison Club were still involved there primarily for economic advancement. Despite the common expressions of ideological and other higher goals as reasons for political participation offered by activists, almost all benefitted directly or indirectly by the ability of the club to reward individuals and families with jobs, contracts and other economic advantages of association with the powerful. Club members treated political patronage and use of influence as an "open secret," seldom openly expressed but always understood.[4] Naturally, the most involved and active were those who stood to gain the most from the success of the club candidates.

## Personal Connections

I had been to the Madison Club on several occasions before coming there to work in the last campaign and I had met many of the club's leaders over the years. My wife's grandfather, Anthony Jordan, had been a president of the club and his youngest son, Anthony Jordan, Jr. had also served as president before resigning to assume a position on the judicial bench. Most of my direct political experience was with "reform" and "independent" candidates who ran against the "regulars." These humble, and often, futile tilts at the machine were regarded by my wife's relatives, I assume, as youthful naivete. Like many other sociologists in the early 70s involved in urban studies, I had helped community groups organize and had done research on local problems or "needs assessments" in order to obtain grant money from government and private agencies. This work occurred during the heyday of the "decentralization" and "citizen participation" movements in New York City and was, therefore, in direct confrontation with the old style regular Democratic political machines.[5]

## The Clubhouse Setting

In the "good old days," the Madison Club was a local community institution. During most of the year, it was open for walk-in business every Monday and Thursday nights. Meetings of the Board of Directors were also held regularly. In addition, there were occasional special meetings and parties which took place there. The clubhouse was used occasionally by other groups such as the Boy Scouts. Therefore the clubhouse had to be accessible to the community and the membership. Over the years, the location of the club was moved several times to reflect skillful redistricting (gerrymandering). Its last location, on Church Avenue, was chosen because its previous Eastern Parkway site, in a predominantly Black area, was seen as "dangerous" by many club patrons. At first, the new area was a stable, white working-class neigborhood. Racial change was, however, only a few years away.

By employing Erving Goffman's perspective of the "dramaturgical method,"[6] the political clubhouse can be analysed as a "stage" upon which members, candidates and constituents, as actors, play out their parts. The Madison Club occupied a slightly shabby two-story building which once contained two street-level stores. It had two entrances from the sidewalk and large display windows. The block where it was located was inactive by Church Avenue standards. The street was, at other nearby parts, a busy retail thoroughfare. Above the storefronts hung a large sign identifying the building as the Madison Club. In the display windows signs announced candidates and up-coming elections. Nothing about the place gave passersby any indication of the powerful who occasionally assembled within.

On the first floor of the building was a narrow corridor leading to two large interior rooms and, off of which, a twisting staircase led to the second floor "offices" and "board room." Those upstairs rooms, and the people who used them, always seemed a bit mysterious as the general and public business of the club took place on the ground floor. The location of the staircase made it possible for people to go upstairs without passing through the more public meeting rooms.

A person entering the club through the corridor would come upon the first room, which was approximately 20x30 feet in size. It was furnished with old, worn, leather covered chairs, wooden office chairs, a few sofas, and tables of equal vintage. A small storage area, housing an obsolete mimeograph machine and office supplies, was in the front, and the men's and women's toilets were in the back of the first room. The most important props in the first room were the coffee pot and the television set built into the front wall, near which several of the chairs were usually arranged.

There were two entrances at either end of the room into the main meeting area. This larger room was arranged either with rows of folding chairs for meetings or as rows of desks along the walls during campaign work. At the head of the room, which was toward the rear of building, was a large wooden table behind which meetings were conducted by club officers. This was also the area of the club where the "big shots" held "court." Throughout the club were metal ashtray stands and clusters of metal file cabinets. On the walls were election district maps, left over campaign posters and a row of portraits of past club presidents, photographs of prominent politicians, and a collection of plaques for various community service awards.

Upstairs in the private offices there was a similar decor, only more crowded and containing more important amenities such as desk phones (downstairs there was a coin-operated phone booth). One might begin to wonder if any of the furniture had ever been new. The floors were uncarpeted and worn but were generally clean until people arrived.

The club was maintained by Cora, an elderly Black woman who lived in the building. She was caretaker of the club for many years, and despite her position was accorded deference, especially by the newcomers, who quickly learned she was not a "servant." She was one of the many regular characters who played out important parts of their lives on the Madison Club Stage.

## Making a "Contract"

I had come to the club in the winter of 1976, as many others had come before me-- to ask for a favor. Because the favor was done, I was destined to return. I had been to the club before for various election victory celebrations, but never on "business." Although there was never any discussion of return for the favor, I knew that a "contract" had been made. In politics, the sense of a contract is that in return for assistance, one is obligated to reciprocate at some future time. For most people it is merely the idea that one ought to vote for the candidate of the club, make a campaign contribution (commensurate to the deed), sign a nominating petition when necessary, or give some other form of support. Due to the relationship of my wife's family to the club I was not personally obliged to return the favor. My fee was charged against the past credit of the family, although I do remember once having typed addresses on envelopes for one of the club's candidates. Despite this, I felt personally obligated because of the immediate and full response I received regarding my problem. In other words "honor" and "reputation" were at stake.

Despite the uniqueness of the situation, one can generalize from my experience about the process of "making a contract." In many ways my experience and observations can be compared, at the abstract level, to the analysis provided by Norbert Elias of the Court Society of Louis XIV, of France.[7] He noted that in the court, power and influence were both determined and represented by one's personal access to those with power, ultimately emanating from the king. Power and privilege was governed by the etiquette of the court and controlled by physical barriers. Being close to the king, or being heard, was equivalent to power and influence. In the court, all were concious of the spatial indications of favoritism and sensitive to shifts in interactions, and etiquette which signified a person's rise or fall from favor. Louis XIV's Court and the Madison Club were complex social as well as political organizations.

As I was not well known at the club, when I arrived I was treated as an "outsider." No one there, other than Stanley Steingut, knew I was coming or who I was. I was just one of many people who might wander in seeking information, help or membership in the club. When I entered the first large room through the corridor, there were several middle-aged and older people standing or sitting about. Most were involved in conversations and a few sat in front of the television watching it rather intensely. It was early evening, around 7:30. No one seemed to notice me, but I was not unnoticed. An older, gray-haired woman, sitting at a table, brusquely called me over and asked what I wanted. I gave her my name and said I had come to speak to Stanley Steingut. She told me that he had not arrived yet, but that I should sit and wait. I took a seat in one of the large leather chairs and waited.

I had met the Speaker several times but was not quite sure that he would recognize me. I was sure he knew I was coming and also why. In any case, I was nervous. I felt out of place. While I sat, I noticed others come into the club. Some looked as uncomfortable as I felt, and I assumed they were there also seeking help. Others came in acting "like they owned the place," and were warmly greeted by those already there. Several moved into the second room, where it was obvious that "business" was conducted.

The club members and guests, the vast majority of whom were men, were dressed in their work clothes; suits and ties for some, overalls for others. A few people, when they arrived, were greeted more warmly and more loudly than others. These were obviously the "big shots" in the organization, I thought. I was later to discover that they were just "nicer" people. The big shots tended to be treated more with deference and respect than familiarity, except by their peers. When the club officers and other important people came into the club, they went directly into the business room without stopping to chat. I also discovered that these "big shots" tended not to simply "hang around," as they had more important business to attend to. These people always appeared to have just come from some important place and were on their way to some place just as important. The big shots also, more than others, furrowed their brows and often appeared to be contemplating serious matters. Later I was to see that these were the "styles" of the leaders, which were imitated by many others in the organization, who also copied their modes of dress and argot. At times, ordinary club members tried hard to look and act important. As a novice, I was easily impressed.

The less important people tended to congregate in the

first room and not in the meeting room. They never went upstairs to the office, referring to that space with some reverence. To the uninitiated, like myself, the "crowd" was quite impressive; they spoke loudly about politics and gave the impression that they knew what was going on. They dropped names in their conversations. In their talk, they spoke of "Stanley (Steingut)," "Abe (Beame)," "Meade (Esposito)," and other powerful members of the party organization. Others more distant to the club or from Brooklyn politics, were referred to by last names (Hugh) Carey, (John) Lindsay, (Ed) Koch, etc.. Those who used first names, it was assumed, knew the individual on a personal basis; familiarity was sign of status. This also, I learned, was a political style of speaking. What was crucial to real power was not who you knew, but who knew you!

Being known on a first, or even a last name basis, by important people was a powerful status symbol and part of the fascination of the political clubhouse world. Such people, an observer would believe, were influential. Newcomers and political climbers tried hard to get close to the powerful. Political clubs are filled with obsequity and sycophancy. Club events were opportunities to meet important people, get to know them and become recognized by them. One attended for immediate or future personal gain. Observationally, a person's power can be measured by the size and tightness of the crowd around him or her, and the relative ease at which its attention can be diverted elsewhere. Proximity to power was clearly something for which to compete. The "big shots," "wheels," or *"machers"* at the Madison Club were seldom left alone; unless of course they wanted to be alone, and then they could be quite rude in dismissing their entourage.

When Stanley Steingut finally arrived at the club with a few associates, the people hanging around in the room took notice. Most conversations stopped and eyes were turned toward him as he walked through, acknowledging some "hellos," and went into the second room. Several individuals from the waiting room quickly followed him inside, abruptly interrupting what had appeared to be deep conversations. I waited a few minutes and also followed inside. He was standing behind the large front table listening to a few people. The room was socially organized that evening as a series of small clusters of people at varying distances from the front of the building.

Someone came over to me and asked why I was there. He took me aside as I explained that I had been sent to see Stanley Steingut. I was quietly told that I would have to wait a while, as other business took place. I then said who it was that sent me and what my relationship was to that person. Then his demeanor changed, and he became quite amicable. He went over to "Stanley," waited for a break in the conversation, and whispered to him. The Speaker looked up and waved for me to come over. He was smiling broadly. I hoped that this meant that he recognized me. I walked over, hesitantly, as I was embarrassed by the reception, but relieved. We shook hands vigorously, (a traditional political ritual of little meaning in most cases) and we moved to the side to talk. One of his assistants stayed with us. He asked how things were at home and we engaged in other "small talk." I had brought my resume with me and I gave it to him. He placed it on the table and we discussed my problem. He listened intently and after thinking about said; "I'll look into it." I was later to understand that politicians never say that anything is guaranteed.

We talked a little while longer and his attention turned to other matters as more people, seeking help, or perhaps who were more important, came into the room. Those seeking help were always escorted over. I felt that I was taking up too much of his time, thanked him, excessively, and left. As I was exiting he said "so long," and used my first name. Although I did not realize it at the time, to those who heard the parting word "Jerry," I had been "made." This definition of me as a person close to the leader provided me with many opportunities, some deference, a little envy on the part of others, and even some hostility, when I came to the a year later to work on what was to be the Madison Club's final campaign.

Because "Stanley" called me "Jerry," club members would speak to me as though I was an "insider" and knew politics well; which I didn't. It was also erroneously assumed that I was aware of "insider secrets." Because I was a willing pupil, though, I learned the styles and mannerisms of the clubhouse scene. Dramaturgically, I could play the role of party "hack" as well as anyone else, when called upon to do so. When I left the club that night, I did not intend to return. I knew that at some point in my life, if Stanley Steingut needed my help, I would gladly lend my assistance. Happily, Stanley Steingut, Speaker of the New York State Assembly and a City power broker, I thought, would never need anybody's aid. What I was unaware of at the time, and perhaps he was too, was that a growing split was in the making at the Madison Club and that this would lead to the greatest primary challenge for the leadership of the district the club ever had.

## Paying Back a Favor

Almost a year later I received a phone call at home. It was the Speaker. We had a short conversation about a problem which had arisen in the district that he felt I could take care of--relatively simple, but delicate. I promised to take care of the problem. I had not learned yet to say, "I'll see what I can do." I learned that the club had split into two factions and that another Democratic organization was

now in the area, led by Ted Silverman, the City Councilman, and his wife, Sandy. Their club, the New Way, was
running candidates against the Madison Club for male
and female district co-leaders and for the New York State
Assembly. Most experts regarded the situation as a minor
irritation. Helene Weinstein, a relatively unknown young
attorney, was Steingut's opponent for the state assembly.
Against good political advice Steingut was also running
for male co-leader against Carl Garritani, a community
leader and retired New York City policeman on disability.
Pearl Anish, a community activist and Steingut's protege
was the Madison Club selection for female co-leader who
was opposed by Sandy Silverman of the New Way Club.
The battle lines were being drawn and the fiercest skirmishes were to take place in the predominantly Jewish and
Italian southern end of the 41st Assembly District, where
the majority of the voters lived in hostile New Way territory.

Steingut asked me to find out who was distributing
New Way campaign literature in a strategic election district; a large apartment complex in a section of Flatbush. I
investigated and discovered who it was and went to the
Madison Club to report to Steingut. When I returned, I
found the club had taken on a new appearance. Campaign
posters covered the display windows. Both rooms were
filled with people, and the business room was arranged
with a long line of desks with people sitting behind them,
busy with all kinds of work and answering the many
phones which were newly installed. Detailed election
district maps were on the walls and boxes of campaign
materials were stacked along the walls. Steingut was surrounded by people I had not seen before. The old timers
were congregating in the social room near the television
set and coffee urn. A new photocopier was in the storage
area. Although the campaign was going on, those as-

sembled appeared to be at ease. I noticed that the business room had quite a rather casual air about it. For example, there were open liquor bottles, and glasses sitting on the desks. Several shirt-sleeved men sat or stood around the desks. The tables were cluttered. Others in the room were chatting and drinking coffee. I also noticed several more women than usual in the business room. They were serving as secretaries; typing and answering phones. I discovered that many of the people in the room were from "upstate," or otherwise outside the district and had come to help in the campaign. These were the "volunteers."

When I came into the club a few people recognized me, but I went directly into the campaign "staff" area. I had no idea of the value of what I had to report and I was reluctant to interrupt the conversation Steingut was having with someone else, so I spoke to one of his aides instead. I told him that Steingut had asked me to look into something and that I was there to report the information. He went immediately over to him and Steingut came over with a few people, shook my hand, and introduced me to them. I then told him what I discovered. It seemed that the person he thought was distributing anti-Steingut literature at the highly voter-registered building complex was not really responsible. He had been asked to cover for someone else. I then said who the other person was. At that point, his smile changed to a frown of disappointment and disbelief. He then quickly turned and walked away without comment, leaving me alone. "What had I said?", I thought to myself. It was as though I brought bad news. I had expected that he would be pleased that the situation was different than he had imagined. I had also arranged for the "falsely accused" to endorse him in the primary. Subsequently I learned that the person who was actually responsible for the problem was a prominent club member and it was assumed he was supporting Steingut in the race.

I hung around for some time in the business room but was totally ignored, so I went into the social room for coffee. I sat around listening to conversations about politics and people, which I did not understand, trying to find a friendly face. A few people came over and I joined in their conversations. After that, I quickly became part of the club. They told me that an organizational meeting was to be held in a few days and I was told to show up for a campaign assignment.

## Campaign Work

A few evenings later the club was packed. In the business room, chairs were arranged auditorium style, the desks pushed to the side. A group of people sat in the front with maps and various sheets of paper in front of them. Several female campaign workers were assisting. Most of the people milled about in the other room, talking or having coffee and a Danish. After about a half-hour of waiting, we were called inside. Steingut gave a short, rather stimulating talk about the issues in the campaign - The Death Penalty and the Nursing Home Scandal, and his performance in the district. The last issue was approached by saying that the community did not realize how much he had done for it and that the New Way was taking credit for his work. His speech was surprisingly lacking in acrimony, given the sometimes vicious tenor I had already observed in the race. In contrast, the small talk at the club painted an horrendous picture of the opposition. Steingut made it seem as though they were only "misguided." This statesmanlike demeanor of the Speaker was an aspect both of his earthy charm and of his vulnerability. He was unwilling, perhaps even unsuited, to be the "dirty" politician he was described as being by the New Way club. It was also obvious to me that he had left most of the local work to people he trusted. This was a fatal mistake; some of his political "friends" had already become his "enemies."

Steingut's brief speech was met with loud applause and the "campaign manager" was introduced. He spoke about what was needed in the campaign. He outlined a "classic" machine operation which relied on a great deal of foot-work and effort by a large cadre of club members. He spoke in terms of "e.d.'s" and "a.d.'s", voter lists, "pull-ing," "lit drops," and other political jargon. No one was to leave without filling out an index card and receiving an assignment. Many of the people assembled were block or precinct "captains" and some were even officers of the club.

When the assignments were given out, a sharp division of labor became clear. Those who were running the cam-paign were not local club members. They were the "up-staters" or Steingut's assembly staff. As the campaign progressed, the club became more segregated along these lines. More and more grumbling was heard. Club mem-bers spoke more frequently about what "they" should be doing. Older members felt they were not given enough respect by the outsiders. All felt that their advice on how the campaign should be run was not wanted.

The "experts" had already made several major errors. In the past the competent machine could eliminate a chal-lenge through the petitioning process, having opposition petitions declared invalid by the courts. The machine could also gerrymander the opponent out of the district, or use some other technical mechanism so that a primary did not have to take place. New Way leader Councilman Silverman had been accused of engaging in such practices several years earlier while he was a member of the Madi-son Club.[8] Having installed most of judges to the county bench and influenced the hiring of people at the Board of Elections made such procedures relatively safe for the county machine. The regulars had also made it difficult for someone, who lost a primary, to continue their fight on an independent line in the general election.

But everything went wrong for the Madison Club in this campaign. First of all they were not up against novices. The people at the New Way were experienced political workers; probably better than the Madison members because they had more recent experience in campaigning for the absorbed Kennedy Club. Secondly, when the Steingut forces successfully challenged the New Way's petitions they made a blunder and left open the possibility of replacement on the ballot by another candidate. Helene Weinstein was replaced by her father Murray. The Weinsteins even gained some sympathy in the process by being "pushed around" by the "machine."

## Nominating Petitions

The petitioning process is basic to a campaign. It provides organizations with lists of voters who are for or against them. Signing a petition creates a minor psychological obligation to vote in the election. If analysed and recorded properly, petitions allow campaign staff to make informed judgements about strategy. The process is a tune up for the election as well as a way to involve club members personally in the political process. Petitions for other than local candidates can also be circulated and become part of the club's contribution to wider political efforts. In a well organized club, signatures are easy to come by, as each election block has a club representative. In the past the Madison Club had many such members. Unfortunately, many of their remaining workers were older, others had long since left the neighborhood and still others had gone over to the New Way. Because the club had not had a real challenge in such a long time and was seen as invincible, members had lost some of their sharpness in political and community activity. The club had also gravitated towards contacts with people through religious and other community institutions. Here too the New Way had picked up supporters. The club had a problem which it was just beginning to realize, but didn't quite appreciate. When people left the club, not just individuals, but temples, parishes and community organizations, were lost.

## Canvassing

My first regular assignment for the campaign was to canvass a number of e.d.s in an area close to Brooklyn College where I worked. An "e.d.", or election district, is a small segment of an assembly district, usually made up of a few city blocks. I was given a list of registered Democratic voters there by street and number listing and was told to visit them personally and talk to them about voting for Stanley Steingut and the rest of the "ticket" in the primary. A good canvasser attempts to identify potential voters and to ascertain for whom they will vote. This information is returned to headquarters and is used to create a list of voters to "pull" (get out to vote) during the election. The experienced canvasser also tries to convince undecided and antagonistic registrants to vote for his candidates. The information can be used to measure the club's degree of support or opposition. The pulling operation focuses on the strongest individual supporters and e.d.s with the greatest number of potential positive votes. The canvasser, if he or she does a proper job, is able to note issues and other items which are important to the voters. This information enables the campaign strategists to plan "lit drops" (distributions of campaign literature) or to fine-tune other efforts to convince voters to come out and vote the club's slate. The canvass also identifies particular polling booths that the club should watch. Less than ethical use of this information includes sabotaging voting machines, delaying the opening of particular polling places or otherwise discouraging high turnout in "enemy" areas. A well-planned and executed canvass is essential to good campaign strategies and operations.

The reason I was asked to take responsibility for that particular district was that there were no "captains" from the club there. This was one of my first indications that the campaign was not going to be as easy as I, and many members of the club, had thought. I discovered later that many more e.d.s were not covered by captains and in many areas there was no one in the club who lived in the areas.

Because of the large territory of single and two-family dwellings I was to cover, I enlisted the aid of several friends who worked with me at Brooklyn College to help out. I gave them instructions and we proceeded to do the canvass. The neighborhoods we walked showed signs of deterioration and racial transition. The registered voter list we carried was a little over a year old. Because the area was "changing," we found that more than half of those on the list no longer lived in the community. We also found that their replacements were not registered voters. Many were resident aliens who were not even eligible to vote. Almost all the newcomers were Black. More important than the lack of eligible voters was the fact that those who were registered as Democrats and seemed likely to vote were anti-Steingut. These were older Jewish, Italian and Irish long-term residents of the community. They cited the "Nursing Home Scandal" and "Capital Punishment" issues and many were vehement in their opposition. We tried to be polite and to discuss the issues but to no avail. Those who seemed in favor of the club slate were generally newly located Black families. The only good point for the club was the paucity of voters in the area. We left campaign literature with the voters and in the mail slots of those not at home.

The best time to canvass is in the early evening when people are at home, or on Saturdays in Gentile areas and Sundays in Jewish areas. Ideally, the canvass is not the first and only contact with the voters. The canvasser should also be someone who knows the neighborhood or lives there. The best person for the job is a local captain who knows the voters well, and is liked by them. One incident demonstrating some problems of local club representatives is illustrative. A canvasser in the last campaign was assigned to a specific e.d. because he had an address there. He neglected to tell the campaign staff that he was no longer living there. Unfortunately, his estranged wife did still live in the neighborhood. The friends and relatives of his spouse were very unhappy with the marital situation, and with him. His identification with the club candidates had a negative effect in that area. The mere mention of his name by canvassers prompted hostile responses. In another instance, novice canvassers were "waylaid" by a resident in the hallway of a large apartment house with many registered voters. The resident, who was working for the New Way Club, used the opportunity to create a scene and when people came out to see what was happening, he went into a loud anti-Steingut diatribe. A person familiar with the building would have known whom to avoid.

## Club Divisions Increase

When I returned to the club, after several evenings of canvassing, things seemed to be worsening. People in the social area talked more openly about problems and resentment toward the outsiders who were running the show. In the campaign room, however, it was a different world entirely. There was no sign of difficulty. When I came in I was told to turn in my canvass to a staff member, but before I left the room to join my friends, Steingut, who was standing with some advisers, came over and asked how things were going. Still not yet aware that I should not be a bearer of bad news, despite my first experience, I replied that he would be "lucky" if he got 30% of the vote. His smile turned to a frown. I felt uncomfortable and feebly tried to put some positive light on the situation by saying that at least there were not very many voters there. This did not help, and my conversation, which was overheard by the advisers, was quickly interrupted and Steingut was ushered away. I went into the next room to discuss my findings with the other workers.

Although only a newcomer in the organization, as the campaign progressed, I became more anxious and personally involved. On several occasions I thought I noticed "enemies" in the club. These were people who, it was believed, worked for the opposition. As things got worse, suspicions and suspects increased. I was reluctant to say anything, as I knew that some of "our" people had infiltrated the New Way and were bringing back information. Perhaps there were also "double agents." "Dirty tricks" were mentioned with greater frequency, such as tearing down enemy posters or distributing false or libelous information. The analogies and metaphors of warfare multiplied.

Because of my extensive community activities I had contacts and familiarity with some parts of the 41st Assembly District. When I tried to offer my advice and expertise as a sociologist to the campaign staff, I was, without exception, rebuffed. Although I took it personally, it was only part of the "professional" political campaigner's *modus operandi*. The paid "experts" try to maintain an air of controlled assuredness, as in a confidence game. Each person competes with others for credit for victory. Therefore the opportunity to give advice is highly coveted. Giving someone else credit for success can result in loss of status and access. People want to be close to the leader when good news is given and remote when the news is bad. Bad news is an indication of failure and someone has to be blamed. A victim, culprit, incompetent, or other scapegoat must be found. The distancing from bad news generally leads to someone, not present, being held blameworthy. This adds to the air of subversion--especially in losing campaigns. No one admits being wrong, or making mistakes. Sometimes the other side is more competent in the contest, but more often their success is attributed to "luck," "deviousness," or some other quality which absolves the losers of responsibility. Experts often cite events "beyond our control." To political professionals, this absolution is necessary as they must later seek new clients for their expert advice.

As the weeks wore on, more excuses were found for failure and more grumbling was heard around the club. The clubhouse was now clearly divided between the regulars and those there only because of the campaign. Recriminations abounded as each side blamed the other for failures. As the day of the primary approached, people became more suspicious of one another and tempers occasionally flared. Divisions also surfaced within the two groups, as each became more segregated from the other. The old timers claimed that, "in their time," they never had problems like now. The outside campaign people complained of the lack of cooperation and the incompetence of club members. The old Madison Clubbers blamed the old Kennedy Club people and *vice versa*. Divisions between Blacks and Whites, Jews and Gentiles, Italians and Irish, solidified and ethnic cliquing was the rule.

When Steingut was in the club, everyone seemed overly friendly toward him but when absent, he was the subject of much negative comment. The old-timers, especially, thought that he had "lost touch" with them. They noted that the real "big wheels," like Mayor Beame, State Controller Arthur Levitt, Surrrogate Sobel, Judge Jordan, and District Attorney Eugene Gold had left the club. Highly respected leaders like Beadie Markowitz had either died, or retired and moved away. Others who had taken advantage of the club contacts and moved out of the neighborhood now were unreachable. Part of the fascination with politics is rubbing shoulders with prominent people. These social contacts gone, cohesiveness depended on favors and declining patronage. The campaign set-backs and the invasion of outsiders made everyone more nostalgic. Defeat was palpable.

## New Style Local Politics

It was clear that the individual and collective "stakes" in the success of the Madison Club's 1978 campaign were diverse and even contradictory. Some of the regulars, overlooked by the campaign staff, were offended and withdrew to the sidelines. Many other people were less dependent on Steingut's personal success or failure. The community organization people, who joined the campaign, could easily switch their allegiance after the campaign. The professionals could always work for someone else after a loss. The other powerful clubs in the Brooklyn organization could benefit by Steingut's defeat and the inevitable realignment of power in the machine that was sure to follow. In fact, after Steingut's loss the neighboring Thomas Jefferson Club of the 39th A.D., led by Meade Esposito, became the home of the new Speaker- Stanley Fink. The Blacks in the club could look forward either to

Steingut's loss or his victory. If he won; he would owe them, if he lost they would fill the vacuum he would leave behind. The remaining Jews, Irish, and Italians would simply move to a different neighborhood.

In the past, traditional campaigning by the Madison Club had been based on years of direct contact with constituents. Each Captain and Lieutenant lived in their districts and personally knew their voters, their problems, their birthdays, etc. The club leadership also tried to insure that the ethnic, religious and racial characteristics of their captains and other workers in the field matched those of the constituents. When petitioning or election time approached, the process went smoothly. Members were rewarded for the efficiency and the volume of the vote. If people hadn't voted club members would phone or go to their homes before closing time and bring them out to the polls to do their "duty." After the polls were closed members would bring preliminary counts back to the club for a victory party. At least this was the way it had worked in the "good old days."

Political campaigning had gone through a revolution since the last time the club waged a battle, but the Madison Club did not change. Because of its power, it felt no need to do so. By limiting the exercise of the franchise and dampening interest in local politics, regular organizations remained in control of the Democratic Party. Reformers and new style politicians operated differently. They were more oriented toward general elections than were regular party officers who focused on primaries. New style politicians virtually ignored the party machinery or they made peace with it for convenience sake. They were more involved in "issues," voter education, and registration drives. The mass media provided them with ways to get their messages directly to potential voters. They also used rallies, demonstrations and debates to expose their candidates to the public. Rather than avoid them, reformers vigorously courted local community organizations.

The competition generated by new style politics also stimulated the entry of new participants in machine campaigning. College-educated professionals, media experts, and pollsters became integral parts of the political scene. Survey and opinion research helped shape issues and stances. Sophisticated analyses of census and voter registration data, combined with telephone surveys, found new potential supporters. The telephone and the questionaire challenged the precinct worker. These methods required larger numbers of workers and much more capital. Campaign financing became more important than the clubhouse. Support of municipal and other unions in the city became a necessity for running phone banks, literature distribution, polling and other work done in the past by club members. The local clubhouse declined in value but the county-wide machine did not. Collecting campaign contributions became more important than rounding up volunteer campaign workers.

In 1978, the Madison Club did not plan on a primary. If the club had not been split by internal conflicts, there would not have been any opposition to confront. At first, the establishment of the New Way Club did not generate much concern, but it gained strength through increasing defections and support from disaffected neighborhoods in the district. Ironically, one source was the Orthodox Jewish groups who felt Steingut had not done enough to protect Bernard Bergman in the Nursing Home Scandal. Another was Carl Garritani, candidate for Male District Leader. Politically unknown, he had built an organization of neighborhood groups in the southern part of the district containing middle and working class Italians and Irish.

Residents in this area were very concerned with neighborhood deterioration, crime, and had recently experi-

enced racial scare tactics such as "block busting" by real
estate agencies. They were, to say the least, politically
conservative. They had also not been involved in Democratic Party politics. Many were not registered voters and
a considerable number of registrants were Republicans or
Independents. In anticipation of the primary, they were re-
registered as Democrats and were therefore not anticipated by the Madison Club strategists. Stanley Steingut
and the Steingut "dynasty" were easy targets for this
active and hostile new coalition of previously quiet communities.

## The Campaign Issues

Corruption, graft, greed, influence peddling and contempt for the community were standard charges against
Steingut during the campaign. Such charges against a
powerful politician in a system which the public takes for
granted as corrupt are as difficult to defend against as they
are to prove. In the surreal world of the political campaign,
fiction and appearances often have greater impact than
reality. Nothing is politically valuable unless attached to
strategies and tactics. In other words, nothing matters
unless you win. The corruption issues were perfect for the
New Way campaign despite the fact that the opposition
was itself a product of the Brooklyn machine.

## The Death Penalty and Abortion

The second major issue in the campaign was Steingut's
stand on the death penalty in New York State. He was
opposed to it. He assumed he had taken the "high ground"
on an important state and national issue for the Democratic Party. Steingut was a "liberal" on most social issues,
such as abortion and rights of minorities. But this again

was out of step with his assembly district. The death penalty issue was a code word for racism in New York politics as was being for "Law and Order" and against "Welfare." The death penalty subsumed all the liberal positions in the 41st A.D..

In New York City as a whole, and especially in the Madison Club district, the Jewish voter is the most important in the primary. Statistically, more Jews were registered, and they voted more frequently in primary elections than did most other groups. During the 1970's the Jewish voter had become nearly as politically conservative as Irish and Italian Catholics but continued to register and vote more frequently than either ethnic group. The fact that Irish Catholic Governor Hugh Carey was also against the death penalty was of no help to Steingut. The Madison Club created for itself a political district which combined Orthodox Jewish congregations, poor and middle-class Black ghettos, blue collar Catholic neighborhoods, and a large number of Caribbean immigrants.

Relatedly, Steingut incensed many Catholic voters by his stand on abortion rights for women in New York State. Although putting increasingly powerful feminists in the Democratic Party on his side, it created problems for him at home. When, for example, Catholic social activist John Hays tried to help Steingut by walking with him in Catholic areas of the district, community residents refused to open their doors to him.

On virtually all issues, Steingut had become a leader of a constituency that did not reside in his district; power sometimes makes it possible for even local leaders to ignore the views of residents. Madison Club members who warned Steingut on his unpopular stands sarcastically remarked that "Stanley had become a statesman." They were concerned because he had placed the organization, and their patronage in jeopardy for "principles."

Perhaps they felt that Steingut the "wheeler-dealer" had become Steingut the "martyr" for social causes. To be successful in politics one must choose stands on issues which give tactical or strategic advantage, or even better, avoid issues altogether. To party hacks, politics is a means to a personal end, not a moral crusade.

The Madison Club's district in the 1970's was rapidly changing its racial composition. The all-White areas of the south, like Canarsie, were now connected to all-Black areas in the north, such as Crown Heights and Bedford Stuyvesant. The district boundaries would not have been the choice of any astute politician, but Steingut had made a personal commitment to always keep within his district the Orthodox and Hasidic Jewish population of Crown Heights which otherwise would be overwhelmed by an allegedly vengeful Black majority. There was growing friction between them, as Blacks began to realize and assert their power. The Madison Club, because of the new political reality, had accepted greater Black participation in the club. Its leaders thought that the future of the Democratic Party in the county was tied to new Black voters.

As correct as this position was later proven to be, no one provided an easy or reliable way to mold the new ethnic and racial mix into a cohesive unit. It had taken decades for the Irish, Jews, and Italians to learn to get along, and they still resented each other's relative success. Steingut's liberal positions and the ethnic composition of the club became an easy target for direct and indirect racist campaign tactics. Although many would disagree, this issue of racial change in the community was the most important one in the campaign and the one on which the fate of the Madison club and Steingut would turn.

## The Big Mistake

One last bit of irony characterized the disastrous 1978 primary. Typically in organization politics, when a regular club fails to prevent a challenge at the local level it relies on the state courts for assistance. Since most judges and the Board of Elections itself are products of the party machinery, regular clubs can in fact "rely" on help. One must also remember that it is the political party which makes its own rules and these rules are enforced by the courts. There are a number of ways of "challenging" the legality of opponents appearing on the primary ballot. Numerous rules exist governing how a candidate becomes certified to appear on a ballot. Although the process may appear simple and peaceful the road to the election is heavily mined. In the interest of maintaining control, party rules provide for many challenges which can only be overcome with legal assistance. Reformers have special problems, for they find little sympathy among election agencies. Election and primary laws tend to be changed with relative frequency, giving advantages to incumbents and party insiders who devise the rules for their own protection. On occasion, reformers and challengers are even unaware of rule changes or do not understand how they will be enforced. There is also variation, by county, for party structure, positions and operation.

It is a common practice that petitions filed by candidates who run against the regular organization are automatically challenged for technical, or even criminal violations. Some challengers can then be quickly eliminated from competition. Weak opponents are those whose petitions barely contain the minimum number of signatures, or those groups who lack an attorney to represent them in challenge proceedings. If the reformer opposition survives the first round, further challenges and appeals use up their limited resources. They must spend time, effort and, perhaps, money to defend their petitions or to file counter-challenges. In Brooklyn almost everyone, reform or regular, files challenges. It has become a political tradition to harass opponents.

In the 1978 primary, the candidacy of Helene Weinstein, for Assembly from the New Way club was challenged. She was to head their ticket against the Madison Club. The stipulation was that she was not, as claimed, a *bona fide* resident of the district, but instead lived in Manhattan. The city-wide newspapers covered the story and also noted that she had a professional relationship with Manhattan Borough President and Steingut nemesis, Andrew Stein. The Madison Club strategists played this up as a "carpet-bagger" issue. Although, as expected, the candidacy of Helene Weinstein was declared invalid, the Madison Club campaign experts had made a huge mistake. As one later explained, the petitions themselves were not declared invalid, only the candidate. Therefore the petition's committee on replacement was permitted to substitute another candidate for the *valid* petitions. Helene Weinstein's father, Murray Weinstein, a local attorney, was selected and the campaign proceeded. Much to their chagrin, and embarrassment, the Madison Club's legal experts had made a crucial error.

They also inadvertently created sympathy for the New Way ticket, which was seen as having survived another devious machination of Stanley Steingut. The press coverage of the challenge gave a sense of "David (the New Way) and Goliath (The Madison Club)." The stage was now set for a surprising "new experience" for the Madison Club; a real primary challenge by a highly motivated and apparently well supported organization.

To the members of the Madison Club, the campaign issues were internal and personal. They wanted to win because their jobs, influence, pride and general well-being were at stake. In the beginning, they had little doubt that they would "bury" the New Way Club and even gleefully planned their revenge. Slowly, however, they got the sense that things were not going to be so easy as the New Way not only persevered but gathered strength. The timing was right for the public issues of the campaign; both those on the surface and those barely submerged by slogans.

The New Way strategy was to launch a two-pronged attack on the Madison Club. One pointed toward winning away supporters of Steingut, and the other, toward generating new voters for the Democratic primary who had previously not been motivated, or even registered, to vote. The strategy of the Madison Club was to proceed as usual, certain that its strength would keep defections to a minimum and prevent the New Way from receiving support from outsiders, which was necessary to carry a campaign against a powerful club. The Madison Club overestimated its own power of intimidation and underestimated the ability of the New Way members to tap into the fears and resentments of the electorate. As the weeks passed, the solid support the Madison Club had received and assumed was theirs gradually eroded with even some of the Jewish groups in Crown Heights siding with the New Way. Club support weakened and suspicions mounted about "sabotage" and "infiltrators" in the club. Only the professional campaigners seemed unfazed by the turmoil.

## Strategy to Win

The Madison Club strategists operated under the assumption that they had won the battle before it was fought. They assumed that there would be no opposition and that they would keep their old friends in line. They had the votes in their pockets, and their debts to call up, when the time came. They undertsood that, as usual, the primary vote would be light and that they would be able to call out their troops, who would vote in unison for the ticket. The professionals had it all figured out, and despite indications of a growing tide against Steingut, and reports of defections, there was no sign of panic. Only among the older club members, who were cut off from the campaign decision making, was there any talk of losing.

The resources available to the Madison Club were enormous. They had union support, bulging campaign chests, professional staff, and endorsements from prominent politicians representing every ethnic group. They also had large civic associations, Catholic parishes, Protestant and Jewish congregations, and even most of the media behind them. The strategy seemed to be; ignore the opposition and act as if there was no contest.

The New Way was working feverishly. It was active at the local level which was the source of its greatest strength. Its members registered many new voters and kept up a barrage of literature and meetings hammering at Steingut for his involvement in the Nursing Home Scandal and his abandonment of the community. When the time came to vote, they pulled out people from places where the Madison Club had no connections. The Madison Club failed to mobilize the masses of Blacks in the district. It was assumed they were not needed, and also not reliable. A victory party was planned at the club-just as it always had been. By primary evening, the last of the campaign posters were going up and the New Way's being torn down; and *vice versa*. The last massive literature distributions and mailings were out; and all the speeches before friendly civic groups had been delivered. Assignments for the election were handed out. Each polling place was to be covered from opening to closing times.

The fact that there was difficulty in finding enough

volunteers to cover all the posts was not seen as much of a problem. The assumption was that since the Madison Club controlled most of the election inspectors, there would be few problems at the polling places. In the "old days" it was easy "to vote from the cemetery," or record multiple votes, but this was not the old days, at least not for the Madison Club. The backing of Andrew Stein was another reason for the reduction in potential voter fraud. The New Way was also not without resources of its own to police the election. Media attention to the campaign would also make it difficult for the machine to operate outside of public view.

## Primary Day

On the day of the primary, I was told to cover a polling place in the southern part of the district. The fact that I had little political experience did not seem to matter. The site was in the heart of "Garritani" country where earlier I had canvassed and discovered a great deal of hostility to Steingut. It was a neighborhood primarily of modest but neat one and two-family homes owned by working class Irish and Italian families who had lived in the area for at least two generations. There was also a sprinkling of older, even more locally established German, Dutch and Scotch families. The edge of the racial transition in the district was located a few blocks north, along a cut for a railroad spur which was bordered by warehouses and light industry plants. The voting booths, for four election districts, were located in the basement of a church.

I was given a certificate which gave me the right to move around the tables where people were checked to see if they were eligible voters, and also to inspect the voting machines. Workers for the opposing sides wore colored buttons to identify themselves to each other. Outside, signs announced the restrictions on electioneering and each camp stationed people along the approaches to the poll. They handed out flyers and told people who to vote for. Printed "palm cards" were facsimiles of the ballot, and voters were allowed to carry them into the booths. I had a clear sense that the Madison Club would lose the vote here as I saw the sneers of some voters as they looked at the club's material and threw it onto the pavement. Most voters, to be polite, simply took the cards, waited until out of sight, and then deposited them in refuse cans near the church. At times during the heavy morning vote, I was the only person from the Madison Club at the poll. After the morning rush of people voting on their way to work, there followed a small surge of mothers who had dropped off their children at school. Then there was a lull until mothers returned to pick up the children in the afternoon. The heaviest voting took place as people returned from work or came out shortly after dinner. Here I met Carl Garritani whose pleasant demeanor contrasted sharply to the club's view of him as the personification of evil.

In the afternoon I was re-assigned to a more eastern part of the assembly district where the population was denser, more middle-class and Jewish in composition. Here the anticipated vote was heavier and more crucial. The polling place was in a large public school with many more voting booths and election districts than my morning post. At this spot I was given the less important job of handing out palm cards. Although the neighborhood in the past had been a bastion of support for the Madison and Kennedy Clubs, the New Way had made significant inroads. The New Way had stationed many of its volunteers around the poll and the Madison Club people were far out-numbered. It was then that I got a real taste of the personal animosity the race had engendered between Madisonians, ex-Madisonians and others, as they squared off on the streets, face-to-face.

Part of the ritual of local elections are visits from head-quarters by people sent to check the polls, bring encour-agement, and perhaps, food and coffee. When the entou-rage arrives, workers become especially vigorous in their electioneering and clashes are more likely to occur, as people attempt to demonstrate their commitment to the candidate.

All morning there had been minor skirmishes- posters were torn down and replaced with opposing ones. The police on duty at the polls were usually asked to intervene. Verbal jousting between palm-carders sharing locations was common, but it was mostly good natured. Toward the late afternoon, however, the skirmishes flared into a real battle.

Andrew Stein, in a chauffer-driven city car, arrived at the school to "inspect" the polls and cheer on the New Way Democrats. While I was outside, he spoke to the poll watchers and inspectors accompanied by several other people. This attracted a crowd as he emerged on the street. The crowd was well within the restricted electioneering area and several Madison Club workers protested. The verbiage escalated into physical contact. Harsh words, cursing and pushing finally ended with shouts of insults and threats of greater physical harm as enemies who once worked together at the Madison Club openly discussed the purported sexual proclivities of each others spouses. The crowd was dispersed at the insistence of the police but for the rest of the afternoon, the friendly bantering be-tween opponents was replaced by silence and glares. Inside the school, another battle took place as some Madi-son Club poll watchers claimed that Stein was not eligible to enter and accused him of jamming a booth. The argu-ment and accusations followed him out unto the sidewalk.

I learned that altercations like these are not uncommon in contested elections and that there are many ways in which interference at the polls can effect outcomes. For example, making it difficult or uncomfortable for people to vote through intimidation is used as a tactic in areas where the opposition is expected to do well. Voting machines can easily be jammed, but in general this is not necessary. Election inspectors control the opening and closing of polls as well as the speed and efficiency of the process. Simply coming in later cuts down on the available time for voting; not having sufficient election employees accomplishes the same task. Raising frequent objections and challenges slows down the process and voters on line often give up and leave. Workers who check signatures against voting cards can easily allow ineligibles to vote and "lose" the cards of opposition voters. New voters are especially vulnerable as they may not know in which election district they are registered. Therefore Board of Election workers, if they are partisan, may ascertain for whom the registrant will vote and decide whether to find a lost card or to provide a "challenge" or substitute ballot. They can also "mar" a paper ballot by filling it out incorrectly, or giving wrong instructions to the voter.

For the above reasons it is important to have "poll watchers." If the election workers are not *your* people, it is even more important. One thing that poll watchers do is check the counters on the machines at the start of voting, and at the end, check the number against the voters who passed through that day. This is not helpful, however, if the poll is not watched and checked throughout the entire day. Political parties control the election process and that is why it is subject to fraud. Modern reforms may have made fraud more difficult than in the past, but it is still possible. Election abuses are a function of the weakness and ignorance of the electorate, multiplied by the power of political organizations. After my first full day of primary election work, I was convinced that the stories told me by old-time Madison Clubbers about how the polls could be controlled decades ago were not so incredible.

Having me act as a poll watcher was like having no one there at all. I did not even know how to "challenge" voters. I could not tell who was or was not eligible. I just sat and tried to look intimidating. For instance, I saw people being assisted inside the booths and was told it was allowed, if the voter requested help due to poor eyesight, or other infirmities. These decisions were made by a particular small "group" of election workers, but, "For whom were they working?", I thought. Some people voted who couldn't read. Some couldn't write their names. This experience helped me to understand how people who were long since dead could have had excellent voting records. The tales I heard of people who would travel from friendly poll to friendly poll, and would vote in place of those registered, but not voted, called "repeaters" became more plausible.

When the polls closed at 9 P.M., poll watchers were expected to scrutinize the reporting of the vote. The machines were opened and the counts called out for each candidate. Forms were filled out by workers and put in sealed boxes to be escorted by uniformed police. Later they would be opened and the official count made. Usually, long before the official count, the outcomes were known, as club members carried the results back to headquarters for unofficial tallies. In some cases results are phoned in. "Key" districts are reported first and after a few of these, the experts already knew the outcome and the margin of victory, or defeat. In the 41st Assembly District, the bulk of the vote, and the key precincts, were in a few locations and the rest was, so to speak, "chopped liver."

At the Madison Club headquarters a large crowd had assembled early. It was traditional to have a big victory celebration even though there was never any doubt as to who would would win. The people at the club were there to hob-nob, give their congratulations, and pay homage to the leader. Attention was always focused on the wider elections and how the club might have contributed to their victory. In past years, club-supported candidates for judge-ships or city-wide offices were the most interested parties in the outcomes, which were received and tallied there from all over the county. Then, people would stay to listen to the radio for election results, or in more recent years, to watch the election returns on television through the night. Presidential elections brought special interest and longer parties. They were great social occasions. Even people only peripherally involved in the club would come for the free food, drinks, and to share the excitement. Often children would be present, which made the election night celebration even more of a family affair.

The election returns were collected in the business room. Early returns were called, or carried in and handed over. They were then written onto large tally sheets and posted on a large display board for all to see. Excitement was generated as each return was put up and people discussed its merits. Those who brought in especially good returns were able to collect attention and compliments on their performance. Rewarded by applause or cheers, they mingled in the crowd, smiling. Others who brought disappointing results, tried to slink out unnoticed. Few in the past faced such disappointment, they merely compared their less favorable returns with others. This night, however, was to be very different from the past.

Actually, many already thought that the club was to be a loser that night. The Madison Club members knew early because of what they heard and saw on the streets. The professionals, whose reputations were at stake, might have known earlier, but they weren't about to let on until they could blame someone else. They knew the club was in trouble when their latest polls showed glaring weaknesses in support. The political leaders had a good sense of the problem because of their interactions with knowledgeable politicos, city officials and important community leaders who had seen the omens. Few wanted to be bearers of bad news so the reckoning was postponed. Perhaps, decades earlier, more drastic action would have been taken to prevent the loss, but the Madison Club and its 1978 candidates had been tamed by time and reform politics. Although still possible, they didn't use all the power at their disposal to rig the election or to have it tampered with.

When I returned to the club, I knew that my returns were not good, but I had predicted it earlier. I was merely hoping that the losing margin would not be greater. My own polling place was not a large voter district, so no one was especially concerned. At the club, people were packed into the business room and spilled into the social room. The food was already uncovered and people were eating and drinking. There was however no din of excitement. I arrived at approximately 9:20 P.M. and already they knew they had lost. It was just a matter of how much. A few, like me waited for a miracle -- perhaps some returns were wrong. Perhaps an area would come out completely different than expected. But it didn't happen. The club lost all races; Steingut lost to Weinstein for Assembly, he lost to Garritani for Male Co-leader and Pearl Anish lost to Sandra Silverman for Female Co-leader. The club also lost most of its County Committee members as well, which would mean a loss of official election inspectors for the general election. People began to leave. Some came in late and simply turned around after hearing the news. Others never came in the building as they heard the news on the street. Few wanted to be around for the *post-mortem*.

Interestingly, many other politicians came to the club to offer condolences. Of special note was the appearance of Stanley Fink, who was later to replace Steingut as Assembly Majority Leader, and Meade Esposito, the Kings County "Boss." Both Esposito and Fink, from the neighboring Jefferson Club assembly district, had the most to gain by the club's losses. The local Republicans, long standing friends of the club, were also there and seemed the most upset. Someone suggested that Steingut could run as a Republican if he wished. Abe Beame was there and so were past club notables who had moved onto the bench. The dwindling crowd hushed as Stanley came in and made a short speech thanking everyone for their efforts. I was miserable. I understood then, better than I ever could from studying texts on machine politics, what blind political loyalty was all about. Politics was still a personal game, despite all the technology. I felt angry at many of the people assembled there whom I knew had more to do with the loss than they would admit; and I was especially upset with those who continued to eat and drink regardless of the mood. I left with a sense of personal loss, barely aware of how much I had actually been deprived of by the defeat. I later understood that I had a great deal to gain if Steingut and the club had won. Right then, I was determined to "get back" at the New Way- people I didn't really know, but whom I had come to despise because of my deepening involvement in the club.

The lessons of the campaign experience demonstrated the depth of personal involvement in urban politics. It was not merely the counting of numbers, but a broad collection of real individual efforts and interests. Politics was no longer simply theoretical to me; it was an intense human activity. I resolved not to give up without a fight. Unashamedly, I even hoped that the club would use its power to contest the election and use every trick to reverse the outcome. Surely something could be done, but nothing happened. The old style machine was no more, at least not at the Madison Club.

## Where and Why Did the Club Lose?:
## North versus the South

An analysis of the returns of the primary election clearly shows the underlying issues of race and neighborhood transition in the campaign.[9] Comparing a map of the returns for the Steingut-Weinstein Assembly race by election districts with a census tract map of the same area highlighting racial composition of residents, one sees a distinct racial pattern- Steingut won overwhelmingly in the Black neighborhoods of Crown Heights (shared with Hasidic Jews), Rugby, and East Flatbush. He was soundly trounced in the predominately Irish, Italian and Jewish districts of Canarsie, Holy Cross and Flatlands. Except for a few of the election districts, Steingut won in the northern neighborhoods and lost in the southern ones. The weakness of the usually monolithic, pro-Steingut Hasidic Jewish vote in Crown Heights made it impossible for him to make up for the losses he expected in the southern districts.

Less obvious was the relatively small turnout of Blacks, versus white voters in all areas. If Blacks had been more heavily registered, the outcome would certainly have been different. The "experts" also did not predict the defections and the new Democratic enrollments in the southern white working-class areas. The strategy of the past-- keeping Black voter participation low, backfired on the club. In fringe areas, where racial transition was occuring, the vote against Steingut was almost two to one. In all-white areas the ratio against him was four to one. The final outcome in the all-important Assembly race was 4,229 votes for Steingut and 4,862 for Weinstein. The New Way margin of victory was provided in the recently annexed sections where community activist Carl Garritani won the male leader position with an even greater margin also over Steingut. It was in these southern areas that the most aggressive and occasionally vicious campaigning took place. The female leadership position was handily won by Sandra Silverman over Madison Club community activist Pearl Anish.

## The Decision to Run as a Liberal

As the leader of the New York State Assembly, Steingut was largely responsible for changing the election law which made it more difficult for candidates to run independently of major party endorsements in general elections. Over the years, reformers had increased their potential strength by creating, and then running on, independent party lines. This diminished the power of the established organizations to control elections. The regulars wanted to make it difficult, if not impossible, for those who lost in primaries to form new parties and get on the ballot for the November general elections. The barriers created by the state legislature became one of the major problems Steingut and the Madison Club officers faced in deciding whether to run in the general election. Steingut had already obtained the Liberal Party designation and would appear on the ballot in any case.

On the first club night after the primary loss, I went to commiserate with the candidates and to find out whether Steingut would run. I also had hoped that I would read in the papers that the election had been challenged, and reversed. That, of course, did not happen and when I arrived Steingut and a few others were discussing their alternatives. I was strongly in favor of an independent line to add to the Liberal one. Others were much more reluctant to take the step. A few intimated that if Steingut won, an arrangement could be made for him to resume his position of Speaker of the Assembly despite the loss of his party designation. It was clear that he was still a power. Few were willing to challenge him openly until after the general elections, and, presumably, the coffin had been nailed shut. The case against the independent line was based on the amount of time and effort involved in obtaining signatures on petitions, and the slight to the party, if he won with that help. The meeting was interesting because of the absence of the "upstaters" and the "professionals," who were probably busy courting the heirs apparent to Steingut's throne. If the election was to be won, the club itself would have to do the work, and Stanley would have to generate a great deal of outside help for the assembly race. This support had to be assured before planning could proceed.

The club officers, and the board of directors, would have to make the decision. As the evening progressed, many more people came to the club. It was clear that most club members were still with Steingut and willing to work in the campaign. I believe that this show of personal support was what led to Steingut's decision to run in a classic "grass roots" campaign. Although it ultimately failed, it was an indicator of the future of Kings County politics. The club decided to continue in the race and also to seek an independent line. However, several days of intensive petitioning efforts proved increasingly futile. For example, in order for a signature on the petitions to be valid, the signer could not have voted in the primary. It was decided to drop the idea of independent line and focus on a more definite, and potentially valuable strategy-- registration of new, primarily Black, voters for the general election. This strategy was to have its own negative consequences as it engendered greater racial conflict both in the club and outside in the community.

## The Liberal Party Endorsement

Even before the primary, Steingut was guaranteed the

endorsement of the Liberal Party and was assured a place on the ballot in the November general election. The Liberal Party in New York is an independent party with its own interesting history but for our purposes it is sufficient to understand that it plays the role of outside supporter, and sometimes spoiler in the battles between the Democratic and Republican parties, in the statewide balloting. The party line also helps to elect officials in New York City, where many of its members reside. Its major source of support is not the numbers of its members but its finances, expertise and manpower in campaigns. The benefit to the party and its members is patronage; the more important its role in an election, the more it gains from the successful candidates it supports. The Liberal Party has a reputation in the state for supporting liberal views, but it has endorsed liberal Republicans, such as U.S. Senator Jacob Javits, as well as Democrats and Independents. In recent years the number of votes cast on the Liberal Line in general elections has decreased and this has put the party in a difficult situation as its potential influence has also decreased proportionally. Other new and independent parties such as the Right-to-Life and the Conservative Party have increased in strength.

In New York State the order of placement on the printed ballot is determined by the number of votes cast for that party in the previous election. This order is a major source of prestige and an indicator of strength. It also is easier for people to vote on the line closest to the left. Much of voting behavior is simply mechanical. Further away toward the right hand, and further down to the bottom of the ballot are more difficult places for voters to record their preferences. There are, in other words, major advantages to ballot location for candidates and parties. Appearing on the Liberal Party column in the general election ballot for Stanley Steingut, presented major practical difficulties and, perhaps, made the difference in his loss.

After meeting with Liberal Party officials, the Steingut campaign swung into high gear. The party was to provide major support in the campaign. Members who lived in the district joined the effort, and party experts were to assist in the campaign. The Liberals probably saw this as an opportunity to vastly increase their influence by being responsible for the election of the Speaker. In addition to the Liberal Party efforts, several unions pledged their political workers and networks, as well as their endorsements. Other unions and organizations, usually tied to the Democratic candidates, agreed to back the Madison Club but were presented with some tactical problems because they generally supported the whole slate of Democratic Party candidates. Large amounts of money needed to be raised and spent in the campaign and several "professionals" were hired to organize and direct the campaign effort. They were to have at their disposal all the resources of the club and its allies, although some of Steingut's allies decided to act independently as part of a coalition, rather than join togther into one large campaign organization. The unions' campaign, for example was run from the club, but in the upstairs offices.

Two newcomers dramatically changed the scene at the Madison Club for the duration of the final campaign; Alan Weintraub and John Ross. Weintraub was presented to the membership as a successful businessman with experience in "grass roots" political organizing and a friend of the Steingut family. John Ross was a political expert with a history of organizing and running difficult campaigns with success. Both were young, and their confidence was matched by a stern, business-like approach to campaigning that was to cause a revolution at the club and produce a classic effort to upset Murray Weinstein in the "impossible" campaign. It was to cost a great deal of money and use enormous numbers of man-hours of volunteer time. The key to the strategy was voter registration, voter education, and pulling of large numbers of Black voters, who were, until that time, a "sleeping giant," and virtually invisible in Brooklyn politics.

## The General Election Campaign

The first meeting called by Weintraub and Ross to start off the general election campaign set a new tone for the Madison Club. The general meeting room of the club was packed with people, most of whom had participated in the primary, but there were numerous others, previously unseen at the club. Many members had been ignored during the primary campaign but had now returned when personally called upon. Others were not even Democrats, but friends of the club or of Steingut. Several were Liberal Party members and representatives of unions. The ethnic composition of the crowd was far more Black than in the past-- evidence that the new political resources were being mobilized. Most of the Black campaigners were active in local community organizations in the northern end of the district.

The meeting was called to order, and Weintraub and Ross took turns addressing the group. They gave the group a sense of the difficulties to be faced and promised hard work as the only way to overcome disadvantages. Club members were also castigated for their poor performance during the primary. Several examples were given of missed opportunities and shortcomings of the primary effort. They were especially critical of the "social" atmosphere of the club. Ross and Weintraub noted that a lot of people came to the club simply to get out of the cold, or to have a free cup of coffee, shoot the breeze, or watch television. New rules were then laid out for the club; no television until after the campaign was over. No one was to hang around in the business room, unless they were there to do work. Everyone was to have specific responsibilites and if they didn't perform, they would be asked to leave. If people didn't volunteer for work, they would be assigned to it.

Many of the club members spoke up at the meeting about what they thought went wrong during the primary. In general the "outsiders" were blamed. The group indicated that they were in general agreement with Weintraub and Ross's evaluation and indicated willingness to work hard in the campaign. The meeting then divided into small groups where people filled out cards indicating where they lived and what they had to offer in the way of time, energy and skills. Most people were given areas of responsibility.

By this time, I had become a Madison Club member and had discussed at great length with Steingut and club officers the possiblity of winning on the Liberal line. We all knew it would take a great deal of effort but we felt we had a "good shot" at an upset. The considerable resources that were available to the club were, it was agreed, dormant. The loss of the primary was seen as a blunder as much as an upset. Because I had become increasingly more personally involved in the club, I became less "objective" about its fortunes. I was especially incensed with the racial overtones of the campaign which the New Way waged during the primary. This I saw as threatening to the increasingly integrated community.

I believed that the aftermath of a racially divisive campaign would destroy any possibility of intergroup cooperation regardless of who was to win. The results of "Divide and Conquer" in racial politics I believed was too high a price to pay for an assembly seat and the district leadership. Yet the only hope for Steingut and the Madison

Club to survive was to go heavily into registering and mobilizing Black voters. This was to have repercussions beyond the assembly district. For the time being, the goal was getting Steingut elected. I believe that after the election, if he had won, he would have taken advantage of the upcoming redistricting to create a racially "safer" district. This possibility also gave politicians in the southern part of Brooklyn more of an incentive to hope, if not insure, that Steingut and the club would lose, as they would be the ones "raided" for white voters by the Madison Club controlled redistricting process.

## Black Voter Registration

The number of registered voters in the 41st Assembly District in 1978 was about 25,000. Registered Democrats made up about half of all registered voters. Approximately 8,000 voted in the primary, and therefore, on a numerical basis, it was still possible to win the general election. The population, 25 years or older, in the district was a little over 100,000. Compared to past decades, the ratio of registered voters to eligible voters was probably at an all time low. Although some have argued that the power of a political club is mainly a function of the *number* of registered voters it controls, it would appear that *control* is the more important part of the equation. Over the decades, party organizations have developed strategies for control which appear, to the politically naive, contrary to logic.

An organization can maintain its party position and retain control of the district despite losing voting strength. In the past, the Madison Club had the best of both worlds; it was one of the largest voting districts and had virtually absolute control over the electorate. As the decades passed and the population and politics of Brooklyn changed, the club was able to consolidate and increase its power by restricting political access to a smaller and smaller circle of "friends." Central control was only possible if the general population refrained from participating in electoral politics.

Political organizations, such as the Madison Club passively discouraged, if not actively prevented, the growth of potentially antagonistic political organizations within its bailiwick. Powerful organizations do not appreciate competition. As the demographic profile of the district, despite gerrymandering, changed, Black residents were the ones increasingly left out. Although Black political organizations developed early on in Brooklyn, they were were very much in the mold of the earlier European "ethnic" satellite club houses. Only when the districts became almost totally Black were these organizations able to take control. Even in these cases, most remained tied to the white ethnic political machinery. This was due in part to the historically low participation of poor Blacks and other low-income groups in politics.

The Madison Club, under the tutelage of reform-minded Stanley Steingut, had welcomed Blacks into the club; if not for moral reasons, at least for appearances. A Black presence at the club was helpful, but developing a viable Black electorate was not a major objective. Jewish, Italian, and Irish factions in the organization saw Black growth as a distinct threat to their own influence or hegemony. As with other ethnic groups, Black club members were connected to their people through activity in numerous community and religious organizations. This generated endorsements and other supports, when they were needed.

Between 1970 and 1980, the Black population in the 41st A.D. increased from 34,743 to 92,653 as the White population decreased from 116,375 to 50,882. Except for pockets of Orthodox and Hasidic Jews, Crown Heights and East Flatbush became almost totally Black communities. Many

Blacks were recent immigrants from the Caribbean who were becoming a major segment of the Brooklyn population. Just as with earlier Europeans, Caribbeans took some time before adjusting to the American political scene, and the absence, at least initially, of persons and organizations helping them to Americanize, diminished their potential influence. As social service and community organizations developed to serve the community, political savvy increased. It was not long thereafter that these racial minorities showed a political sophistication equal to their Americanized counterparts. The Madison Club developed ties with these new groups by serving as an intermediary for the groups receiving government assistance. A major disadvantage of the Caribbean Blacks was the large number of "illegal" or "undocumented" aliens who lived among those with registration papers and visas. In any case, a large proportion of this population was ineligible to vote because they were not citizens. However, this did not prevent the groups however from peripheral involvement in politics through monetary or manpower support.

It is important to note the wide rift between American and Caribbean Blacks if one is to understand the relative lack of Black empowerment in Brooklyn. Each of these subcommunities tended to resent the other, and this made political and community cooperation between them difficult. Together, they would be a potent political force. The economic and educational profile of some of the Caribbean groups was in many cases higher than for American-born Blacks. But Caribbeans from some of the Islands, such as Jamaica and Barbados, also had political values which were rooted in different historical experiences that were very different from those of American Blacks. Many Caribbeans were less willing to accept a second-class political status. The two groups, especially business people and those with job skills, saw each other in direct competition for economic rewards in Brooklyn. The competition, of course, was political as well. While they operated together at the Madison Club during the 1978 campaign, it was obvious that relations between the groups were not amicable. The two groups did not mix well and made disparaging remarks about each other to white ethnic club members. When Steingut lost the primary, both American and Caribbean Blacks became the potential saviors of the organization.

As might be expected, most of the white members in the organization would have preferred that this not be the case. They knew that the increased reliance on Blacks would diminish their own influence. Some even began to think that they would be better off if the club lost. These feelings were not openly expressed. They were reflected, unfortunately, in performance, and commitment to the campaign. The decision then, to go full scale into registration and courting Blacks voters in the 41st Assembly District, was not without its dangers. When the primary was lost, and the club committed itself to the general election, there was no other choice. To accomplish a major voter registration drive, many people and resources were needed. Even though the club had the support of Liberal Party members and many unions, especially those with large minority group memberships, a substantial cadre of local people was still needed. Whites were needed for White areas, and Blacks for Black areas; Jews for Jewish areas and Gentiles for Gentile areas, and so on.

The club's strategy and resources included sympathetic Republican voters and their leaders who might benefit by helping to reseat Steingut in the Assembly. In New York State, it is not unusual for Republicans and Democrats to have "cozy" local relationships; for example, informal agreements would be made not to challenge one another in "hopeless" campaigns. The 41st had long been a virtually non-partisan area. The perennial Republican assembly candidate, Frank D. Petrizzo, was a good friend of Steingut and was one of the first to offer his condolences at the club when Steingut lost the primary. Some people present said that the young man was actually in tears at the time. A few members of the Madison Club itself were registered in the Republican Party. Despite Steingut's liberal positions on issues, even Conservative Party members were prepared to give him assistance. The assumption was, of course, that if he won, he would owe them more favors. Others still feared him and the club because club members would still hold powerful positions in government and the private sector despite his election loss. Republican, Conservative, and Liberal Party friends agreed to approach their constituents and entreat them to vote for Steingut on the Liberal Party line in the upcoming election.

The registration campaign included many activities; sound trucks roamed the neighborhoods urging people to register and vote, fliers were circulated almost daily, announcements were made from friendly pulpits, and at other public forums, club members and friends heralded the voter registration campaign. All ethnic and religious associations were called in to help, but the focus was primarily on Blacks. As there was a rush to register voters in time for the elections, personal approaches were reinforced with massive drives. Folding tables were set up in busy shopping areas, and at rush hours; near subway and bus stops, and other strategic locations. Campaign workers stopped people and asked if they were registered. Loud speakers were used to address crowds. Well-known Black politicians and other Black public figures also made appearances to attract people and urge them to register. The support of Black community organizations was easily obtained as they saw the campaign as a "community," as well as a political, struggle. Many were watching the arena as a test case for the future of Black political organizing in Brooklyn. Few of those involved in the drive were interested only in the welfare of the Madison Club or Steingut. They had their own political agendas. Some Black leaders noted the irony of being urged to participate by those who made it so difficult in the past.

The campaign also brought in political leaders from other parts of the city. Popular Bronx Borough President Robert Abrams toured Jewish areas with Steingut and Bronx Congressman Mario Biaggi tried to help Steingut in Italian American neighborhoods by making personal appeals and going to Italian American community clubs with Steingut. Steingut also got the endorsements of prominent Black leaders Charles Rangel and Percy Sutton.

Frequently in the registration effort there was contact with people who were ineligible to vote, as they were not citizens. Even these contacts, however, were of benefit for those who came after Steingut, as the campaign was a vehicle for political awareness and organization among Blacks. The strengths, as well as the weaknesses, of the Black community became apparent during the effort. Many eligible voters simply had never thought of registering, or gave weak reasons for their dereliction. Not unexpectedly, a large proportion were unaware of the conflict, the candidates, or even what an assembly race was. They had no experience with politics. At least for the present, this experience was not as important as getting them registered and maintaining contact with them until the day of the election. Then, if possible, they would be pulled and instructed to vote for Steingut on the Liberal Line.

## Campaigning in High Gear

The registration effort was a major success. Over four thousand new voters, assumedly voters for Steingut, were registered and copies of their registration forms retained to send them Steingut literature and contact them when necessary. The Steingut campaign took on new life as a major political crusade. Liberal Party and liberal voters, union activists and minority organizations were pulled together to forge a formidable, organization. The successful registration effort also nurtured the belief among once-downtrodden club members that it was possible to win, and attracted more political support in the form of contributions. It also kept some of the party wolves at bay, who were waiting in the wings for Steingut to lose, express their condolences, and then rejoice. The new support made it unlikely that major defections among regulars would take place before the general election. Steingut was seriously wounded but still alive.

John Ross and Allan Weintraub ran a tight ship at the club. Many of the oldtimers greatly appreciated it. They remembered when people like Nat Sobel, Abe Beame, and Tony Jordan worked the elections. No nonsense. Everyone had a task and each was held accountable. John Ross was particularly militaristic in his approach to the street work. People were frequently told, "shape up or ship out," or some similar expression was used to indicate that he had little tolerance for loitering in the club.

Since a great deal of discussion took place out in the open during the campaign, this restriction on casual workers was also important to prevent sabotage by opponents. Ross and Weintraub recognized that several members of the club were, in all likelihood, working for the other side or, at least, working both sides of the fence. People reported many times that they had seen one person or another at the New Way, or in conversation with the opposition. As the campaign progressed, paranoia increased. The campaign leadership believed that such mistrust was natural in politics. Precautions could be taken, but resolving the problem was impossible. They also had their own people working the other side. The most important aspects of the campaign were seldom discussed in public anyway.

To prevent repeating the mistakes of the primary, a new list of voters was generated and checked. The names and addresses of new voters were added to the list regularly. Each election district was assigned at least one "captain," and the assembly district was covered with the most reliable and active people that could be found, regardless of political affiliation and prior activity at the club. Many oldtimers were put back into action, and given tasks which would not overtax them. If possible, captains were given workers. At the club, volunteers were available for literature distributions, clerical work, mailings, etc.. Often there was a large amount of work to do and members brought friends, relatives or children in to help out. Work such as folding campaign flyers and stuffing thousands of envelopes with pro-Steingut materials took a great deal of manpower. After meetings, the organizers tried to keep people behind to do these labor-intensive tasks. In this work a certain and quite sexist "pecking order" could be observed. Some people seemed to feel that such busy work was "beneath" them. Repetitious, simple tasks were for the most part performed by women, children and the otherwise "less able." When I involved myself in these activities I tried to organize them in a more rational format, as there were mountains of paper to mail out or put in mailboxes or under doors. This supervisory role allowed me to maintain some of my limited prestige within the group.

The club was open for campaign work every day, except Saturdays, from early morning through late at night, during the campaign. I was there almost every day, and sometimes twice a day, and participated in every facet of the campaign. My education in political campaigning was thorough. In order to make sure that the mail would be delivered in a timely fashion at a bulk rate, it was necessary to deliver it to the Central Brooklyn Post Office. Each piece had to be assembled into bunches, by zip code, tied together, and tagged. Otherwise it would not be accepted for delivery. Additionally, it was said that in order to guarantee the smooth operation of the process, palms had to be "greased."

The campaign generated huge volumes of literature. Each side countered the other's mailings and distributions--accusations and counter--accusations. By the end of the campaign it seemed as if mailings and "lit drops" were a daily occurence. The cost of this paper war was enormous. Literature was "dropped" throughout the A.D. but not randomly. Some specific neighborhoods, or sections, were known to be particularly sensitive to certain issues and so literature was designed to focus on those issues. The greatest areas of contention were the southern parts of the district, where the battle of words was especially personalized and nasty.

Distributing literature gave an idea of where voters were located. One day I "leafletted" blocks in the center of the A.D.. At the time we had little idea about the number of registered voters there. I went from door-to-door along the many streets of small multi-family houses, sticking folded flyers into mailboxes. In the process I was able to see the names on the boxes and check them against the voter registration roles. The names did not match. The Eastern European, Irish and Italian names had been replaced by French names. The area had become the home of immigrants from Haiti, legal and illegal. I recommended to Ross and Weintraub, therefore, that we stop spending resources on the area, except for those voters actually confirmed as there.

On other "lit drops" in other sections, particularly in the anti-Steingut south, I met a great deal of hostility. For example, in order to distribute flyers inside of apartment houses, I had to be let in through locked doors and I was frequently refused entry after identifying myself as someone from the Steingut campaign. On these forays, I also picked up the literature being distributed by the other side. One piece was particularly enlightening concerning tactics of the Weinstein-Silverman group. In a totally white working-class section a cheaply done copy of an *Amsterdam News* (a city-wide Black newspaper) article with a picture of Steingut surrounded by prominent Blacks who were endorsing him, had been distributed. The Madison Club people had, of course, not dropped them there. The flyer had no identification and appeared to be an official Madison Club distribution. Needless to say, the effect was not good for Steingut. Even more scurrilous, literature had been circulated in other areas. Some pieces made accusations of criminal conduct or claimed that Steingut had ruined the neighborhood in a multitude of ways. This sort of campaigning had occurred in the primary as well.

The campaign in Crown Heights had become more and more difficult as there was a significant split in the Jewish community, stimulated by the Steingut opposition and aggravated by Black-Jewish conflicts on the Community Planning Board. Despite these problems, Black voter registration continued apace in the Crown Heights, and Steingut travelled with prominent Blacks throughout the area who exhorted crowds of Blacks to vote for him. In Black areas, the alleged "racism" of the opposition was frequently alluded to. Although these activities certainly increased Black support for Steingut, they had a negative effect on white ethnic voters and raised suspicions among some of their community leaders. Others were concerned with the nursing home scandal which involved Rabbi

Bernard Bergman. A few were openly critical of Steingut for not protecting Bergman. Even the Black support for Steingut was not monolithic. Some Blacks had sided with the New Way, and it was clear to all, that regardless of Steingut's fate, the A.D. would be a Black area in a year or two, and the power vacuum would be filled by minority politicians.

## Election Eve

The night before the election, I worked late at the club on last minute arrangements, getting my assignments for the next day-- what polls to open, which ones to check, who to work with, which polls to close, and being available for emergency trouble-shooting. Ross and Weintraub had wrought a miracle, or so it seemed to me. Confidence was high. On election day we were assured that there would be legions of workers available. Despite all the good signs, I had my doubts about "union" volunteers. From my obser-vations, they seemed to be just putting in time for the union, not for the club. They were not reliable, and I overheard many of them talking about the campaign in negative terms. Many of the white workers seemed to especially disagree with Steingut's positions on capital punishment and abortion and their comments could be clearly heard by anyone within earshot. Finally, the union-supplied work groups themselves did not seem very inte-grated, and race, or so it appeared to me, was the main issue in the campaign.

Sound trucks were to criss-cross the A.D. all day. Food and drinks were to be brought to poll workers. Car pools were formed to pick up voters and baby sitting was arranged for mothers. The club was going all out. A large fund was established to pay some workers' expenses. I found out later that virtually everyone was putting in expense vouchers. Many were people I thought were "volunteers" like myself. Perhaps in clubhouse politics "volunteerism" has a different meaning.

On election day morning, I opened a poll in the southern part of the A.D. and on the way back to the club, checked for problems at other polling places. If necessary, I was to call headquarters for assistance. For the rest of the day I worked with Lenny Dwoskin, a long-time captain and, I believe, one of the last, really dedicated, Madison Club members. The experience was a graduate course in grass-roots political work. I had spent a great deal of time with him at the club and he had taken me under his wing.

Lenny knew virtually everyone in his election district, who was registered, who supported or was against, Steingut. He was active in all aspects of the community and always tried to involve the club and Steingut in what went on there. If someone had a problem, he would bring them to the club or offer help. He knew that although not many people were in favor of Steingut this time around, they would vote for him because he had asked them to, as a favor. This was the old way, and it worked. He spoke to everyone several times during the campaign. He knew who would make it to the polls without a reminder, who had to work during the day and therefore would vote in the evening, what times voters ate, who had voting age children, who had children to look after, and who needed a ride.

He called on them at home and asked if they had voted, but first he checked their cards at the polls. He did this at least three times during the day, and again in the evening. As a result of this meticulous process, almost everyone he expected to vote for Steingut had voted. As he walked through the neighborhood, it was clear that everybody knew him and what he expected. There was a great deal of friendly banter, and some not so friendly. Lenny would comment to me as to what people actually meant by what they said, and who was on what side in the election-- despite what they said. Like the gentleman he was, if he had a disagreement with someone, he would politely smile and quietly walk away with a shrug of his shoulders.

## Who Lost, Who Won

When the polls closed, we were elated by the results. Because we were in "key" precincts, we drove quickly to the club. But, when we arrived it was clear that we were too little, too late. Already people were leaving and muttering about the loss. Other key districts were not reporting well for Steingut. I still expected a miracle, but it didn't happen. The longer I stayed at the club, the gloomier the rooms became. For the second time, I became angry as workers ate the food for the victory party. Soon only the most devoted club members remained to wait for Steingut and his family. In a repeat performance, the party "big shots" also came to offer their condolences, despite benefiting from his loss. The old timers looked worn out. Steingut came down from the board room and gave another "thank you for all your support" speech, and he and his wife appeared relieved that the ordeal was over. There was nothing more I could do, so I left, but, melodramatically, I promised myself that someday I would be a "winner." Obviously I had personalized the whole experience. What began as a minor obligation became a moral crusade.

There was some gratuitous talk of challenging the election because of irregularities. The New Way had controlled the polls because of their primary victory. They had employed the same tactics as the Madison Club. However, it was decided that the election irregularities were insufficient to reverse the outcome. Some club diehards argued that a reversal could be "pulled off," but the guaranteed media scrutiny, and, more importantly, the fact that powerful politicians stood to gain by Steingut's loss meant that any efforts would be futile.

The final vote count was 10,179 votes for Murray Weinstein, 1,889 for Republican candidate Frank D. Petrizzo and 8,530 for Stanley Steingut on the Liberal line. The geographic distribution of the votes followed the same pattern as the primary: Steingut won in Black areas but lost by greater margins in White areas. The Orthodox and Hasidic Jewish vote in Crown Heights was split. Black registration efforts increased Steingut's identification with Black voters, but, more critically, a large number of new Black voters had difficulties voting for Steingut at the polls. Many votes were lost by simple errors. Because Steingut appeared only on the Liberal line on a complicated ballot, voters had to search to find him. A large number of first time Black voters simply voted "Democratic." They voted straight down the column for Democratic candidates. Steingut was not one of them. The high turnout of Blacks did, however, ultimately matter. In later years, Black voters and Black political organizations would eventually take over the neighborhoods as an unanticipated consequence of trying to save a vestige of the white ethnic political past. By trying to prevent change, the Madison Club had unwittingly heralded the future of New York City politics.

## Footnotes

1.  For discussion of the "dramaturgical method" see: " Erving Goffman, *The Presentation of Self in Everyday Life*, Garden City: Doubleday and Company, 1959. For discussions of phenomenology and the notion of "taken for granted" see: Alfred Schutz, *Collected Papers II: Studies in Social Theory*. The Hague: Martinus Nijhoff, 1964.
2.  For discussions of these methods see: George Psathas, *Phenomenological Sociology*, New York: John Wiley and Sons, 1973 and Robert

W. Jones, "A Note on Phases of the Community Role of the Participant Observer," *American Sociological Review*, 1961, 26: 446-50.

3.  In many ways, the political club is like a "Secret Society." For a discussion see: Georg Simmel, *The Sociology of Georg Simmel*, London: The Free Press, 1950. Translated and Edited by Kurt Wolff. Part Four: "The Secret and the Secret Society," Pp. 307-75.

4.  For a discussion of "secrets" see: Goffman *op. cit.*, pp. 142-65.

5.  For analyses of New York City decentralization see: Alan Altschuler, *Community Control*. New York: Frederick A. Prager, 1970, Maurice R. Berube and Marilyn Gittel, *Confrontation at Ocean-Hill Brownsville*. New York: Frederick A. Praeger, 1969, and Diane Ravitch, "Community Control Revisited," *Commentary* (1972) 53, pp. 69-74.

6.  Goffman, *op. cit.*

7.  Norbert Elias, *The Court Society*. New York: Pantheon Books, 1983. Especially Chapter V. "Etiquette and Ceremony," pp. 78-116.

8.  Verbatim Excerpt of the Meeting of the City Council Committee on Rules, Privileges and Elections," City Hall, City of New York, March 31, 1977. Hon. Edward V. Curry, Chairman, Presiding.

9.  Election returns were compiled by Charles Posner for use in the last campaign. I am grateful to him for the use of the material. The analysis is my own. Other sources. *U.S. Census of Population and Housing*, 1980. See Appendices for assembly and census districts maps and table of 1978 primary election returns.

### Appendix A.
### Voter Registration 1900-1980
### New York City, City Counties and Madison Club Assembly District

| | 1900 | | | 1905 | | |
|---|---|---|---|---|---|---|
| | Dem.s | Rep.s | Total | Dem.s | Rep.s | Total |
| New York | 173,476 | 112,806 | 300,275 | 202,775 | 142,64 | 369,495 |
| Bronx | | | | | | |
| Kings | 101,526 | 83,146 | 189,478 | 119,347 | 105,887 | 237,436 |
| Queens | 13,049 | 9,715 | 23,849 | 18,958 | 13,350 | 34,063 |
| Richmond | 6,723 | 4,577 | 11,752 | 7,413 | 6,485 | 14,364 |
| Total | 294,774 | 210,244 | 525,354 | 348,493 | 268,362 | 655,358 |
| A.D. | 4,702 | 5,099 | 10,000 | 9,145 | 9,006 | 18,827 |
| | % | % | % | % | % | % |
| New York | 58.8 | 53.6 | 57.2 | 58.2 | 53.1 | 56.4 |
| Bronx | | | | | | |
| Kings | 34.4 | 39.5 | 36.0 | 34.2 | 39.4 | 36.2 |
| Queens | 4.4 | 4.6 | 4.5 | 5.4 | 5.0 | 5.2 |
| Richmond | 2.2 | 2.2 | 2.2 | 2.1 | 2.4 | 2.2 |
| A.D. | 1.6 | 2.4 | 1.9 | 2.6 | 3.3 | 2.8 |

| | 1910 | | | 1915 | | |
|---|---|---|---|---|---|---|
| | Dem.s | Rep.s | Total | Dem.s | Rep.s | Total |
| New York | 181,325 | 132,091 | 351,009 | 137,626 | 68,061 | 251,619 |
| Bronx | 50,741 | 20,311 | 87,179 | | | |
| Kings | 109,832 | 105,598 | 240,679 | 124,198 | 92,058 | 247,282 |
| Queens | 22,315 | 17,275 | 44,491 | 44,556 | 14,120 | 64,518 |
| Richmond | 7,818 | 6,422 | 15,234 | 10,718 | 4,250 | 16,736 |
| Total | 321,290 | 261,386 | 651,413 | 367,839 | 198,800 | 667,334 |
| A.D. | 4,937 | 8,376 | 13,944 | 8,528 | 9,994 | 21,229 |
| | % | % | % | % | % | % |
| New York | 56.4 | 50.5 | 53.8 | 37.4 | 34.2 | 37.7 |
| Bronx | 13.8 | 10.2 | 13.0 | | | |
| Kings | 34.2 | 40.4 | 36.9 | 33.8 | 46.3 | 37.0 |
| Queens | 6.9 | 6.6 | 6.8 | 12.1 | 7.1 | 9.6 |
| Richmond | 2.4 | 2.4 | 2.3 | 2.9 | 2.1 | 2.5 |
| A.D. | 1.5 | 3.2 | 2.1 | 2.3 | 5.0 | 3.2 |

| | 1920 | | | 1925 | | |
|---|---|---|---|---|---|---|
| | Dem.s | Rep.s | Total | Dem.s | Rep.s | Total |
| New York | 189,155 | 229,188 | 503,820 | 247,008 | 108,092 | 387,686 |
| Bronx | 79,461 | 76,829 | 199,358 | 141,477 | 40,320 | 199,715 |
| Kings | 178,628 | 259,402 | 494,926 | 254,723 | 154,262 | 434,477 |
| Queens | 68,025 | 65,954 | 145,106 | 114,126 | 53,898 | 175,831 |
| Richmond | 15,898 | 12,257 | 30,336 | 27,255 | 7,995 | 36,410 |
| Total | 531,167 | 643,630 | 1,373,546 | 784,599 | 364,567 | 1,234,119 |
| A.D. | 8,778 | 14,053 | 26,969 | 18,709 | 9,686 | 30,909 |
| | % | % | % | % | % | % |
| New York | 35.6 | 35.6 | 36.6 | 31.4 | 29.6 | 31.4 |
| Bronx | 14.9 | 11.9 | 14.5 | 18.0 | 11.0 | 16.2 |
| Kings | 33.6 | 40.3 | 36.0 | 32.4 | 42.3 | 35.2 |
| Queens | 12.8 | 10.2 | 10.6 | 14.5 | 14.7 | 14.2 |
| Richmond | 2.9 | 1.9 | 2.2 | 3.4 | 2.2 | 3.0 |
| A.D. | 1.6 | 2.2 | 2.0 | 2.4 | 2.6 | 2.5 |

## Appendix A., Cont'd

|  | 1930 | | | | | 1935 |
|---|---|---|---|---|---|---|
|  | Dem.s | Rep.s | Total | Dem.s | Rep.s | Total |
| New York | 259,817 | 100,561 | 405,582 | 367,683 | 91,041 | 500,436 |
| Bronx | 210,407 | 95,917 | 291,548 | 296,213 | 27,565 | 354,315 |
| Kings | 356,778 | 144,033 | 549,310 | 557,314 | 102,345 | 701,810 |
| Queens | 182,943 | 78,684 | 275,431 | 278,420 | 61,594 | 354,662 |
| Richmond | 35,525 | 9,041 | 56,434 | 46,689 | 8,076 | 56,646 |
| Total | 1,045,440 | 428,236 | 1,568,305 | 1,546,322 | 290,621 | 1,967,869 |
| A.D. | 33,489 | 12,263 | 52,874 | 52,764 | 7,542 | 66,017 |

|  | % | % | % | % | % | % |
|---|---|---|---|---|---|---|
| New York | 24.8 | 23.4 | 25.8 | 23.8 | 31.3 | 25.4 |
| Bronx | 20.1 | 22.4 | 18.6 | 19.2 | 9.4 | 18.0 |
| Kings | 34.1 | 33.6 | 35.0 | 36.0 | 35.2 | 35.6 |
| Queens | 17.4 | 18.4 | 17.6 | 18.0 | 21.2 | 18.0 |
| Richmond | 3.4 | 2.1 |  | 3.6 | 3.0 | 2.8 |
| 2.8 |  |  |  |  |  |  |
| A.D. | 3.2 | 2.8 | 3.4 | 3.4 | 2.6 | 3.4 |

|  | 1940 | | | | | 1945 |
|---|---|---|---|---|---|---|
|  | Dem.s | Rep.s | Total | Dem.s | Rep.s | Total |
| New York | 352,764 | 102,881 | 508,375 | 308,837 | 93,338 | 511,497 |
| Bronx | 297,016 | 37,265 | 395,917 | 300,794 | 50,573 | 461,667 |
| Kings | 528,376 | 13,123 | 730,804 | 513,468 | 105,120 | 766,618 |
| Queens | 276,835 | 76,487 | 353,322 | 277,421 | 89,740 | 412,697 |
| Richmond | 48,879 | 7,748 | 55,612 | 36,408 | 10,361 | 49,679 |
| Total | 1,503,870 | 337,504 | 2,065,261 | 1,436,928 | 349,132 | 2,202,158 |
| A.D. | 53,361 | 7,696 | 74,391 | 31,012 | 3,482 | 34,728 |

|  | % | % | % | % | % | % |
|---|---|---|---|---|---|---|
| New York | 23.4 | 30.4 | 24.6 | 21.4 | 26.7 | 23.2 |
| Bronx | 19.8 | 11.0 | 19.2 | 20.9 | 14.4 | 21.0 |
| Kings | 35.1 | 33.5 | 35.4 | 35.7 | 30.1 | 34.8 |
| Queens | 18.4 | 22.6 | 17.1 | 19.3 | 25.7 | 18.7 |
| Richmond | 3.2 | 2.2 | 2.6 | 2.5 | 3.0 | 2.2 |
| A.D. | 3.5 | 2.2 | 3.6 | 2.2 | 0.9 | 1.5 |

|  | 1950 | | | | | 1955 |
|---|---|---|---|---|---|---|
|  | Dem.s | Rep.s | Total | Dem.s | Rep.s | Total |
| New York | 387,758 | 143,928 | 666,372 | 258,884 | 79,775 | 368,827 |
| Bronx | 385,175 | 78,643 | 556,695 | 239,281 | 47,301 | 315,203 |
| Kings | 651,145 | 162,206 | 941,862 | 409,546 | 100,093 | 545,949 |
| Queens | 356,303 | 163,155 | 577,095 | 264,457 | 116,078 | 403,331 |
| Richmond | 44,886 | 18,140 | 66,570 | 39,285 | 16,279 | 57,764 |
| Total | 1,825,267 | 566,072 | 2,808,694 | 1,211,453 | 359,526 | 1,691,074 |
| A.D. | 29,181 | 4,839 | 39,888 | 12,268 | 11,183 | 25,280 |

|  | % | % | % | % | % | % |
|---|---|---|---|---|---|---|
| New York | 28.0 | 25.4 | 23.7 | 21.4 | 22.2 | 21.8 |
| Bronx | 21.1 | 13.8 | 19.8 | 19.8 | 13.2 | 18.6 |
| Kings | 35.6 | 28.6 | 33.5 | 33.8 | 27.8 | 32.2 |
| Queens | 19.5 | 8.9 | 20.5 | 21.8 | 32.2 | 23.8 |
| Richmond | 2.4 | 3.2 | 2.4 | 3.2 | 4.5 | 3.4 |
| A.D. | 1.6 | 0.8 | 1.4 | 1.0 | 3.1 | 1.4 |

## Appendix A., Cont'd

| | 1960 | | | | | 1965 |
|---|---|---|---|---|---|---|
| | Dem.s | Rep.s | Total | Dem.s | Rep.s | Total |
| New York | 406,016 | 146,881 | 618,232 | 481,349 | 145,633 | 706,865 |
| Bronx | 357,822 | 85,769 | 489,435 | 449,198 | 102,628 | 606,596 |
| Kings | 650,581 | 170,626 | 886,731 | 781,109 | 186,292 | 1,048,907 |
| Queens | 455,900 | 208,759 | 717,702 | 600,345 | 232,900 | 915,171 |
| Richmond | 46,912 | 22,129 | 72,424 | 65,890 | 30,141 | 101,917 |
| Total | 1,917,231 | 634,164 | 2,784,524 | 2,377,891 | 697,594 | 3,379,456 |
| A.D. | 21,578 | 10,263 | 36,820 | 26,706 | 5,992 | 35,579 |

| | % | % | % | % | % | % |
|---|---|---|---|---|---|---|
| New York | 21.2 | 23.2 | 22.2 | 20.2 | 20.8 | 20.9 |
| Bronx | 18.6 | 13.5 | 17.6 | 18.8 | 14.7 | 17.9 |
| Kings | 33.9 | 26.9 | 31.8 | 32.8 | 26.7 | 31.0 |
| Queens | 23.8 | 32.9 | 25.8 | 25.2 | 33.4 | 27.0 |
| Richmond | 2.4 | 3.4 | 2.6 | 2.8 | 4.3 | 3.0 |
| A.D. | 1.1 | 1.6 | 1.3 | 1.1 | 0.8 | 1.0 |

| | 1970 | | | | | 1975 |
|---|---|---|---|---|---|---|
| | Dem.s | Rep.s | Total | Dem.s | Rep.s | Total |
| New York | 405,938 | 125,621 | 625,498 | 415,022 | 95,293 | 594,445 |
| Bronx | 365,418 | 85,654 | 507,807 | 361,407 | 72,053 | 487,187 |
| Kings | 670,428 | 158,322 | 920,024 | 661,676 | 140,325 | 902,183 |
| Queens | 559,062 | 201,655 | 862,211 | 531,640 | 173,074 | 806,470 |
| Richmond | 67,270 | 33,246 | 112,174 | 71,087 | 34,552 | 121,841 |
| Total | 2,068,116 | 604,498 | 3,027,714 | 2,040,832 | 515,297 | 2,912,126 |
| A.D. | 18,496 | 14,765 | 43,433 | 18,034 | 5,533 | 28,477 |

| | % | % | % | % | % | % |
|---|---|---|---|---|---|---|
| New York | 19.6 | 20.8 | 20.6 | 20.3 | 18.4 | 20.4 |
| Bronx | 17.6 | 14.2 | 16.8 | 17.7 | 14.0 | 16.7 |
| Kings | 32.4 | 26.2 | 30.4 | 32.4 | 27.2 | 31.0 |
| Queens | 27.0 | 33.4 | 28.4 | 26.0 | 33.6 | 27.6 |
| Richmond | 3.2 | 5.4 | 3.7 | 3.4 | 6.7 | 4.2 |
| A.D. | 0.8 | 2.4 | 1.4 | 0.8 | 1.0 | 0.9 |

| | 1980 | | |
|---|---|---|---|
| | Dem.s | Rep.s | Total |
| New York | 342,635 | 57,691 | 473,452 |
| Bronx | 268,695 | 38,696 | 349,533 |
| Kings | 491,369 | 79,655 | 647,667 |
| Queens | 439,917 | 117,763 | 653,783 |
| Richmond | 66,996 | 28,147 | 112,755 |
| Total | 1,609,612 | 321,952 | 2,237,190 |
| A.D. | 12,947 | 4,997 | 23,830 |

| | % | % | % |
|---|---|---|---|
| New York | 21.2 | 17.9 | 21.1 |
| Bronx | 16.6 | 12.0 | 15.6 |
| Kings | 30.5 | 24.7 | 29.0 |
| Queens | 27.3 | 36.6 | 29.2 |
| Richmond | 4.1 | 8.7 | 5.0 |
| A.D. | 0.8 | 1.5 | 1.0 |

Source: *New York State Assembly Legislative Manuals* and *Reports* of the New York City Board of Elections.

**Appendix B.**
**New York State Population**
**Selected Characteristics, 1900-1970**

| | 1900 | 1910 | 1920 | 1930 |
|---|---|---|---|---|
| Total Population | 7,268,894 | 9,113,614 | 10,385,227 | 12,588,066 |
| White | 7,156,881 | 8,966,845 | 10,172,027 | 12,153,191 |
| Black | 99,232 | 134,191 | 198,483 | 412,814 |
| Other | 12,781 | 12,578 | 14,717 | 22,061 |
| Native Born | 5,267,358 | 6,237,573 | 7,385,915 | 8,959,249 |
| Foreign Born | 1,889,523 | 2,729,272 | 2,786,112 | 3,193,942 |
| **Country of Origin*** | | | | |
| United Kingdom | | 153,930 | 142,068 | 153,522 |
| Ireland | | 367,877 | 284,747 | 293,225 |
| Germany | | 410,839 | 295,650 | 349,196 |
| Poland | | 167,379 | 247,519 | 350,383 |
| Austria | | 189,052 | 151,172 | 142,298 |
| Hungary | | 96,841 | 78,374 | 70,631 |
| Russia/USSR | | 473,551 | 529,240 | 481,306 |
| Italy | | 472,192 | 545,173 | 629,322 |
| Latin America & Caribbean | | 9,569 | 19,859 | 35,584 |

| | 1940 | 1950 | 1960 | 1970 |
|---|---|---|---|---|
| Total Population | 13,479,142 | 14,830,192 | 16,783,360 | 18,236,882 |
| White | 12,879,546 | 13,757,033 | 15,289,158 | 15,837,512 |
| Black | 571,221 | 918,191 | 1,495,446 | 2,163,263 |
| Other | 28,375 | 39,906 | 77,040 | |
| Native Born | 10,026,016 | 11,371,666 | 10,296,160 | 12,241,661 |
| Foreign Born | 2,853,530 | 2,500,429 | 2,289,314 | 2,109,776 |
| Foreign Stock | 4,198,130 | 3,890,445 | | |
| **Country of Origin*** | | | | |
| United Kingdom | 122,122 | 104,875 | 432,578 | 334,424 |
| Ireland | 235,755 | 186,752 | 492,041 | 386,503 |
| Germany | 316,844 | 270,661 | 674,215 | 516,216 |
| Poland | 281,080 | 254,065 | 683,610 | 557,478 |
| Austria | 172,347 | 149,955 | 315,796 | 237,836 |
| Hungary | 75,254 | 65,276 | 142,834 | 115,474 |
| USSR | 436,028 | 353,835 | 738,514 | 569,813 |
| Italy | 584,075 | 503,175 | 1,476,946 | 1,330,057 |
| Latin America & Caribbean | 32,875 | 48,423 | 243,345 | 526 634 |

* Where figures for Foreign Stock are given, data for Country of Origin is for Foreign Stock and not for Foreign Born.

Source: *United States Census of Population 1900, 1910, 1920, 1930, 1940, 1950, 1960, and 1970.*

### Appendix C.
### New York City Population
### Selected Characteristics, 1900-1970

| | 1900 | 1910 | 1920 | 1930 |
|---|---|---|---|---|
| Total Population | 3,437,202 | 4,766,883 | 5,620,048 | 6,930,446 |
| White | 3,369,898 | 4,669,162 | 5,459,463 | 6,587,225 |
| Black | 60,666 | 91,709 | 152,467 | 327,706 |
| Other | 6,638 | 6,012 | 8,118 | 15,515 |
| Native Born | 2,167,122 | 2,822,526 | 3,591,888 | 4,687,046 |
| Foreign Born | 1,270,080 | 1,944,357 | 2,028,160 | 2,293,400 |
| **Country of Origin*** | | | | |
| United Kingdom | | 103,395 | 94,668 | 146,262 |
| Ireland | | 252,662 | 203,450 | 192,810 |
| Germany | | 278,114 | 194,154 | 237,588 |
| Poland | | 145,679 | 238,339 | |
| Austria | | 190,246 | 126,702 | 127,169 |
| Hungary | | 76,627 | 64,393 | 59,883 |
| Russia/USSR | | 484,193 | 479,800 | 442,250 |
| Italy | | 340,770 | 390,832 | 440,250 |
| Latin America & Caribbean | | 46,401 | 73,815 | NA |

| | 1940 | 1950 | 1960 | 1970 |
|---|---|---|---|---|
| Total Population | 7,454,995 | 7,891,957 | 7,781,984 | 7,894,798 |
| White | 6,977,511 | 5,332,235 | 6,640,662 | 6,091,988 |
| Black | 458,444 | 747,547 | 1,087,931 | 1,664,574 |
| Other | 19,040 | 27,900 | 53,391 | 138,236 |
| Native Born | 5,374,975 | 6,107,751 | 6,223,294 | 6,467,740 |
| Foreign Born | 2,080,020 | 1,784,206 | 1,558,690 | 1,437,058 |
| Foreign Stock | 3,785,451 | 3,306,012 | | |
| **Country of Origin*** | | | | |
| United Kingdom | 85,812 | 53,614 | 175,024 | 116,342 |
| Ireland | 160,325 | 143,808 | 311,638 | 220,622 |
| Germany | 224,749 | 185,467 | 324,231 | 210,040 |
| Poland | 194,163 | 179,878 | 389,353 | 292,319 |
| Austria | 145,106 | 124,256 | 219,574 | 145,981 |
| Hungary | 62,588 | 51,968 | 96,815 | 72,071 |
| Russia/USSR | 395,696 | 314,603 | 563,943 | 393,918 |
| Italy | 207,096 | 344,115 | 858,601 | 682,613 |
| Latin America & Caribbean | 28,746 | 41,529 | 91,115 | 375,140 |

* Where figures for Foreign Stock are given, data for Country of Origin is for Foreign Stock and not for Foreign Born.

Source: *United States Census of Population 1900, 1910, 1920, 1930, 1940, 1950, 1960, and 1970.*

**Appendix D.**
**Brooklyn Population**
**Selected Characteristics, 1900-1980**

|  | 1900 | 1910 | 1920 | 1930 |
|---|---|---|---|---|
| Total Population | 1,166,582 | 1,634,351 | 2,018,356 | 2,560,401 |
| White | 1,145,603 | 1,610,487 | 1,984,953 | 2,488,448 |
| Black | 19,673 | 22,708 | 31,912 | 68,921 |
| Other | 1,306 | 1,156 | 1,491 |  |
| Native Born | 810,885 | 375.548 | 456,240 | 492,725 |
| Foreign Born | 355,697 | 571,356 | 659,287 | 686,770 |
| **Country of Origin*** |  |  |  |  |
| United Kingdom |  | 28,213 | 25,003 | 47,458 |
| Ireland |  | 70,653 | 53,660 | 45,299 |
| Germany |  | 87,912 | 56,778 | 56,134 |
| Poland |  | 51,928 | 106,714 |  |
| Austria |  | 35,913 | 31,981 | 47,471 |
| Hungary |  | 8,795 | 11,198 |  |
| Russia/USSR |  | 160,596 | 189,421 | 219,483 |
| Italy |  | 100,424 | 138,245 | 193,435 |
| Latin America & Caribbean |  | 46,401 | 73,815 | NA |

|  | 1940 | 1950 | 1960 | 1970 |
|---|---|---|---|---|
| Total Population | 2,698,285 | 2,738,175 | 2,627,319 | 2,602,012 |
| White | 2,587,951 | 2,525,118 | 2,245,859 | 1,905,788 |
| Black | 106,263 | 208,478 | 371,405 | 656,194 |
| Other | 3,071 | 4,579 | 10,055 |  |
| Native Born | 1,820,313 | 1,894,592 | 2,110,970 | 1,524,838 |
| Foreign Born | 767,638 | 630,526 | 516,349 | 456,636 |
| Foreign Stock | 1,319,575 | 1,077,136 |  |  |
| **Country of Origin*** |  |  |  |  |
| United Kingdom | 24,391 | 15,451 | 47,010 | 28,416 |
| Ireland | 34,775 | 29,714 | 70,484 | 42,862 |
| Germany | 42,111 | 29,038 | 56,001 | 33,951 |
| Poland | 87,980 | 79,582 | 167,070 | 122,336 |
| Austria | 53,621 | 42,729 | 75,031 | 44,898 |
| Hungary | 12,010 | 10,661 | 25,354 | 20,758 |
| Russia/USSR | 201,961 | 154,949 | 245,912 | 153,540 |
| Italy | 183,712 | 153,727 | 372,518 | 277,927 |
| Latin America & Caribbean | 5,924 | 7,143 | NA | 151,433 |

**Appendix D., Cont'd**
**1980**

| | |
|---|---|
| Total Population | 2,230,936 |
| White | 1,265,769 |
| Black | 723,748 |
| Native Born | 1,699,963 |
| Foreign Born | 530,973 |
| **Country of Origin\*** | |
| United Kingdom | 8,223 |
| Ireland | 6,572 |
| Germany | 8,594 |
| Poland | 36,097 |
| Austria | 6,647 |
| Hungary | 6,803 |
| Russia/USSR | 40,460 |
| Italy | 62,106 |
| Latin America&Caribbean | 201,154 |

\* Where figures for Foreign Stock are given, data for Country of Origin is for Foreign Stock and not for Foreign Born.

Source: *United States Census of Population 1900, 1910, 1920, 1930, 1940, 1950, 1960, 1970, and 1980.*

### Appendix E.
### Assembly District Population
### Selected Characteristics, 1900-1980

| | 1900 | 1910 | 1920 | 1940** |
|---|---|---|---|---|
| Total Population | 73,564 | 86,014 | 98,100 | 330,220 |
| White | 69,928 | 84,645 | 97,458 | 319,589 |
| Black | 3,524 | 1,281 | 635 | 10,477 |
| Other | 112 | 78 | 7 | 154 |
| Native Born | 53,521 | 65,727 | 64,039 | 224,267 |
| Foreign Born | 20,043 | 20,287 | 34,061 | 105,953 |
| **Country of Origin*** | | | | |
| United Kingdom | | 2,248 | 1,399 | 1,619 |
| Ireland | | 4,986 | 2,388 | 1,448 |
| Germany | | 4,131 | 2,001 | 1,238 |
| Poland | | 1,891 | 6,314 | |
| Austria | | 470 | 2,057 | 3,923 |
| Hungary | | 404 | 638 | |
| Russia/USSR | | 1,064 | 18,274 | 24,455 |
| Italy | | 2,290 | 2,194 | 2,511 |
| Latin America &Caribbean | | 188 | | |

| | 1950 | 1960 | 1970 | 1980 |
|---|---|---|---|---|
| Total Population | 109,747 | 129,519 | 150,555 | 152,936 |
| White | 108,667 | 122,769 | 116,375 | 50,882 |
| Black | 1,003 | 6,361 | 34,743 | 92,653 |
| Other | 90 | 389 | 837 | 9,434 |
| Native Born | 82,867 | 97,035 | 74,986 | 96,209 |
| Foreign Born | 26,880 | 32,484 | 31,220 | 56,727 |
| Foreign Stock | 51,447 | 44,349 | | |
| **Country of Origin*** | | | | |
| United Kingdom | 815 | 3,294 | 2,050 | |
| Ireland | 1,753 | 5,565 | 3,643 | 5,815 |
| Germany | 1,002 | 2,943 | 2,602 | 2,998 |
| Poland | 3,741 | 14,858 | 12,330 | 6,065 |
| Austria | 2,514 | 6,461 | 3,766 | |
| Hungary | 605 | 1,968 | 1,117 | |
| Russia/USSR | 10,861 | 25,985 | 16,685 | 4,697 |
| Italy | 2,443 | 9,792 | 10,307 | 10,592 |
| Latin America &Caribbean | 14,343 | 10,928 | | |

\* Where figures for Foreign Stock are given, data for Country of Origin is for Foreign Stock and not for Foreign Born.
\*\* 1930 N/A

Source: *United States Census of Population 1900, 1910, 1920, 1930, 1940, 1950, 1960, 1970, and 1980.*

## Appendix F.
### 41st A. D.Primary Election Returns by Election District, 1978

| Votes For Neighborhood | E.D. | Steingut | Weinstein | | E.D. | Steingut | Weinstein |
|---|---|---|---|---|---|---|---|
| Crown Heights | 1 | 126 | 65 | Holy Cross | 14 | 16 | 39 |
| | 2 | 137 | 58 | | 23 | 46 | 21 |
| | 3 | 128 | 63 | | 31 | 49 | 71 |
| | 4 | 24 | 19 | | 32 | 31 | 43 |
| | 5 | 125 | 43 | | 33 | 56 | 95 |
| | 6 | 52 | 45 | | 34 | 35 | 66 |
| | 69 | 51 | 45 | | 35 | 20 | 51 |
| | 72 | 27 | 32 | | 36 | 18 | 34 |
| | 75 | 102 | 39 | | 37 | 10 | 13 |
| | 76 | 57 | 13 | | 38 | 10 | 29 |
| Total | | 829 | 400 | | 39 | 52 | 172 |
| | | | | | 68 | 9 | 28 |
| East Flatbush | 7 | 125 | 45 | | 73 | 13 | 79 |
| | 8 | 85 | 24 | | 74 | 6 | 11 |
| | 9 | 34 | 6 | | 80 | 13 | 77 |
| | 10 | 71 | 59 | Total | | 384 | 829 |
| | 11 | 69 | 26 | | | | |
| | 12 | 30 | 19 | Flatlands | 40 | 176 | 261 |
| | 13 | 62 | 29 | | 41 | 9 | 23 |
| | 15 | 59 | 19 | | 42 | 42 | 109 |
| | 16 | 16 | 8 | | 43 | 13 | 96 |
| | 17 | 40 | 19 | | 44 | 33 | 100 |
| | 18 | 21 | 21 | | 45 | 29 | 75 |
| | 19 | 52 | 18 | | 46 | 129 | 154 |
| | 20 | 29 | 24 | | 47 | 52 | 156 |
| | 21 | 53 | 39 | | 48 | 117 | 121 |
| | 22 | 18 | 6 | | 49 | 122 | 83 |
| | | | | | 50 | 106 | 83 |
| Total | | 764 | 362 | | 51 | 32 | 73 |
| | | | | | 52 | 115 | 79 |
| Rugby | 24 | 21 | 40 | | 53 | 58 | 91 |
| | 25 | 69 | 31 | | 54 | 92 | 153 |
| | 26 | 69 | 54 | | 55 | 70 | 122 |
| | 27 | 94 | 32 | | 56 | 98 | 118 |
| | 29 | 95 | 42 | | 57 | 54 | 147 |
| | 30 | 73 | 96 | | 71 | 0 | 5 |
| | 78 | 61 | 20 | Total | | 1347 | 2049 |
| Total | | 482 | 315 | | | | |
| | | | | Canarsie | 58 | 49 | 193 |
| Remsen | 60 | 77 | 126 | | 59 | 25 | 152 |
| Village | 61 | 71 | 85 | | 70 | 3 | 19 |
| | 62 | 41 | 105 | | 77 | 25 | 112 |
| | 63 | 66 | 67 | Total | | 102 | 476 |
| | 64 | 66 | 48 | | | | |
| Total | | 321 | 431 | | | | |

Total, All E.D.s: Steingut-4,229 (46.5%) Weinstein 4,862 (53.4%)

Sources:Data collected by Madison Club member Charles Posner for use in the last campaign. Available also from the New York City Board of Elections

**Appendix G.**
**18th Assembly District 1900**

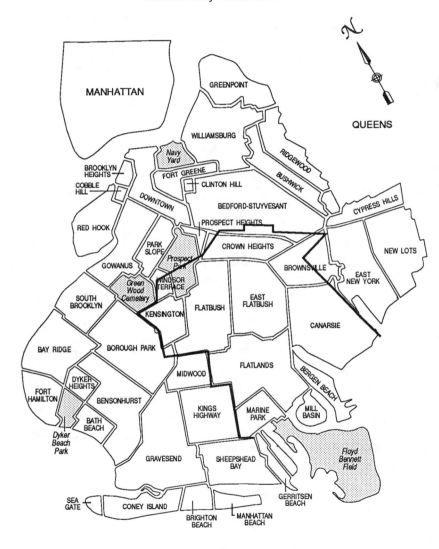

Source: New York State Assembly *Legislative Manual*

## Appendix H.
## 18th Assembly District 1910

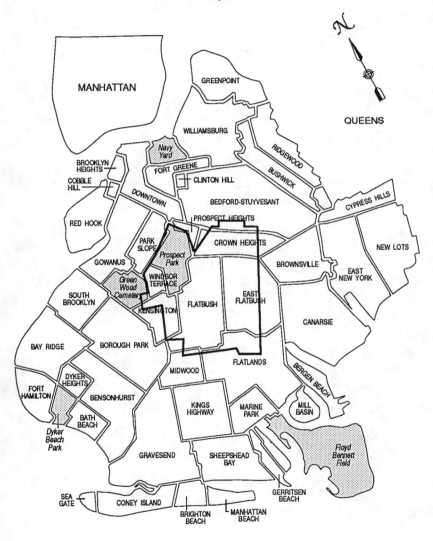

**Appendix I.**
**18th Assembly District 1920**

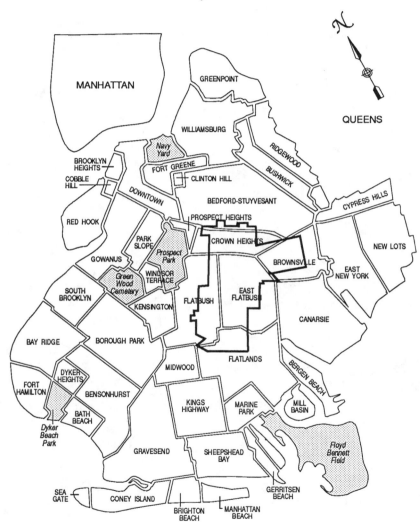

Source: New York State Assembly *Legislative Manual*

## Appendix J.
### 18th Assembly District 1930, 1940

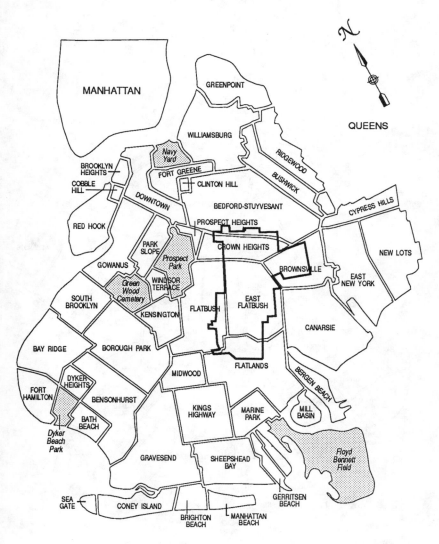

## Appendix K.
### 41st Assembly District 1950

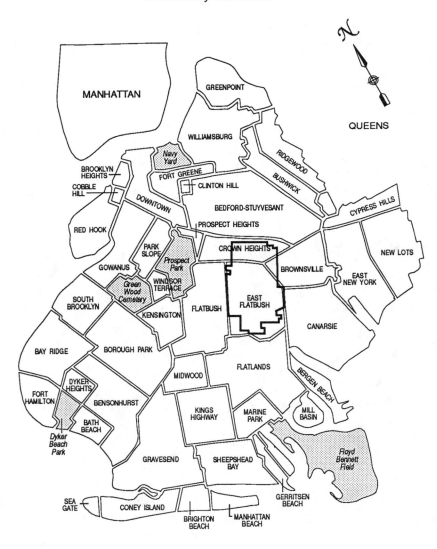

## Appendix L.
### 41st Assembly District 1960

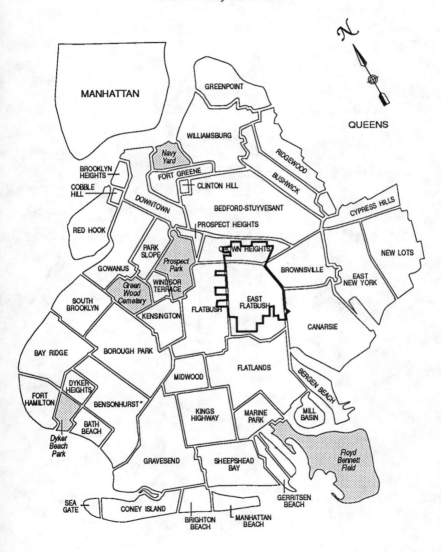

Source: New York State Assembly *Legislative Manual*

**Appendix M.**
**41st Assembly District 1970**

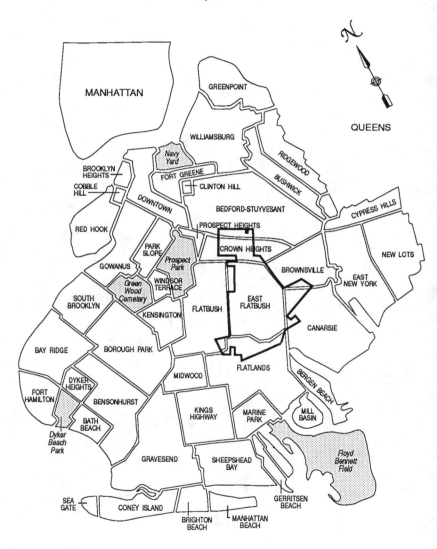

Source: New York State Assembly *Legislative Manual*

**Appendix N**
**Census Tracts by Race**
**41st Assembly District 1970**

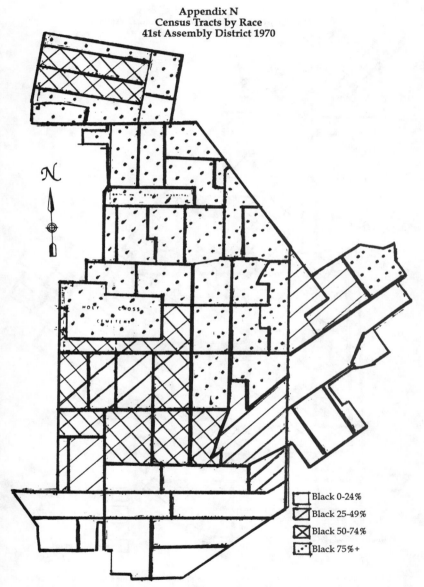

Black 0-24%
Black 25-49%
Black 50-74%
Black 75%+

Source: New York City Board of Elections and U.S. Census of Population 1970

**Appendix O**
**Primary Election Returns by Election District**
**41st Assembly District 1978**

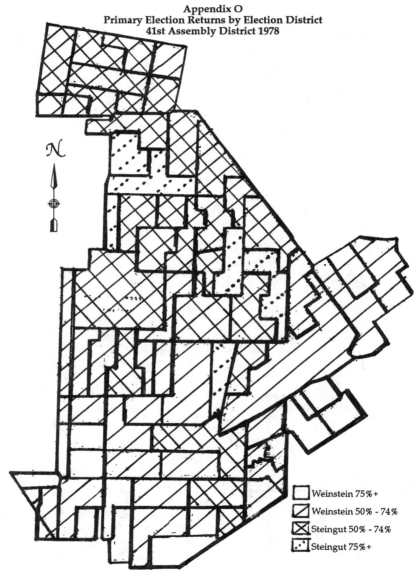

$\mathcal{N}$

Weinstein 75% +
Weinstein 50% - 74%
Steingut 50% - 74%
Steingut 75% +

Sources: Data collected by Madison Club member Charles Posner for use in the last campaign. Available also from the New York City Board of Elections

# A

# B